FIGHTING BACK

FIGHTING BACK

The War on Terrorism—
from Inside the Bush White House

Bill Sammon

Since 1947
REGNERY
PUBLISHING, INC.
An Eagle Publishing Company • Washington, DC

Lyric excerpt from "Dirty Work" by Donald Fagen and Walter Becker
Copyright © 1972
Universal-MCA Music Publishing on behalf of itself and Red Giant, Inc.
    (ASCAP)
All rights reserved. Used by permission.

Library of Congress Cataloging-in-Publication Data

Sammon, Bill.
  Fighting back : the War on Terrorism—from inside the Bush White House
/ Bill Sammon.
      p. cm.
Includes bibliographical references and index.
  ISBN 0-89526-149-9
  1. United States—Foreign relations—2001– 2. Terrorism—Government
policy—United States. 3. War on Terrorism, 2001– I. Title.
  E902 .S36 2002
  973.931—dc21
                                    2002012395

Published in the United States by
Regnery Publishing, Inc.
An Eagle Publishing Company
One Massachusetts Avenue, NW
Washington, DC 20001

Visit us at www.regnery.com

Distributed to the trade by
National Book Network
4720-A Boston Way
Lanham, MD 20706

Printed on acid-free paper
Manufactured in the United States of America

10 9 8 7 6 5 4 3 2 1

Books are available in quantity for promotional or premium use. Write to Director of Special Sales, Regnery Publishing, Inc., One Massachusetts Avenue, NW, Washington, DC 20001, for information on discounts and terms or call (202) 216-0600.

To my witty and wonderful mother, Teresa, and the memory of my father, Art, a brave fireman who will always be my hero.

Contents

We have a chance to write the story of our times,
a story of courage defeating cruelty
and light overcoming darkness.
This calling is worthy of any life.

—President George W. Bush
Address to the United Nations
November 10, 2001

Prologue

Two-Headed Calf

A PAIR OF TURKEY BUZZARDS circled high above Prairie Chapel Ranch as a white pickup truck appeared on the horizon, followed by half a dozen SUVs.

"Here we go," called out a photographer in the familiar signal that President Bush was approaching.

A ripple of excitement swept through the small group of journalists who had been standing around for an hour, waiting for the morning sun to warm the Texas prairie that seemed to stretch endlessly in all directions. We had passed the time swapping stories and comparing questions we hoped to ask the commander in chief on this, the 109th day of the War Against Terrorism.

The little caravan crawled along the horizon for a while and then turned down a long gravel path toward the old governor's house. This is where Bush had stayed while his newer home was being built clear on the other side of the 1,600-acre spread. From this vantage point there was no sign of the thick woods or picturesque canyons the president liked to roam in his spare time, savoring a waterfall or chainsawing through the stubborn cedar that seemed to spring up like weeds.

The big Ford pickup crunched to a stop in front of the house and Bush clambered out of the driver's seat. That was another reason he loved this sprawling, dusty ranch—it was the only place on earth where he could still drive his own truck. Clinton had gone eight years without driving anything bigger than a golf cart. But down here, in the wide-open spaces of Crawford, Bush could do things that seemed impossible in Washington, where the White House was hemmed in on all sides by a teeming, noisy metropolis. It's not that he didn't treasure his life at 1600 Pennsylvania Avenue, which he began each morning by taking his dogs into the Rose Garden to, well, water the roses. But he also understood that he was only a temporary tenant of the White House; it was, after all, "the people's house." When Bush stopped being president, he would return to his beloved Texas, where he had been raised since the age of two, to live out his remaining years. He had already decided that this was where he wanted to be buried. In the meantime, the president was determined to visit his ranch as much as possible. He had come down here two days before, arriving December 26, and planned to stick around long enough to celebrate the New Year. Bush had been so busy prosecuting the war that this was his first trip to the ranch since a month-long hiatus in August. Back then, Democrats and the press had savaged him for spending too much time away from Washington, even though the nation was at peace. Ironically, now that America was at war, these same critics were silent about the commander in chief's taking another Texas vacation.

Bush wore cowboy boots, blue jeans, and a brown work jacket over a charcoal plaid shirt, unbuttoned at the neck to reveal the top of a white undershirt. As he approached us, his dog Spot, an English springer spaniel, bounded out of the cab and began a thorough reconnaissance of the area. Meanwhile, the passenger door opened and

Army General Tommy Franks, ground commander of the war, stepped out. Having just returned from the Afghanistan theater, Franks was still dressed for battle—tan army boots, laced up high over his desert fatigues. He also wore a black jacket and matching beret, the latter laden with four silvery stars.

Under a crisp blue sky, the two men ambled over to a skinny lectern adorned with the presidential seal. They stood in the shadow of an elevated screen that White House staffers had erected just out of camera range so that the president wouldn't have to squint at the morning sun as he addressed the press. Bush folded his hands on the podium and casually crossed one leg behind the other as he began his exchange with the Fourth Estate. Franks stood off to the side with his hands on his hips, although at one point he crouched down to pet Spot.

Bush was clearly tickled to be hosting Tommy, a fellow Texan whom he lauded as "a down-to-earth, no-nonsense guy." The president pointed out with pride that Tommy had attended Midland Lee High School in Texas around the same time as First Lady Laura Bush. Bush enjoyed saying the name Tommy, repeating it dozens of times in the course of his remarks. The name itself seemed to reinforce Tommy's salt-of-the-earth nature, which the president obviously valued. Truth be told, Bush was showing off his prized general to the press corps, basking in the reflected success of a warrior fresh from battle. At the same time, he was showing off the press corps to Tommy, the way a rancher might show off a two-headed calf to a curious visitor. When the discussion turned to the war in Afghanistan, Bush was eager to bring Tommy into the mix.

"He's got a lot to say on that if you want him to talk about it," the president suggested. "Okay, bring the man to the mike."

As Tommy stepped forward, I asked, "General Franks, could you talk about how you took evasive action when you were fired upon the other day? There was a report yesterday that your helicopter was fired upon."

Tommy paused. Then with great reluctance and maximum modesty, he said, "I have been told since I took that helicopter ride that someone took a shot at the helicopter. I didn't see it when it happened, and I believe it may have happened, but then again, this is Afghanistan and we have pockets of Taliban still in that country. And that's one of the reasons that we're going to stay there until we have mopped all that up."

The performance seemed to please Bush, a former pilot in the Texas Air National Guard, and he soon went back to fielding most of the questions. The president talked about the latest Osama bin Laden videotape, mounting tensions between India and Pakistan, Argentina's financial crisis, even the collapse of Enron—a subject he had not previously been asked about in public. When I asked him whether he would make recess appointments, Bush said he was "thinking about it" and expressed disappointment "that a lot of my appointments were stalled in the United States Senate, weren't given a hearing." When I asked him whether he was upset that an Arab-American member of his Secret Service detail had been barred from a commercial flight bound for Texas, Bush said, "Yes, I was. I talked to the man this morning. I told him how proud I was that he was by my side. He's here on the ranch, and he's guarding me." The president added, "If he was treated that way because of his ethnicity, that will make me madder than heck."

While the questions covered a wide range of disparate subjects, they had one thing in common—they were highly topical. Bush was being asked about the headlines of the day, events that had occurred within the last twenty-four-hour news cycle. He had become so adept at this practice that on any given day he could anticipate the media's questions with remarkable accuracy. In fact, Bush was conducting today's news conference as if he had been given an advance peek at the script. He even seemed to anticipate the obligatory softballs about his favorite pastimes—fishing, jogging, and working the land.

So it was perhaps not surprising that the president became flummoxed when I decided to throw him a curve ball.

"Mr. President," I began, "some say the events of 2001 have changed you, while others say that you're the same person you always were."

"Yes," the president said tentatively.

"Who's right?" I asked. "Or is it fair to say there's some truth in both arguments?"

Bush looked at me as if I were, indeed, a two-headed calf. He was not about to get all touchy-feely in the middle of a boot-stompin' tour of his ranch with fellow Texan Tommy Franks, who had just dodged death in Afghanistan.

"Talk to my wife," Bush said dismissively and turned to another reporter.

As the small gathering chuckled at the president's flip reply, I tried to bring him back to the topic, although it was obvious he was in no mood for introspection.

"I don't know," the president chafed. "I don't spend a lot of time looking in the mirror—except when I comb my hair."

Again he turned to the next reporter, although he seemed to sense his answer was unsatisfactory. Unlike former president Bill Clinton, who pontificated about his feelings at the drop of a hat, Bush was uncomfortable stepping onto such Oprahesque terrain. "I am not very good at psychoanalyzing myself," he once told an interviewer. Years later, he wrote derisively of reporters, "They worship at the altar of public confession." In this respect he was much more like his father, who once responded to a similarly navel-gazing query by admonishing the questioner, "Don't put me on the couch."

Still, I considered it an important question. Democrats and the press were claiming the events of September 11 had utterly transformed Bush from a bumbling lightweight into a steely-eyed statesman. But the president's closest aides and friends, those who had known him the longest, insisted Bush hadn't changed a whit. They suspected the president's critics had come up with the spin about transformation as a way to rationalize their earlier criticism of Bush as a nincompoop. Otherwise, the detractors would be forced to admit they had been wrong about Bush in the first place. I figured it was fair to ask the president himself to settle the issue once and for all. So I kept sputtering until he finally took pity on me.

"Listen, I'll give you a hint," Bush said with a slight air of exasperation. "I liked coming to the ranch before September the 11th; I like coming to the ranch after September 11th."

And with that, he turned away, this time for good. At first I thought I had failed to get a meaningful answer to the question. But as I stood there on the chilly grass of Prairie Chapel Ranch, watching Bush and Tommy Franks clomp away down the gravel path and disappear under the tin roof of the old governor's house, it began to dawn on me that he *had* answered the question, albeit elliptically.

No American who lived through September 11 could claim to be wholly unchanged by the tragedy. This was especially true of two groups of people—those who were directly affected by the attacks and those who were deeply involved in America's response. George W. Bush, by virtue of his presidency, was uniquely positioned with one foot in each of these camps.

For starters, he was more directly affected than most Americans by the attacks themselves. As a husband, father, and president, Bush had a day that was nothing short of harrowing. He feared for the safety of his wife, who was on Capitol Hill when it was reportedly being targeted by suicidal terrorists. He was so worried about his twin daughters—whom he described as "freaked out"—that he ordered them whisked to secure locations on their college campuses. At various points throughout the day, the president was informed that hijacked airliners were hurtling toward the three sacrosanct places he called home—the White House, Camp David, and Prairie Chapel Ranch. There were even credible threats of attack against Air Force One as it hopscotched the country, ferrying the president and anxious aides from one bunker to another. To suggest these events had no lasting impact on Bush would be naive.

Secondly, few people were more deeply involved in America's response than the commander in chief himself. It was Bush who decided when and how to unleash the punishing, relentless counterattacks. It was Bush who took responsibility for sending young Americans into harm's way, knowing that some would surely die. It was Bush whose very presidency had been turned upside down by this unwelcome war. To argue that he was somehow impervious to these cataclysmic changes was, to put it mildly, fatuous.

And yet that is not to say the president's core character and fundamental personality underwent some profound seismic shift. Bush fervently believed that a man either possessed leadership or he didn't. It was not a trait that could be magically acquired in the midst of a sudden crisis. As far as the president was concerned, he was handling the war against terrorism the same way he had handled the governorship of Texas and the ownership of his various business interests—namely, by working on a problem diligently, surrounding himself with thoughtful people, soliciting their advice, and then making decisions without a lot of anguished second-guessing. More often than not, this strategy had proven successful.

But Bush wasn't the kind of guy who could just explain all that right there in the middle of Prairie Chapel Ranch, at least not with Tommy Franks by his side. So he was sardonic and cryptic instead. And yet he got his point across. In fact, he imparted more information about himself by dancing around that one question than by answering all the others.

Of course September 11 was a transforming event for Bush, just as it was for every other American. And *obviously* his presidency had been changed into something he never imagined.

Still, as the president himself observed three days after the attack, "adversity introduces us to ourselves." Just as America was reminded of its true character by September 11, so too was Bush reminded that deep down, he was the same man who had raised his right hand a scant eight months earlier and sworn to uphold the Constitution. He was the same president who had declared in his inaugural address, "Sometimes in life we are called to do great things." He was the same softy who wept at the drop of a hat.

The turkey buzzards were still circling when the deceptively simple answer slowly dawned on me.

George W. Bush was still, well—George W. Bush.

Chapter One

This Had Better Be Good

ON THE MORNING OF SEPTEMBER 11, 2001, George W. Bush awoke in a bed whose last famous occupant was Al Gore. Blinking into consciousness in the predawn darkness, the president of the United States found himself alone in a massive luxury penthouse suite on the island of Longboat Key, Florida. To his left was a wall of windows overlooking the Gulf of Mexico, where a pair of heavily armed boats patrolled the murky surf. To his right was Sarasota Bay and, beyond that, the city of Sarasota itself, where Bush was scheduled to give an unremarkable speech on education later in the morning.

Swaddled in the finest Frette linens and matching duvet, the president was stretched out on the same king-sized bed that Gore had slept in nearly five years earlier, the night before he battled Jack Kemp in the 1996 vice presidential debate in nearby St. Petersburg. Gore had liked the Colony Beach & Tennis Resort so much that he returned there in 2000 to prepare for his presidential debates with Bush, although the vice president stayed in a beachfront cottage instead of the penthouse now occupied by the president. In fact, as Bush swung his six-foot frame out of bed and padded across the olive Berber carpet in front of the sliding glass doors, he could see the cottage down there on the beach. So that was where Gore had plotted his overly aggressive performance for the first debate. Thank God for those sighs! If it hadn't been for Gore's exasperated sighing throughout that first, fateful debate, the press might have awarded the vice president a victory on debating points alone. Even Bush conceded that Gore was the superior debater. But those sighs had shifted the focus to stylistics and Gore had taken a beating in the all-important court of public opinion. *Saturday Night Live* had a field day with those sighs, mercilessly lampooning Gore as an insufferable, microphone-hogging smarty-pants who oozed smarmy condescension. The vice president's aides had actually forced him to watch a tape of the withering send-up. Afterward, Gore felt compelled to promise "a few less sighs, absolutely" for the second debate. It was a remarkable nod to the power of popular culture. An irreverent skit on a late-night comedy show had more influence on a major presidential candidate than all the long-winded blowhards in the political press.

Of course, Bush did not exactly escape unscathed from that skit. As usual, he was portrayed as a vacuous frat boy who was so incapable of pronouncing or remembering the names of heads of state that he resorted to the shorthand "Leader One" and "Leader Two." Try as he might, Bush had never been able to shake his reputation as a foreign policy lightweight, which was hopelessly cemented when he flunked a humiliating pop quiz at a Boston TV station a full year before the election. Why on earth had he ever allowed himself to get drawn into that reporter's brazen demand that he recite the names of four world leaders? Who the hell knew the name of the president of Chechnya anyhow? It wasn't even a country! Bush tried to look on the bright side. At least the stereotype of him as an airhead was becoming so stale that it was overshadowed in the first debate by

Gore's pompous sighing—not to mention his penchant for exaggeration. That gave the comedy writers and political pundits some fresh material to chew over, shunting the caricature of Bush the Brainless to the back burner.

Gore had returned to that squat brown cottage in the sand, now illuminated by the flickering flames of tiki torches, to bone up on his briefing book for the second debate. Chastened by the mockers, the vice president was determined to eradicate his image as a boorish know-it-all. But he ended up overcompensating in Round Two. He was overly subdued, almost docile, as if he were biting his tongue when he really wanted to lash out at the increasingly confident Bush. *Saturday Night Live* portrayed the vice president as a self-shackled sycophant who took pains to agree with everything his opponent said. Bush, miraculously, had dodged another bullet.

Perhaps that was why Gore had fled the Colony to recalibrate yet again before the third and final debate. Whatever the reason, the vice president finally managed to win one, fair and square. But by then it was too late. Even Gore's own pollster, Stanley Greenberg, conceded the vice president never regained the national lead that had slipped away after the first debate. As far as the public was concerned, the presidential debates of 2000 could be summed up in a single sound bite of political shorthand: Bush the underdog had beaten Gore the favorite.

Of course, Bush had gone on to vanquish the vice president in the election and again in the Florida recount wars. And yet he seemed unable to shake Gore's political ghost. Even now, as the president pulled on a white T-shirt and tan running shorts, he was aware that Gore was plotting a political comeback. Having withdrawn from public view after those nightmarish thirty-six days of dimpled chads, Gore had purposely kept a low profile for nine months. But lately he had begun meeting with small groups of supporters to test out privately a new line of attack on Bush. He planned to make this attack public in a major coming-out speech at the annual Jefferson-Jackson Day Dinner in Iowa on September 29. The political reporters were already salivating at the prospect of Gore's tearing into Bush all over again.

And then there was the Mother of All Media Recounts, which, in the parlance of cyberjournalist Matt Drudge, was about to "impact." Never mind that *USA Today* and the *Miami Herald* had published the muddled results of their own statewide recount months ago. Never mind that more than a dozen other media outlets had also tallied various batches of ballots, with wildly disparate results. Never mind that the overwhelming majority of Americans desperately wanted to move on from this endless rehashing and second-guessing of a painfully contentious chapter in U.S. history. None of this seemed to matter to the *New York Times*, the *Washington Post*, CNN, and the host of other media outlets that had formed a consortium and anointed themselves the last word on recounts. They had already poured more than a million dollars into the project, which was originally scheduled to be published no later than Easter. But the consortium had so many big-name participants that it turned into a lumbering bureaucracy that could not reach decisions without anguished and protracted consultations among a tangle of outsized egos. Deadlines slipped left and right. By late summer the consortium had settled on September 17 as the day on which the whole mess would finally be published. But in just the last week, that deadline had slipped yet again and the consortium was now looking at late September as a target. Would the madness never end?

Bush tugged on a pair of white, ankle-high athletic socks. What he needed was a good run. In addition to clearing his head, it would burn off some of the calories he had packed on at dinner the night before. It had been a veritable feast of his beloved Tex-Mex cuisine—or at least Florida's idea of Tex-Mex. Truth be told, Red Snapper Ranchero would be considered a bit froufrou at a barbecue in Crawford, Texas, the landlocked site of Bush's 1,600-acre ranch. Still, the president enjoyed the Texas Tortilla Soup and the Lone Star Tenderloin. The resort had made up a special presidential menu just for the occasion. Under the extremely watchful eyes of the Secret Service, the Colony's chefs had begun preparing the food as soon as Bush rolled up in his limousine at 6:30 P.M. on Monday, September 10. The president bounded out of the backseat and strode into the small lobby, where he was greeted by a poised, impeccably dressed blonde with chiseled cheekbones named Katie Klauber Moulton, then the Colony's general manager. After greeting Moulton and two of her family members, Bush spotted a group of maids, gardeners, and other menial workers who had obviously been shooed away from the president's trajectory. He immediately sized up the situation and made a beeline for these startled employees, pumping their hands and thanking them for their hospitality. He took his good old time, making sure he didn't forget anyone, before finally getting into a cramped, aging elevator with a couple of Secret Service agents.

A sixty-year-old maintenance man named Kenneth Kufahl had been instructed in advance to take the elevator directly to the fifth-floor penthouse. Not that Bush was in any danger of running into unscreened members of the public. All guests had been cleared out of the building to make way for the invasion of White House staffers, aides, communications technicians—even an antiterrorism unit. Still, the Secret Service was taking no chances. Kufahl was under strict orders to take the president directly to the penthouse.

The proximity of the most powerful person in the world, however, unnerved the maintenance man, who fumbled with the various keys, switches, and buttons on the elevator's control panel. Several seconds ticked by.

"Son, you're makin' my men nervous," Bush said. "And that makes me nervous. Calm down and this whole thing's gonna come off real easy."

The president cut a glance at the agents, a couple of tough-looking hombres with coiled wires coming out of their ears and walkie-talkie microphones up their sleeves. They remained expressionless, a pair of stone-cold Terminators in off-the-rack suits.

Bush then studied the elevator operator, who struggled to regain his composure. The president was accustomed to encountering citizens who were overwhelmed by the power of his office. Some literally quaked in the presence of the leader of the free world. Their palms went clammy, their voices quavered, they fumbled with whatever they were holding. They weren't so much intimidated by Bush himself, who in fact was remarkably down-to-earth, as they were by the raw power of the presidency. Bush understood this and actually spent a surprising amount of his time just trying to put ordinary people at ease. He sensed that Kufahl was the sort of no-nonsense guy who responded well to straight talk. Indeed, the 6-foot-4-inch maintenance worker fancied himself a "man's man" with a disdain for "plastic people."

Sure enough, Kufahl calmed down and got the proper elevator key to work, which allowed him to flip the necessary switches and press the necessary buttons to get Bush up to the fifth floor. The dark green elevator disgorged the president into a narrow hallway, directly opposite a table that contained a large vase of exotic flowers—ti, protea, and birds-of-paradise. The hall contained the doors to three suites. One was the permanent home of Klauber's father, Murray, who founded the Colony after tiring of his orthodontics practice in Buffalo back in 1969. Another was for Bush's personal assistant, Blake Gottesman. Bush turned right and walked a few paces to the end of the corridor, where he entered the third door, Suite 503.

Once inside, the president proceeded down a short hall that opened into the living room, which had a panoramic view of the Gulf of Mexico along the western exposure. The sun was already descending toward the aqua surf, where dolphins frolicked near a sand bar and pelicans cruised low in search of easy meals. Another bank of windows lined the northern exposure, although the Secret Service had loaded up the balcony with enough heavy ficus trees to block the view from anyone who might try to catch a glimpse of the president from the condominiums to the north. The room contained a plush gray couch that was upholstered in the softest, supplest leather imaginable. A thick slab of glass topped a table of brushed stainless steel. In one corner stood a trio of tall, slender, weather-beaten planks that had been carved into crude human totems—one smiling, one frowning, one poker-faced. They were African grave markers that had been brought to America as souvenirs. In the opposite corner stood a big-screen TV, topped by a curiously outdated stereo system, the kind that contained a turntable for vinyl record albums. As he surveyed his surroundings, Bush walked across a floor of off-white Italian tile topped by a multicolored rug that was done up in the style of an old-fashioned hooked rug, although this one seemed a lot more expensive.

The eastern half of the suite consisted of a dining room and a kitchen, which, like the living room, were brightened by fresh flowers that had been specifically chosen for their lack of fragrance. Cobalt blue ginger jars overflowed with gerber daisies and snapdragons, all set in "spring arrangements" of warm pink and peach tones.

Another batch of ficus trees had been placed along the balcony out-side the dining room and kitchen. Through the branches, Bush could look out over a sea of tennis courts. The Colony didn't have a single golf green, but it had so many tennis courts that it had been dubbed America's top resort by *Tennis Magazine*. Just beyond the courts, across Gulf of Mexico Drive, were the roofs of spectacular mansions that faced Sarasota Bay. One of them was the home of Florida Secretary of State Katherine Harris, who had been savaged by the press for upholding Bush's victory in the recount wars. Harris, who also kept a home in Tallahassee in order to fulfill her duties in the state's capital, had recently decided to move back to Longboat Key and run for Congress, which was a pretty safe bet, considering the strong Republican makeup of Florida's 13th District.

Bush then retraced his steps, veering right just before he reached the entrance door of his suite. This placed him in another short hall-way that opened first to a small bathroom and then to the master bedroom. The headboard of the bed was set into a slight recess along the south wall. Opposite the bed stood an exquisite antique armoire of worm-eaten English pine, which concealed another television. The eastern wall was dominated by an elaborate ceiling-high bookshelf that had been built to match the armoire, complete with artificially "fatigued" wood, although there was no way to replicate the tiny wormholes of the armoire. The shelves of this particular piece of furniture, which had set the Colony back more than $10,000, were lined with vases, rare seashells, and a row of paperback books, all in German, that had been left behind by a family from Munich who rented the suite once a year. Bush freshened up in the master bathroom, a dark, expansive chamber of highly polished marble the color of chocolate. Off to one side was a low doorway that led to an even darker shower stall built for two people, each of whom would have three shower heads strategically aimed at their head, chest, and derriere. Vases of orchids had been placed in both the bathroom and bedroom.

Within twenty minutes of entering his 2,800-square-foot suite, which the Colony rented out at $1,300 a night, Bush was back in the elevator, which Kufahl had no trouble operating this time.

"You got it down pat?" Bush said.

"Yep—it's as easy as up and down," replied the maintenance man, who decided Bush was the kind of guy to whom he could relate. When they reached the first floor, Kufahl said, "Enjoy the food."

Bush traversed the small lobby, passing doormen who wore pith helmets and white, short-sleeved uniforms of the sort found on policemen in the Caribbean. He walked across the driveway to the resort's beachfront restaurant, entering a small, private dining room just inside the main entrance, where he was warmly received by thirteen dinner companions, mostly warriors in the postelection struggle. The most prominent of these was his younger brother, Florida Governor Jeb Bush, whom the Democrats had accused of somehow rigging the recounts, even though he had recused himself from the entire mess. There was also Marsha Nippert, who had chaired the 2000 Bush campaign in Sarasota County. Nippert was one of the slate of twenty-five Florida electors who cast the decisive votes for Bush in the electoral college, despite harassment from Gore loyalists who demanded they defect to the Democratic side. At one point the phone lines at her house had been cut. Two other electors were present—Florida House Speaker Tom Feeney and Senate President John McKay—both of whom had threatened to invoke the GOP-controlled legislature to restore themselves and the rest of the Bush slate to the electoral college in the event a rogue Gore slate was installed by one of the courts entangled in that historic debacle.

Florida State Senator Lisa Carlton, chairman of the powerful Appropriations Committee, was there. So was John Delaney, mayor of Jacksonville, where Bush had given an education speech earlier in the day. Former Florida governor Bob Martinez had made a point of showing up. The Republican Party was represented at the state level by Chairman Al Cardenas and at the Sarasota County level by Chairman Tramm Hudson, a local banker. About the only guest who didn't have an overt political title was Carlos Alfonso, president of a Tampa architectural firm, who had been generous to the Bush campaign. Rounding out the dinner list were three men the president had brought with him from Washington: trusty White House Chief of Staff Andy Card, top political advisor Karl Rove, and Education Secretary Rod Paige.

Although they all expected the president to sit at one end of the long table, he chose a seat halfway down one side. That allowed him to face a large bay window, bathed in warm sepia tones, that looked back toward his hotel. He pulled out a carved wooden chair—with a seat upholstered in a pattern of monkeys eating grapes—and sat down directly across from his brother.

Seeking to put everyone at ease as quickly as possible, Bush announced to the waiters, "Bring out those menus—I'm starving." When a platter of chili con queso was placed near him as an appetizer intended for consumption by several people, the president pulled it close and began double-dipping tortilla chips into the concoction in a manner that signaled this would be an extremely informal dinner. Before long, he had single-handedly cleared the platter and moved on to other items on the menus, which were brought out by a pair of waiters who had emigrated to the United States from Southeast Asia. When one of them produced a wine list and began to take drink orders, he was discreetly pulled aside by Hudson and reminded that Bush was a teetotaler. The waiter nodded and brought Bush the first of several nonalcoholic beers.

For the next two hours, the president enjoyed a relaxed, carefree dinner with people whose company he seemed genuinely to enjoy. He recounted a funny story about getting Jeb a summer job that turned out to be a disaster. Jeb made sure there was plenty of good-natured irony in his voice when he addressed his big brother as "Mr. President." This fraternal razzing prompted appreciative laughter all around. Inevitably, the conversation turned to sports, which suited Bush, a former owner of the Texas Rangers. The president reeled off obscure statistics that only a true baseball nut would know.

As the evening progressed, the president talked about books, movies, restaurants, families, growing up in Texas, and his recent life as a "windshield rancher." More than once he threw his head back and laughed with the abandon of a man with a clear conscience. He spoke of his attachment to Barney, the Scottish terrier who had been given to him by Christie Todd Whitman, head of the Environmental Protection Agency. The jet black dog had legs so short that Bush had to carry him off the presidential helicopter, Marine One, whenever the first family touched down on the South Lawn of the White House after a weekend at Camp David. The press joked that Bush must be secure enough in his masculinity to be filmed awkwardly toting a small dog under his arm.

"My wife sort of likes the dog, but the neat thing is that he's crazy about me," the president confided to his dinner companions. "I've never had a dog so crazy about me as this dog. He just follows me everywhere."

By and by, the talk turned to politics. There were analyses of Jeb's reelection chances against Janet Reno, the former attorney general

under Bill Clinton, who had just thrown her hat into the ring. Someone complained about the disarray of the Republican Party in California, a state that had voted overwhelmingly for Gore. Before long
the diners were plotting to regain Republican control of the U.S.
Senate, which had swung to the Democrats after the defection of
Vermont Senator Jim Jeffords in May. Complicating the task was the
fact that several longtime GOP senators had announced their intentions to retire, including Phil Gramm of Texas and Jesse Helms of
North Carolina. Bush speculated on who might run in New Jersey
and which sitting Republicans could be persuaded to keep their seats
in two or three other key states. If things broke the right way, he
believed the Senate might return to GOP control after all. But
Tramm Hudson pointed out pessimistically that Republican Senator
Fred Thompson of Tennessee was talking about getting out of the
game.

"I'll bet you five dollars that he does not run," said Hudson,
emboldened by the aura of presidential bonhomie.

He stood up and extended his hand across the table. Several people, struck by the local pol's brazenness, looked on disapprovingly.

Bush smiled, shook his hand, and said, "We'll see what happens."

Hudson had been the heir apparent to Representative Dan Miller,
the local congressman who was planning to retire at the end of 2002.
But the banker eventually found himself eclipsed by Harris, who had
become an overnight sensation in the national GOP after her performance in the recount wars. Seeing the handwriting on the wall, Hudson agreed to place his own congressional aspirations on hold. But
not every Republican at the table was happy about this turn of events.
McKay, who had often locked horns with the secretary of state, saw
an opportunity to stir the pot in her absence.

"Mr. President, why don't you appoint Katherine Harris as ambassador somewhere so Tramm can run for Congress?" the Florida State Senate president suggested.

Jeb rolled his eyes at Hudson and laughed.

The president said, "Well, the chairman *should* go to Congress," and left it at that. He wasn't about to run down the woman who had taken so much heat for him.

As with most dinner parties, there were times when a single participant held the floor and other periods when several smaller conversations took place simultaneously. During one of these latter interludes, Bush acknowledged to former governor Martinez, who sat next to him, his growing concerns about the nation's economy. The downturn had begun to accelerate in recent weeks. The dot-com bubble, which had swollen to such enormous size during the Clinton era before beginning its spectacular implosion in the final ten months of the outgoing administration, continued to deflate throughout the first eight months of the Bush administration. The Nasdaq had lost a shocking two-thirds of its value. That included a drop of 12 percent since the new president's inauguration. The Standard & Poor's 500 had plummeted some 18 percent since Bush took office and was nearing a three-year low. Unemployment had just jumped to 4.9 percent, the highest rate in four years. And consumer confidence was sinking just as retailers were gearing up for the crucial Christmas season.

The press was beginning to hammer Bush on the economy. Although no one had announced that the nation was technically in a recession, journalists began tossing the word around with increasing abandon. Worse yet, they were starting to hint it was Bush's fault. Although the economic slowdown began in March 2000, the press waited until a Republican was in office before making the economy a major political issue. The slump had been the top story in the *New York Times* for the last three days. That very morning, when Bush had visited a Jacksonville grammar school, the White House press corps that accompanied him ignored the education message of the day and focused instead on the economy. Bush himself refused to answer questions on the topic, although his aides were forced to fan out and defend the administration against Democratic attacks that blamed the president for the slowdown. No wonder Bush's job approval rating, as measured by Gallup, had slipped to 51 percent, the lowest level of his presidency, that very day.

Bush told Martinez he was fully aware of the rough road that lay ahead. He would take a beating in the press for sixty to ninety days because the economy would almost certainly get worse before it got better. And yet Bush expressed a stoic confidence that his tax cuts, which had been enacted over the summer, would eventually help turn the economy around. Rebate checks of up to $600 were already being mailed to millions of American families. Not that the press believed this would help. Reporters were already parroting Democratic claims that the tax cut would merely obliterate the federal budget surplus and force a "raid" on Social Security funds. This earned Bush a "down" arrow in *Newsweek*'s "Conventional Wisdom" on September 3. "Adios, surplus," the magazine smugly stated. "When retired boomers dine on dog food, will they say thanks for that $600?"

Meanwhile, there was some skittish talk from congressional Republicans back in Washington about the need for additional cuts, perhaps in the capital gains tax, to provide a more immediate economic boost than the income tax reductions, which were scheduled to phase in over ten years. Although Bush had not ruled out additional cuts, he seemed to prefer sticking to his original plan and riding out the storm, which he believed would begin to clear by the end of the first quarter or, at the very latest, the beginning of the second quarter of 2002. In the meantime, the president was quietly acknowledging to Martinez that the tough economy might make it difficult for him to get much traction on some of his other agenda items.

"There's beginning to become an undercurrent in Washington that Bush was to blame, Bush's tax cuts were to blame for the deficit," the president later told me. "And therefore, it looked like we were going to fall into the old 'he's against Social Security; I'm for Social Security'—the old-style political game.

"I recognized the reality. And I was confident the facts would eventually bear us out—that the cause for the slowdown in revenues was not tax relief, but was, in fact, recession," he explained. "And that history would verify that. Because the tax relief part of the loss of revenue is minor compared to the economic slowdown. And then I was prepared to fully fight off criticism based upon the sound economic theory that a tax relief plan is good for actually restarting the economy."

But Bush realized if he spent all his time fighting off criticism, he would make no progress on another top priority—school reform. That's why he had made a point of leaving Washington that morning on a two-day trip to promote his education bill. The Republican-controlled House had passed the measure, but it was languishing in the Democrat-controlled Senate. To remedy the situation, the conservative president had struck up an unlikely alliance with Senator Ted Kennedy, a strident liberal who wanted the legislation as badly as Bush did. The Massachusetts Democrat was to hear testimony on the subject the next morning from Laura Bush, whose appearance was anticipated as something of a coming-out for a First Lady who until now had kept a low public profile. Confident in his wife's quiet charm and undaunted by the lukewarm reception to his own education speech that morning in Jacksonville, Bush had pressed on to

Sarasota intending to do it all over again the next morning at another elementary school.

At length, the dinner dishes were cleared away and the waiters began taking orders for dessert—baked Alaska. Bush insisted he couldn't possibly eat another bite, but then began poaching off other people's plates. Finally, he relented and ordered his own slice, which he consumed with obvious relish.

At 9 P.M., a White House photographer came in and began to snap pictures of the dinner party. All the guests passed their menus down to Bush for autographs. Then the president got up and walked into the main restaurant, where he spent another ten or fifteen minutes shaking hands and posing for pictures with waiters, busboys, hostesses, and other employees. Eventually he made his way back across the driveway and stepped into the now familiar green elevator.

"How was the food?" Kufahl asked as he flipped the switch.

"Very good," Bush answered.

So good, in fact, that the president had eaten too much of it. He had hoped to take a jog on the beach the next morning, but that region of the Gulf Coast had just been hit with an unusually nasty outbreak of red tide, a sudden bloom of algae that produces neurotoxins potent enough to kill enormous schools of fish. A day earlier, to the horror of Katie Klauber Moulton and her staff, thousands of dead fish had washed up on the Colony's 800-foot beach. Workers had spent the entire day hauling away tons of rotting fish carcasses that stank to high heaven. Bush, who could still smell a strong odor of fish in the air, decided against a jog on the beach. Anticipating just such a possibility, the Colony had turned one of the bedrooms in the president's suite—yes, there were two more bedrooms and another full bath on the second floor of the penthouse—into a mini-fitness center. That had entailed hauling out the twin beds and other furniture and lugging up a treadmill, which was so bulky that workmen had to remove the wrought-iron banisters in order to get the machine upstairs. But it was all for naught. Bush didn't feel like running on a treadmill in an air-conditioned bedroom. He wanted to get out and enjoy one of the last mornings of summer. He alerted his Secret Service detail that he would be jogging at a nearby golf course.

"Six o'clock we run," Bush said to one of the agents in the elevator.

"It's not light till 6:30," the agent protested.

"Then we run at 6:31," the president said.

As was his custom, Bush went to bed early. Snipers kept watch over the president from the roofs of the Colony and adjacent structures. The Coast Guard and the Longboat Key Police Department manned boats that patrolled the surf in front of the resort all night. Security trucks with enough men and arms to stop a small army parked right on the beach. An Airborne Warning and Control System (AWACS) plane circled high overhead in the clear night sky.

Bush stretched out on the bed once occupied by Gore. He fell asleep before his nightly mocking by Jay Leno on the *Tonight Show*.

"President Bush has called an emergency economic summit to deal with this recession," the comedian cracked. "Bush said he's really worried about job loss—yeah, his own."

The next morning, after lacing up a pair of white sneakers with black rubber soles, Bush headed for the elevator.

"Good morning," the president said to the elevator operator. "How we doin'?"

"Good morning," Kufahl replied. "We're doin' good."

"Were you up all night?" Bush inquired.

"No," Kufahl nodded. "I took a nap, too."

With little fanfare, the president hopped into his armor-plated limousine and headed for the Longboat Key Golf Club, which was two miles down Gulf of Mexico Drive. Bush traveled in an elaborate motorcade, which included everyone from Secret Service agents to the ubiquitous military aide who carried the "football"—a briefcase bulging with codes the president would need in the event he had to order a nuclear attack. Bringing up the rear of this long caravan of vehicles barreling down Gulf of Mexico Drive in the darkness were two vans containing a dozen members of the White House press corps. While many more journalists had accompanied Bush on this trip to Florida, only this small pool of reporters was required for such mundane tasks as coverage of a presidential jog. Each member of the larger group of journalists took his or her turn pulling pool duty, after which they would share any presidential news or atmospherics with the rest of the press corps, often in the form of irreverently written "pool reports."

These reports, almost always penned by a newspaper reporter, were e-mailed to White House press aide Rachael Sunbarger, who then electronically distributed them to the rest of the press. But she also sent copies to top White House officials, who eagerly perused them as unvarnished barometers of what the press really thought of POTUS, the acronym for President of the United States. These documents were especially insightful because they contained raw, unedited observations by journalists who were writing for their peers, not their newspaper editors or readers, and therefore expressed themselves more candidly. Because White House correspondents framed America's perceptions of the president, their unguarded reports were closely read by top administration officials, and, on occasion, the president himself. Bush had been irked by what he considered a particularly sarcastic pool report in July, when he paid a routine call on the House Republican caucus.

"Our protagonist departed the White House near unto 9:20 this morning, bound for the Capitol in a determined effort to find Gary Condit," began Dana Milbank of the *Washington Post*, who archly recounted Bush telling the pool, "We're going to get a lot of things done for America."

"The president and the caucus got so many things done for America so quickly that the hour-long meeting lasted only 45 minutes," the reporter wrote. "The big news of the day was made when our protagonist spoke about education. He declared that education 'is a passion for me.'"

Milbank called this a "startling revelation" from "our hero." He said Bush "controversially" called for a Patients' Bill of Rights that "honors patients."

The reporter deadpanned, "'We're 90 percent there,' quoth he."

Bush aides were livid. They felt Milbank, one of the most influential members of the press corps, had crossed the line by writing a snarky, condescending pool report that fairly dripped with contempt for the president. Unfazed, Milbank mischievously reacted to this criticism in his next pool report, which was written less than a month before the president's trip to Sarasota.

"The handsome armored presidential Chevrolet Suburban carrying our charge from the YMCA camp hurtled at 50 miles per hour through Estes Park and down the twisting mountain road. The motion set your pooler's stomach a-churning, but the twisting doubtless had no adverse impact on our POTUS, who has a constitution greater than your correspondent's."

With mock obsequiousness, Milbank called Bush "our maximum leader" and "the compassionate president." He lauded everything from "the president's good judgment" to his eyesight, which "is better than your pooler's."

"Your pooler hesitates to point out that the president was 25 minutes late," the reporter wrote. "Doubtless this was not the fault of our usually punctual POTUS."

Bush aides were astonished by such insolence, which seemed limitless.

"The president, in plaid workshirt, worked the crowd under the watchful but respectful eye of your representative," Milbank continued. "Running late, our charge shrewdly decided to go straight from the fundraiser to the ballpark."

Fortunately for Bush, such sarcasm would be missing from this morning's pool report, since Milbank had not accompanied him on the trip to Florida. In fact, this morning's pool contained one of the president's favorite reporters—Dick Keil of Bloomberg News Service. The tall, lanky, forty-year-old, who had been an All-American runner in college, was once invited to jog with Bush during the presidential campaign. But the deadline duties of a wire reporter interfered and Keil had to decline the offer. Now he hoped to get another chance. Last night, Keil's boss, David Morris, had run into White House Press Secretary Ari Fleischer at a Sarasota watering hole. Fleischer had alerted Morris that Bush might be running in the morning. Morris, on a lark, wondered aloud whether Bush might allow a certain Bloomberg reporter to accompany him. Fleischer thought for a moment and then replied that if a certain reporter were to show up in running clothes the next morning, there was a distinct possibility he would get to run with the president. Morris had relayed all this to Keil, who was now the only journalist in the press vans dressed in running shorts. Unfortunately, by the time the tail end of the motorcade rolled to a stop in front of the golf clubhouse at the Longboat Key Club's Islandside Course, Bush was already out of his limousine and running for all he was worth. Keil barely glimpsed the reflective heels of the president's sneakers before he disappeared into the gloom at 6:32 A.M. So the reporter schlepped his morning newspapers and coffee over to the edge of the golf course with the other journalists and waited for the president to finish his jog.

Bush was immediately glad he hadn't run on the bedroom treadmill or the smelly beach. The air here at the golf course was rich with the fragrance of bougainvillea and freshly cut Bermuda grass, which the grounds crew was already mowing to the persnickety height of 150 one-thousandths of an inch. Bush ran along gently meandering asphalt golf cart paths that were still wet from a predawn sprinkling, which made the smell of the cut grass all the more lush and invigorating.

"I vividly remember that run," he told me later. "I remember feeling great and feeling kind of purged because of the humidity."

But he added, "It was kind of dark."

It was so dark, in fact, that a Secret Service agent rode a bicycle in front of the president and shone a flashlight to illuminate the way. Another agent was already huffing and puffing as he ran ahead of Bush. Three more ran just to the rear. Behind them puttered a caravan of three electric golf carts, each carrying additional Secret Service agents in suits and ties who were armed to the teeth. A second cycling agent brought up the rear of this odd little presidential entourage.

The Longboat Key Club resort, along with its Islandside Golf Course, was part of a gated community that also included a dazzling array of luxury condos and beachfront villas. Bush could make out the lights of fabulous high-rises with French names like L'Ambiance and Pierre, where individual condos went for a cool $2 million. The price doubled in newer buildings like the Regent. But even that was chump change compared with the stupendous sums that were regularly shelled out for the ostentatious mansions in the shadows of the high-rises. There was one under construction right across from the golf course that had already set its owner back a whopping $20 million. Bush got an eyeful of this breathtaking opulence as he hustled up and down the little hills and crossed the picturesque footbridges that spanned the various ponds and canals of the golf course, earning it the clunky nickname "Watery Challenge."

The brackish water was not the only challenge to golfers on this course, who also had to contend with 1,700 cabbage palm trees that lined the fairways and were forever spoiling good shots. The groundskeepers had painstakingly landscaped the trees in beds of crushed white shells. The cost of trimming the picturesque palm fronds—solely for the benefit of aesthetically discerning golfers—was a staggering $28,000 a pop.

At the fifth tee, Bush hollered "good morning" to a maintenance worker hunched over an irrigation pipe. The man looked up and was dumbfounded to see the president of the United States breeze by.

The crickets were still chirping and the sky was just starting to morph from black to a deep royal blue when Bush circled back toward the clubhouse, where the press pool waited.

"Hey," called one of the reporters as Bush approached. The president's shirt, which said AUSTIN RACE FOR THE CURE, was soaked with sweat and plastered to his skin.

"Just warming up," Bush said. Without slowing down, he waved his arm at Keil and called, "C'mon, Stretch! C'mon!"

In a flash, the president had passed the pool, whose members exhorted the stunned Keil, "Go! Go!" The reporter managed to hand his coffee and newspapers to colleagues and dashed to catch up with the president, who was already heading to the front nine for another loop.

"C'mon, Stretch!" Bush called again over his right shoulder.

Approaching a fork in the golf cart path, the president ordered one of the cycling Secret Service agents to "keep going." The man started pedaling like mad, his gun clearly visible beneath his warm-up jacket.

"Run yet, Stretch?" Bush said to Keil, whose long legs had propelled him to the president's side in mere moments. Notorious for giving out nicknames, Bush had long ago chosen "Stretch" as the moniker for Keil, who was 6-feet-6-inches tall.

"No, sir," said Keil, whose eyes had not yet adjusted to the darkness. "How are you finding your way out here?"

"Oh, well, he's got a flashlight," Bush said, gesturing to the gun-toting cyclist up ahead. Actually, the agent had just switched it off because there was now enough ambient light for Bush to see the path. Every once in a while, the cyclist would call out "splits"—the distance they had covered and the time it had taken. Hours earlier, the Secret Service had carefully measured the route and marked various intervals with chalk so that Bush could keep track of his speed.

For a fifty-five-year-old man in the second half of an extremely brisk, four-mile run, Bush was astonishingly talkative. He told Keil his goal was someday to run three miles in under twenty-one minutes, or less than seven minutes per mile. Keil, who had never lost the accuracy of the internal clock he had developed in college, told Bush they were already running at a pace of seven minutes and fifteen to twenty seconds per mile. Judging by the lack of presidential wheezing during this high-speed, extended conversation—which would tax the lungs of lesser athletes—Keil assured Bush he would have no trouble reaching his goal.

"Are we going a little faster now?" the president said to the agent the next time a split was called.

"Yes, sir," the agent answered.

Dawn was beginning to break on this typically humid Florida day, with very little breeze. Bush was sweating profusely and enjoying every minute of it. The light was now revealing countless shades of lush green vegetation, punctuated here and there by brilliant flashes of hibiscus, daisies, oleander, crotons, and gardenias. The bougainvillea seemed to grow more fragrant with each footfall.

Somehow or other the men got talking about dogs, and Bush asked Keil whether he preferred big ones or little ones. The reporter said he didn't have any particular preference but happened to own a pug that he liked quite a bit. The pug was about Barney's size.

"Ever take him running?" Bush inquired.

"No," Keil said. "He always wants to go, but the vet says it wouldn't be good for him."

"Yeah, same thing with Barney," Bush said. "They're not built for that kind of thing."

The president, who fancied himself something of an arborist back on his ranch, puffed past century-old banyan trees—massive, gnarly things with countless secondary trunks that descended from branches and plunged into the earth among a tangle of lizard-covered roots. As he ran, he listened to the reporter talk about his nine-year-old son, Reid, who had made his Little League pitching debut the previous Sunday and struck out five of the six kids he faced. In the second inning—the kids were limited to two innings—Reid had finished the job with a mere eleven pitches.

"Really?" said Bush, who sixteen days earlier had become the first president inducted into the Little League Hall of Fame. "That's a proud moment for a papa."

Bush genuinely like Keil, a quiet, intense reporter who wasn't afraid to respectfully question the most powerful man in the world. The president shared his thoughts on the worsening economy, although he expressed confidence he had figured out a way to manage it. Bush was upbeat, even chipper, as he sketched out the political realities that awaited him back in Washington. He acknowledged that Congress would reject some of his policies and defeat legislation he supported, but he was convinced that even these failures could redound to the advantage of Republicans. By the end of the run, Keil, who agreed to keep the specifics of the conversation off the record, was struck by the new president's mastery of so many subjects, including one of particular importance—how the political game was played in Washington.

Bush stopped running when he crossed the final chalk line, several hundred yards shy of the clubhouse. A Secret Service agent in a golf cart brought him and Keil plastic bottles of water as they cooled down on the walk back.

"The representative of the press corps acquitted himself quite well," Bush announced as he approached the pool.

"I was beggin' for mercy out there," Keil said modestly.

"Thank you, Stretch," the president said with a deferential gesture to the towering journalist, who beamed appreciatively.

"How far'd you go, altogether?" asked Scott Lindlaw of the Associated Press. At mundane events like presidential jogs, it was customary for the press to refrain from hard-hitting questions in lieu of lighthearted banter. At least that's how these conversations usually started out.

"About four and a half," Bush said.

"Four and a half *miles*?" said Lindlaw, evidently making sure the president hadn't suddenly begun measuring his jogs in kilometers.

"I think so," said Bush, motioning to Keil for confirmation. The president bowed his head distractedly and scratched his scalp as he continued walking.

"It was a very solid, 7:15-, 7:20-a-mile pace," Keil reported.

"Was that more than usual?" asked Steve Holland of Reuters. The reporters were trying to lull Bush into a friendly, casual conversation, whereupon they might get him to actually commit news.

"Well, he spurred me on to new heights," said the president, finally stopping. He added playfully, "I knew he'd come back and brief you all, so—"

"He held his pace from the moment we left," Keil said, as if to assure Bush this was the only briefing the reporters would get.

"Thank you, Stretch," said the president as he began to make his getaway.

Bush was well aware that these friendly chats could turn treacherous. During a similar encounter on a golf course five weeks earlier, Francine Kiefer of the *Christian Science Monitor* repeatedly asked him if he was "taking any naps in the afternoon." Bush saw it as an attempt to perpetuate the widely reported story that he was spending too much time vacationing on his Texas ranch. *USA Today* had even commissioned a poll showing that 55 percent of Americans believed the four-week break was too long. The president knew that if he acknowledged taking even an occasional nap, the press would have a field day. So he refused to rise to the bait. Instead of answering the question, Bush suggested the elitist press resented having to cover his working vacation. "I know a lot of you wish you were on the East Coast, lounging on the beaches, sucking in the salt air," he told the reporters. "But I'm getting a lot done and it's good to be on my ranch. It's good to be home."

Hoping to avoid a repeat of that exchange, Bush decided to wrap up his visit to the Longboat Key Golf Club quickly. The reporters sensed their opportunity for news was slipping away.

Lindlaw gamely jumped in. "Can we talk about tax cuts?"

"Not right now," said Bush, smiling and putting his hand up in the gesture that politely says: Back off. "You can talk about it at the next event."

"Very good," said Lindlaw, backing off.

"Okay," chimed in Holland, the picture of reasonableness.

Bush then turned around and stopped again, causing the sweat-soaked Secret Service agent who had been walking fifteen feet in front of him to stop as well. Three agents in suits were also nearby, silently waiting for the maximum leader to terminate this bull session with the Fourth Estate. The president stood there with a mischievous smile playing across his face, as if debating whether to continue his trademark ironic banter with the press. A full three beats elapsed.

"I may talk about it, too," he finally said. "I haven't made up my mind yet."

He added, a bit more seriously, "I am gonna talk about education, though."

"Any news?" said Lindlaw, abandoning the pretense of cozy questions.

"On education?" Bush said, stalling for time.

"Yeah."

Bush nodded his head, adding cryptically, "Pay attention."

"Always."

"Only facts; no opinions," said Bush, now in full stride to the motorcade. Then to Keil, "Stretch, thank you. I appreciate it."

"Thanks, Mr. President."

The phalanx of Secret Service agents fell in around Bush, who took a swig from his water bottle as he headed toward the limo. The military aide with the football followed close at his heels. One of the sweaty agents opened the car door and relinquished it to an even sweatier agent, who held it for the commander in chief—the sweatiest of them all. Bush settled back in the blue leather upholstery and the agent closed the door with a heavy metallic *clunk*.

Back at the Colony, Bush dined on fresh berries and fruit juices. While he had no compunction about eating fatty foods for dinner, he tried to keep breakfast as healthy as possible. He hit the three-headed shower and got dressed for the day. The president put on a pale blue shirt, a crimson monochrome tie, and a charcoal, two-button wool suit of the sort worn by reserved American business executives. Bush was not considered a dapper dresser. He shunned the trendy, three-button suits favored by Gore. He avoided the fancy French cuffs preferred by Clinton. He didn't care for the pronounced pinstripes that had looked so robust on Ronald Reagan. In fact, Bush wouldn't be caught dead in anything so daring as a double-breasted suit or a jacket with pointed lapels or absolutely any garment that looked remotely European. Even a handkerchief peeking out of a breast pocket was too flashy for this corporate-bred Texan, who preferred plain, muted garments that, if anything, were not very memorable.

For the next hour, Bush met with a stream of advisors in his penthouse suite. He received his usual CIA briefing, although he would have to wait until the next day to receive a special briefing that his staff had just completed on how to dismantle the al Qaeda terrorist network, headed by Osama bin Laden in Afghanistan. As he prepared for his education speech in the penthouse suite, Bush also received informal updates on overnight political developments. He was given a thick sheaf of articles, columns, and editorials that had been reprinted from the morning newspapers, including the *Washington Times*, the *Los Angeles Times*, *USA Today*, and the *Washington Post*.

For the fourth day in a row, the "darkening economic outlook" was the top story in the *New York Times*. "Pressure mounted on President Bush to drop his cautious approach to dealing with the weakening economy," the story intoned. The paper's lead editorial, in describing the GOP's handling of the economy, opined, "There is a whiff of panic in the air." A front-page headline in the *Washington Post* warned, "Poll Finds Public Wary on Tax Cut: Majority Hold Bush Responsible for Dwindling Budget Surplus." The front page also hammered the White House on two favorite Democratic themes—arsenic levels in drinking water and a dearth of human stem cells for medical research.

By 8:30 A.M., the presidential advisors had cleared out of the sumptuous penthouse. Bush headed for one last trip down the elevator, accompanied by several sharpshooters who had just descended from the roof.

"What do these fellas do?" Kufahl asked.

"They help protect me," Bush said.

"Were they up there all night?" persisted the maintenance man, no longer cowed by the power of the presidency.

"Yeah," Bush said.

Then, remarking on the red tide, which still stank up the place, Kufahl said, "Mr. President, do you think you're ever gonna eat fish again?"

"My friend, *none of us* are ever gonna eat fish again," Bush said with a twinkle.

Spotting a White House photographer as he stepped out of the elevator, Bush told Kufahl, "C'mon, get your picture taken."

The photographer snapped a shot of Kufahl with the president and promised to send a print to the Colony later. But Kufahl wanted another photo with his own camera, which he pulled from his pocket in slow motion so the Secret Service wouldn't mistake it for a weapon.

"Can you take my picture?" Kufahl asked.

"I can't," said the photographer, who often got such requests.

"Take his picture," Bush growled good-naturedly, whereupon the White House photographer hopped to it.

After much shaking of hands and posing for pictures and saying pleasant things to local VIPs who had been invited to the Colony to see him off, Bush clambered into his Cadillac limousine, which set off for the city of Sarasota at 8:39 A.M.

When Gore's motorcade had passed through the city less than a year ago, local police shut down traffic along the route, but only the lanes in which Gore was traveling. The police did not consider a vice president important enough to merit blocking traffic from oncoming lanes. But now that a full-fledged president was in town, the police shut down traffic in both directions, leaving the roads utterly deserted for Bush's long motorcade, which barreled along at 40 mph, running red lights with impunity.

This particular motorcade was longer than usual, because all the local police agencies wanted in on the act. Taking the lead were two Florida Highway Patrol cruisers with flashing blue lights on top. Then came a decoy limousine, followed by the real McCoy. Both were long and black and adorned on the sides with discreet presidential seals. Each had a small American flag mounted on one front corner of the hood, and a blue presidential flag on the other. The president's limo was newer, more modern, with heavier cladding around the blue-tinted windows. Five small black antennae sprouted from the lid of the trunk in order to give Bush the best mobile communications money could buy. Behind the presidential limo was a black Chevy

Suburban, its backseat windows open so that Secret Service agents could rest their arms on the outside edge of the doors, the better to spring into action should the need arise. Another agent sat in the back with the glass hatchback open. Next came another Suburban full of agents, a dark minivan with the football-toting military aide, a long line of vans filled with all manner of White House functionaries, and at the end, the press pool. Bringing up the rear were row after row of local motorcycle cops, riding two and three abreast.

In fact, the motorcade was so long that Bush was already well on his way down Gulf of Mexico Drive by the time the tail end of the caravan snaked its way out of the Colony's parking lot. The president settled back for the brief, nine-mile ride, which would take him from the richest and whitest part of Sarasota County to the poorest and blackest. He passed the Longboat Key Club and the golf course where he had been jogging just two hours earlier. He traversed a short bridge that took him to Lido Key, home of the Mote Marine Laboratory, a marine-research facility. That's where Gore had practiced for the debates against Bush, standing in an auditorium beneath a fiberglass shark that he adopted as sort of a debate mascot. Not that it did him much good.

"Manatee zone," read the sign on a short causeway that took Bush to yet another island, this one called St. Armands Key. He entered St. Armands Circle, a palm-studded roundabout wreathed by upscale shops. The motorcade was so long that it arced around nearly three-quarters of the circle before turning onto John Ringling Boulevard, built by the "Circus King" who moved the winter quarters of the Ringling Bros. and Barnum & Bailey Circus to Sarasota from Bridgeport, Connecticut, in 1927. Another short causeway and the president was on Coon Key, the smallest of the five interconnected islands on this glorious morning jaunt. Palm trees rose up from the grassy median and lined both sides of the road. After passing a posh retirement home and the Sarasota Yacht Club, Bush approached a bridge to the final island, Bird Key, and could already see the Sarasota skyline looming in the distance.

It was 8:46 A.M. when the president headed for that last stretch of causeway that had been built with timbers hauled by circus elephants three-quarters of a century earlier. Sailboats lined Sarasota Bay on the left and right, a brilliant blue sky arced overhead, and the shimmering office towers of the city rose up in the distance. What could possibly go wrong on a day such as this?

Crossing over to the mainland, the motorcade turned left on North Tamiani Trail and then immediately cut east on Third Street, which took Bush through a portion of downtown. A few dozen protesters lined the street, some of whom waved banners that demanded, "No Offshore Drilling." This was a reference to the president's recent decision to allow limited drilling off Florida's coast—a compromise he hammered out with Jeb, who had wanted all drilling banned.

The motorcade turned north on Washington Boulevard, which took Bush through the seedier part of town, past the tattoo parlors, liquor stores, adult boutiques, bail bondsmen, and pawnshops, including one called Presidential Pawn. The procession of cars continued until it reached what police considered the worst street in the county, Martin Luther King Jr. Way, where the elementary school was located. To the president's left was a vacant lot that served as a hangout for young black toughs dressed in the ghetto garb of the day— sleeveless "wife beater" undershirts, low-slung shorts with absurdly drooping crotches, enormous rubber sneakers, and jet black do-rags tied tightly across their crania. The edge of the lot was jammed with hulking, rusting pimpmobiles—Lincolns, Caddys, Buicks—as big and lumbering as ocean liners. Some of the young men zigzagged idly down the street on stripped-down bicycles. Their expressions ranged from supreme boredom to pure menace. For block after block to the west, drug dealers infested this street named after America's most revered civil rights leader. Iron bars were bolted over the doors and windows of squat, ramshackle apartments, beer-and-wine stores, Tex-Mex food joints, check-cashing cages, and blighted urban churches.

Bush did not have to run the worst of this gauntlet. In fact, the reason the motorcade had jogged over to Washington Boulevard instead of staying north on Tamiani was to avoid the most crime-infested portion of Martin Luther King, which stretched out to the president's immediate left. The motorcade turned right for the final blocks of the journey, which were not exactly scenic either. Another knot of protesters appeared near a beer-and-wine grocery. One held a sign that read, "Got Arsenic?" Another placard said, "Counting votes is elementary," a reminder that some still bitterly clung to the belief that Gore would have won the election if only all the votes had been counted. As if Bush needed another reminder.

At 8:55 A.M., the president arrived at Emma E. Booker Elementary School, named for an early black Sarasota educator. It was the most modern and well-maintained building on Martin Luther King Jr. Way. The limousine pulled past the main portico and then backed into a sheltered space that separated the administration side of the building from the classrooms. As Secret Service agents scrambled out of the Suburbans and the military aide with the football hustled out of the minivan to catch up, Bush stepped from his limousine.

"We're on time—I like to stay on time; I like to be crisp," he told me later. "I'm heading into the event and somebody is whispering in my ear."

He was referring to his personal assistant, Blake Gottesman, who was giving the president some final stage directions.

"'Here's what you're going to be doing; you're going to meet so-and-so, such-and-such,'" Bush recalled being told. "And Andy Card says, 'By the way, an aircraft flew into the World Trade Center.'"

"And my first reaction was—as an old pilot—how could the guy have gotten so off course to hit the towers? What a terrible accident that is. The first report I heard was a light airplane, twin-engine airplane."

The president was told that National Security Advisor Condoleezza Rice was at the White House, waiting to talk with him on a secure phone line that had been installed in a holding room just off the school's portico. Standing outside the door to that room was the school principal, a black woman named Gwendolyn Tosé-Rigell, who now greeted Bush. But before she could introduce him to the five dignitaries who were lined up next to her, the president explained that he needed to take an urgent phone call. He excused himself and disappeared into the adjacent room, which had been secured by the White House advance team. Bush picked up the phone and talked with Rice, who was sitting in her office in the West Wing, watching live television coverage of the stricken building belch black smoke into a cloudless sky.

"There's one terrible pilot," Bush muttered.

Turning to Card, the president speculated that the pilot must have suffered a heart attack. How else does one crash into the tallest building in New York without a single cloud to obstruct the view? Not that Bush had actually seen images of the burning building yet—there was no TV in the room. But he figured that even a small plane could cause significant damage. Some lives had undoubtedly been lost on impact and fire probably now endangered many others. Bush would need to reassure the public as soon as possible. He decided to pledge the full resources of the government, including the Federal Emergency Management Agency, to cope with the disaster. Since his speech on education was still thirty minutes away, the president would comment on the accident at the conclusion of a second-grade reading drill, which was scheduled to begin momentarily. He and his aides hammered out a statement that would form the basis of his answer to the inevitable question from the journalists, who were already waiting in the classroom.

Bush went back out to the portico and apologized again to Gwendolyn Tosé-Rigell. She was a Democrat who had voted for Gore and privately considered Bush a "phony." Still, her school had been chosen for a presidential visit, which was a great honor—regardless of whether it happened to be a president she supported. So she smiled and began the introductions. There was Booker Teacher of the Year Edwina Oliver; Florida Lieutenant Governor Frank Brogan; Sarasota County School Superintendent Wilma Hamilton; the retiring congressman Dan Miller; and a red-haired, fresh-faced kid in a suit who looked like a teenage White House intern. In fact, he was Representative Adam Putnam, twenty-six, of nearby Bartow, Florida, the youngest member of the 107th Congress. When Bush finished shaking all these hands, he went back inside the holding room, this time accompanied by Tosé-Rigell. She led him past the presidential advisors, who were still trying to nail down more information about the plane crash, and approached a door at the other end of the room, which led to the second-grade class of Sandra Kay Daniels. The teacher was seated up by the chalkboard, facing sixteen uniformed children, mostly black. They all craned around for a glimpse of the usually punctual president, who was two minutes late for this 9 A.M. appointment.

"Good morning, boys and girls," said Tosé-Rigell as she entered the room from the left side. She was followed by Bush. The president's appearance set off a flurry of snapping and clicking from the cameras of the press pool, who were crammed behind some low tables at the back of the room. *Ksht, ksht, ksht, ksht!*

"Good morning, Mrs. Rigell," Daniels said in the sort of singsongy voice a teacher uses when she wants her students to follow suit. But all they could manage was, "Good morning."

"Mornin'," Bush said affably as he approached the front of the class.

"I have brought with you to meet—me—the most wonderful guest," began Tosé-Rigell, already tongue-tied by the proximity of such power. "Would you please stand and recognize the president of the United States—President Bush."

"Good morning," Bush said again.

"Good morning," said the children, even less unified for this second salutation.

They stood up, and the president shook the hand of a little girl directly in front of him.

"How are you?" he said. Gesturing to a black man in a blue suit who had followed him into the room, he added, "I'd also like you to meet the Secretary of Education—"

"Hello, boys and girls," Rod Paige said mildly, his hands crossed in front of him as he took his position at the side of the room. The girl who had just shaken Bush's hand waved at Paige.

"—and the lieutenant governor of Florida," said Bush, motioning to Brogan.

"We met, didn't we?" Brogan said to the class in a cheery voice as he took his post next to Paige.

"Yeah," a few of the children murmured.

"Good to meet you all," said Bush, who turned to Daniels and added, "Hi." He walked toward her with his right hand extended.

Beep, beep, beep, beep! A pager or cell phone went off in the back of the room. This was a major pet peeve of the president's, who was known to stare daggers at any journalists who failed to switch their cell phones and beepers to the silent "vibrate" mode in his presence. The offender quickly quieted the device.

"And this is Mrs. Daniels," Tosé-Rigell said belatedly.

Bush crossed in front of the principal and shook hands with Daniels, a black, bespectacled woman with a dazzling smile.

"Hi, Ms. Daniels, how are you?" he said, putting his left arm around her and facing the class as if posing for a photo. "Great to meet everybody."

"Eric," said a hushed voice from the back of room, "what're ya doin'?"

It was the press pool again. One of the cameramen was upset at a soundman named Eric, whose boom microphone had dipped into the camera shot.

Bush, who was accustomed to the rustlings and jostlings and rootings of the noisy journalists who shadowed him everywhere, ignored this latest outburst. Instead he looked at one of the kids, who was saying something to him in a soft voice. Bush shrugged at the child and said, "Yeah, I know it."

"Eric!" the voice hissed. This time it was loud enough to cause both Bush and Daniels to shift their gaze to the rear of the room, although they didn't allow the distraction to break their smiles. The president glanced at the pool as if it were the repository of particularly unruly students.

"Good to meet you all," Bush said to the children as he stepped away from Daniels.

The president noticed a little girl over to his left, in the front row, whose face was frozen with fear. He stopped, cocked his head, and drew back in a playful half-crouch.

"You okay?" he said with a reassuring smile.

The petrified child nodded.

"That's good," Bush chuckled. This seemed to break the ice and the entire room let out a relieved laugh. After a pause of several seconds, the president looked at Daniels expectantly. "Well? Shall we—?"

"We shall begin," Daniels said absently.

"Sit down, please," Bush instructed the children as he pulled up a maroon chair that rolled on plastic casters. The president had learned long ago that if he didn't take charge in situations like this, he would be hanging around all day.

"Thank you for standing up. Good to meet you all," said Bush, clasping his hands and rolling forward a few inches. "It's really exciting for me to be here. I want to thank Ms. Daniels for being a teacher. I want to thank Gwen for being a principal."

Mindful of his propensity to trip over his own tongue, Bush was not about to attempt the name Tosé-Rigell, although he felt safe enough with Daniels.

"And I want to thank you all for practicing reading so much," he added. "It's really important."

He then gave Daniels another expectant look, as if to say, "Well, take it away." He had been in the room for just under a minute, but that didn't change the fact that he had a schedule to keep.

"And this morning we do have a lesson that we've been preparing for you," Daniels managed.

"Good," Bush said, pleased that they were finally getting down to brass tacks. It was 9:03 A.M.

"And it's lesson 60 of our SRA reading book," she said, referring to a phonics-heavy instructional guide that was also used in the Houston School District, where Paige had been superintendent before Bush tapped him for education secretary.

"I know very well where that came from," Bush said, prompting an audible chuckle from Paige.

"Are you ready, my butterflies?" said Daniels, suddenly coming to life.

"Yes," they answered, this time in unison. The shock of having the president in their midst was already beginning to fade.

Slam! Someone at the back of the room had dropped something heavy on the floor, causing a student to look back at the press pool.

"Eyes on me—one, two, three," Daniels called out. "Get ready to read all the words on this page without making a mistake."

She gestured to a flip chart of words on a pink easel. One of the boys prematurely read the word "park," which Bush found terribly amusing. He grinned from ear to ear.

"Read this word the fast way," Daniels said. "Get ready."

"Park," the children said.

"Yes, park. What do these two letters say?"

"Ar."

"Yes, ar. Sound it out. Get ready."

"Ar."

"What word?"

"Park."

"Yes, park. What do these two letters say?"

"Ba."

"Yes, ba. Read this word the fast way. Get ready."

"Ball."

"Yes, ball. What do these two letters say?"

Bush marveled at the scene before him. Daniels was a gentle, pleasant woman, but now that she was immersed in the act of teaching, she took on the efficiency of a drill instructor. Over and over, in a rapid-fire voice, she commanded the students to sound out words "the fast way." The children responded like grunts in boot camp, calling out the answers in clear, loud, unified voices. The president's rapt gaze bounced from teacher to students and back again. After all those years of teacher's unions pushing the "whole language" method of learning—large doses of trial and error mixed with even larger doses of vague talk about a child's "inner motivation"—the pendulum had finally swung back to good old-fashioned phonics. The truth of the matter was that reading test scores had dropped so precipitously that the unions could no longer defend the "whole language" method. Bush was delighted to see these children learn to read the same way he had learned back in Texas—by sounding out the individual components of words.

"Remember what you say when there's an E at the end of the word," Daniels said. "Get ready."

"Cane."

"Yes, cane. Get ready."

"Can."

"Yes, can. Get ready."

"Made."

"Yes, made," the teacher said. "Give yourselves a pat on the back."

"Yeah!" Bush called out approvingly, clapping his hands together. This triggered chuckles from the adults in the room, although the children remained quiet. That was another thing about being president—the lamest utterance imaginable was always treated as some profound witticism.

Soon Daniels was off to the races again, drilling the kids for all they were worth. The president was utterly transfixed, smiling as if he were about to burst with happiness. Education! His top domestic priority! The economy would just have to wait a few more minutes. And, of course, there was that statement he needed to make about the plane crash.

"I was concentrating on the program at this point, thinking about what I was going to say," Bush told me later. "Obviously, I felt it was an accident. I was concerned about it, but there were no alarm bells."

"Get ready to read all these words on this page without making a mistake," Daniels said. "Look at the letter at the end and remember the sound it makes. Get ready."

"Kite."

"Yes, kite. Get ready to read this word the fast way. Get ready."

"Kit."

"Yes, kit."

As Daniels said the word "kit," Bush heard a noise behind him. It was the sound of a door closing—the door through which the president had entered the room. Someone must have just walked in, although Bush didn't bother looking around. His eyes were still pinned on the reading drill.

"Sound it out," Daniels commanded. "Get ready."

"Kit," the children mumbled.

"Sound it out," repeated Daniels, unsatisfied. "Get ready."

"Kit," they said, still a little weakly.

"What word?"

"Kit!" they practically shouted.

"Yes, kit. Boys and girls, sound this word out. Get ready."

"S-t-ea-l."

"What word?"

"Steal."

"Yes, steal. Read these words the fast way. Get ready."

"Playing."

"Yes, playing. Get ready."

"Must."

"Yes, must," said Daniels, concluding the first half of the lesson. "Boys and girls, pick your reader up from under your seat."

The children bent down to retrieve their textbooks, which were lying on the floor. Through his peripheral vision, Bush noticed someone taking advantage of this pause to approach him. He swiveled slightly in his chair and was surprised to discover it was Card, who had not even been in the room when the president entered. Now he was walking right up to him in the middle of a public event. This was highly unusual. Didn't Card realize the cameras of the national press corps were capturing this breach of protocol? Sure enough, the shutters came clattering to life. *Ksht, ksht, ksht!* The press was suddenly on high alert, obviously stimulated by this departure from the day's carefully choreographed stage directions.

"Open your book up to lesson 60 on page 153," said Daniels, oblivious to the curious little drama being played out in her classroom at 9:07 A.M.

Now Card was leaning over to whisper something in Bush's ear. The president cocked his head to listen. The shutters went into extended spasms, clicking and whirring like mad. *Ksht, ksht, ksht, ksht!* The children blithely flipped through their books for the correct page. Bush didn't pick up the copy of the book that had been placed on the easel for him. He was no longer engrossed in the reading drill. His smile had vanished.

Card drew closer. The pages flipped. The cameras clicked. *Ksht, ksht, ksht, ksht, ksht!* The press was drinking it all in. The chief of staff's mouth was mere inches from the president's right ear. The tops of their heads were practically touching. Card opened his lips to speak. Bush strained to hear. This had better be good. The spasms rose....

Ksht, ksht, ksht, ksht, ksht, ksht, ksht, ksht, ksht, ksht, ksht!

Chapter Two

"In Over His Head!"

STANLEY GREENBERG WAS IN his element. Armed with a sheaf of fresh polling data and surrounded by a scrum of newspaper reporters who were scarfing down a free breakfast, the Democratic pollster painted a gloomy picture indeed for one George W. Bush.

"...and that is the context in which people are turning away from the president," Greenberg was saying. "It is very striking, the pullback from the tax cut. Fifty-four percent of the people in this poll said they got the tax cut. And yet what you see is now 45 percent of the country oppose the tax cut...."

Greenberg was in full number-crunching mode, feverishly pontificating on the statistical nuances of his latest poll for Democracy Corps, an organization that, according to its web site, was "born out of outrage over the impeachment of President Clinton." That outrage only intensified when Greenberg's former boss, Al Gore, lost the 2000 election. As its web site bitterly explained, "Democracy Corps rededicated itself after the presidential candidate with the most votes and the most popular policy agenda did not become the President of the United States." The angry white males who had founded and now

constituted Democracy Corps were Greenberg, Democratic consul-
tant Bob Shrum, and former Clinton strategist James Carville.
Together, they were the most formidable cabal of partisan Democratic firepower in American politics.

"—so we're moving toward a budget debate in which I think the
president and Republicans have a lot of difficulties," Greenberg said,
finally coming up for air.

Seizing on this pause, a reporter began to ask Greenberg a question. But Godfrey "Budge" Sperling, an eighty-six-year-old columnist
for the *Christian Science Monitor,* cut him off. He had been hosting
these breakfast meetings for thirty-five years. The Sperling Breakfast
had become something of a Washington institution since it began on
February 8, 1966. It was also something of an insult to television
reporters, who were expressly barred from attending. Only print
reporters—those who worked for newspapers or magazines—were
ever invited to a Sperling Breakfast. In the world of the Washington
press corps, print reporters considered themselves—how to put this—
a bit more serious, a shade more reflective, a tad more thoughtful than
their counterparts in the broadcast world. They fancied themselves a
collection of noble, rumpled, ink-stained wordsmiths who, when you
got right down to it, were just plain smarter than the blow-dried airheads who regularly resorted to verbal food fights on TV. Naturally,
no one in the press corps would come right out and say such a thing.
But every journalist inside the Beltway knew it to be true. It was also
true that while print reporters looked down on broadcast reporters
from an intellectual standpoint, they ached with envy and resentment
over the fabulous salaries hauled in by the TV types. Some of these
airheads made seven-figure salaries, while most of the ink-stained
wretches remained hopelessly mired in the five-figure range. It was
nothing less than a travesty.

Such were the vanities and resentments that oozed up and down the media food chain. But they were never discussed at the Sperling Breakfast, a high-minded affair that generally stuck to public policy and presidential politics. In fact, over the years, Sperling had landed some pretty big political names at his breakfast table. In 1968, Robert F. Kennedy began a Sperling Breakfast by insisting he would not run for president. By the time the meal ended, however, the eleven reporters who had been grilling Kennedy came away convinced he didn't mean it. At another Sperling Breakfast, Republican strategist Ed Rollins bragged he had passed out $500,000 in "walking-around money" to suppress the black vote in New Jersey and help put Christie Todd Whitman in the governor's mansion. He later said he fabricated the whole thing in a "sin of arrogance." At still another Sperling Breakfast, House Speaker Newt Gingrich famously complained that President Clinton had made him board Air Force One through a rear door and sit in the aft of the plane. Some believe that complaint, which the press portrayed as petty, was the beginning of Gingrich's fall from power.

But perhaps the most infamous Sperling Breakfast of them all occurred in September 1991, when Arkansas Governor Bill Clinton tried preemptively to neutralize the "womanizing" issue. Clinton wanted to run for president, but only if he could avoid the fate of Gary Hart, who dropped out of the 1988 race after he was caught lying to the press about his "Monkey Business" affair with Donna Rice. So Clinton dragged his wife, Hillary, to the Sperling Breakfast, where he told Budge and the other print journalists that while he had experienced "problems" in his marriage, he had most definitely turned over a new leaf. The reporters didn't seem terribly exercised about the whole thing, so Clinton took that as a green light to press ahead with his presidential bid.

Ten years had passed since that fateful meeting, and now Sperling was coming to the end of his long run as host of the breakfasts that bore his name. In fact, today's breakfast with Greenberg, Shrum, and Carville would be one of his last. After hosting more than 3,200 of the get-togethers over three and a half decades, he would turn the institution over to a younger journalist at the *Christian Science Monitor* at the end of the year. Of course, everyone emphasized that Sperling would continue to attend these breakfasts. But it just wouldn't be the same without him as the moderator, gently guiding the discussion as reporters and pols wolfed down scrambled eggs, home fries, sausage, and bacon. The food was packed with so much cholesterol it should have been served with a rib-spreader. Sperling interrupted the reporter who was trying to pose a question to Greenberg just after the tender hour of 8 A.M. on Tuesday, September 11.

"Stan, um—" the reporter began.

Sperling jumped in and directed the room's attention instead to Carville. The "Ragin' Cajun" had shown up late and taken his seat while Greenberg was speaking. Carville and Greenberg may have been equal partners in Democracy Corps, but in the world of Washington journalism, Carville's star power rendered poor Greenberg practically invisible.

"James, you got anything you want to say?" Sperling offered.

"Yeah, I'm for the sales tax for transportation in northern Virginia," Carville said.

The reporters chuckled at this reference to the traffic gridlock that paralyzed Washington and its suburbs every morning.

"Tax-raising Democrat!" the jovial Shrum trumpeted in a tone of mock accusation.

Another round of good-natured laughter filled the Mount Vernon Room in the basement of the St. Regis Hotel on Sixteenth Street, just two blocks from the White House. When the merriment died down, the reporter was finally allowed to pose his question to Greenberg. He wanted to know why Democracy Corps was needed in the first place.

"What are the Democratic institutions that you found timid and therefore of necessity to form this organization?" he said. "Is it Congress you're talking about?"

Greenberg explained that Democracy Corps was formed at a time when "you had the White House under challenge in the impeachment process. And you had the Democrats in Congress trying to deal with it. We thought there was an opportunity for Democrats to use the impeachment issue. We had lots of evidence that that was true. But it was late in that election. We advised some candidates who did use it successfully."

But not enough Democrats were wielding impeachment as a political weapon, according to Greenberg, Shrum, and Carville, who decided to take matters into their own hands.

"So we thought, independent of both the White House and the Congress, to press the issue," Greenberg continued. "We paid for the organization ourselves and then we institutionalized ourselves and have gotten ourselves funded."

"But you're not currently expressing dissatisfaction with the Democratic leadership—" the reporter began again.

"No," said Greenberg.

"No," said Shrum.

"No," said Carville.

"—of Congress or the DNC?" he added. The Democratic National Committee was headed by Clinton's best friend, Terry McAuliffe.

"No, no, no," Greenberg insisted. "All I'm saying is what we believe is there's a need for an organization like ourselves, which is independent of everybody. We can say whatever we think on these questions and press the Democrats to take the most advantage. We're not locked into a short-term battle in 2002, which Congress needs to be. We're not working for a particular presidential candidate of 2004—well, James certainly won't be. And so we can speak quite freely."

After a pause, he added, "This is not a hard time, by the way, to talk freely if you're a Democrat. It's not like you look at the polls and say, 'Oh my goodness, what am I gonna come speak about next?'"

Truth be told, there had never been a time in Greenberg's career when he had trouble coming up with things to speak about, especially after conducting one of his polls. And Greenberg had been taking polls ever since the mid-1960s, back when he was a member of the Young Democrats at Miami University in Ohio, where he wrote screeds in the student newspaper against the "White Christian Republic." His first poll—on whether women, like men, should be allowed to live off campus—was enough to get Greenberg hooked. After graduation, he landed a polling gig with Bobby Kennedy's presidential campaign. And yet, as a liberal intellectual, Greenberg always felt embarrassed about his status as a lowly political pollster. He eventually abandoned it to immerse himself in the Ivy League, picking up a doctorate from Harvard and teaching Marxist theory at Yale. But the lure of polling and the tantalizing possibility of playing a small role in political history was simply too intoxicating.

In 1980, Greenberg chucked academia and set up a polling firm in his basement—just in time to witness the Reagan Revolution. Ironically, it was Reagan's landslide rout of Democrats in 1984 that put Greenberg on the path toward national prominence. He was hired by the Michigan Democratic Party and the United Auto Workers to find out why the Detroit suburbs of Macomb County had voted 2-to-1 for Reagan after decades of solidly supporting Democrats. Countless polls and focus groups later, Greenberg discovered what Reagan, himself a former Democrat, had instinctively known all along: that middle-class voters felt abandoned by the Democratic Party, which was cheerfully giving away their hard-earned tax dollars to ethnic minorities and special interest groups. Greenberg realized that if liberals wanted to take back the White House, they would have to hitch their wagon to a "New Democrat," which is why he gravitated toward Arkansas Governor Bill Clinton in the late 1980s.

The Clinton experience was not altogether pleasant for the idealistic pollster. In February 1992, when New Hampshire voters learned of Clinton's draft dodging and affair with Gennifer Flowers, Greenberg watched the campaign's numbers collapse. He broke the bad news to his boss with a single word: "Meltdown." But he and the rest of the "war room" somehow managed to save the candidate's hide, a feat they went on to repeat countless times during Clinton's first two years in the White House. During those heady, preimpeachment days, Greenberg could afford to look back on the Gennifer Flowers scandal and laugh. Greenberg's wife, Democratic Congresswoman Rosa DeLauro of Connecticut, even gave him a large neon sculpture proclaiming, MELTDOWN. Greenberg displayed it with self-referential pride in the couple's D.C. townhouse. And why shouldn't he? After all, he, Stanley Greenberg, had risen from a middle-class neighborhood and the lowly public school system right there in Washington to become the powerful, poll-taking Svengali of the Clinton White House.

But after Democrats took a shellacking in the midterm elections of 1994, Clinton fired Greenberg, deciding his old friend lacked decisiveness. He was replaced by the decidedly more decisive Dick Morris, who ended up conducting another crucial "bimbo poll"—this one to see whether Clinton should lie about Monica Lewinsky. The ignominy of it all! Greenberg was reduced to polling for foreign liberals who wanted a touch of the old Clinton magic—Nelson Mandela of South Africa, Tony Blair of Britain, Gerhard Schroeder of Germany, Ehud Barak of Israel. He finally got a shot at redemption in 2000, when he was hired as chief pollster for Al Gore's presidential campaign. But alas, that too ended in wrenching, heartbreaking, infuriating defeat. Which was why Greenberg, fifty-six, was down here in the Mount Vernon room, answering questions from a gaggle of rumpled reporters, instead of down the street at his rightful place in the Oval Office, helping shape history.

Greenberg emitted a small sigh and launched into a discussion of his latest batch of focus group findings on George W. Bush.

"He was born wealthy and privileged and elite—that's taken for granted," Greenberg said. "In this poll, 45 percent say he's in over his head. Now this is the *president of the United States!* Forty-five percent of the American people, in this survey, say he's *in over his head!* There is a fundamental doubt about his competence.

"But they also want him to succeed," he added with a trace of disappointment. "The public is not looking for a failed president. They would like him to succeed. Their lives would be better if he succeeds, so they're not going to draw conclusions about him before they are forced to."

Greenberg added, "Right now, as the economy weakens, his problem is leadership and confidence in the sense that he really knows how to handle the economy. With the surplus disappearing, it looks like the government's finances are a mess and the country lacks wealth."

"Doesn't that lower the bar for him, though?" a reporter asked. "Doesn't it give him a chance to exceed the old expectations?"

"Um—" said Greenberg.

"I think *he* lowered the bar," interjected Shrum, chuckling to himself. "He's the one who lowered the bar, so I don't think he gets—"

"But if people think he's in over his head and the country doesn't collapse in an obvious way, doesn't that kind of redound to him?" the reporter continued. "And they want him to succeed."

Greenberg, who by this time had mentally marshaled another batch of demographic data, directed the reporters to the seventeen pages of poll results they had been given.

"Look at the graph on the right-direction, wrong-track numbers in the country," he instructed. "This is not just in the most recent period, where we've seen the sharp increase in unemployment. This is over the entire period of his presidency, from the moment of his joint session speech, where he established his personal numbers and a sense of direction for the country. It has gone steadily down since that time."

"Where does he come out on likability?" a journalist asked. "And how much influence would that have on elections?"

"I don't think they're going to vote for him on likability," Greenberg said defensively. "I think they'll vote on job approval. And the correlations are much, much stronger on job approval—you know, with votes. And his disapproval has been steadily rising.

"But there is a reality that is: He is seen as honest, a person of good character, honest and moral," the pollster added. "And that is one of the pieces, you know, that holds him up."

This clearly annoyed Greenberg.

"We rush into these focus groups with these doubts that people have about him, and I'm wanting them to turn against him," he admitted. The pollster added with a chuckle of disbelief, "They don't want him to fail. I mean, they think it matters if the president of the United States fails. It'll affect their lives; it's bad for the country; it'll be bad for their lives. And I think they're holding him up."

Greenberg concluded, "They're scared to turn away from him."

One of the reporters suggested that despite all these gloomy poll numbers, Bush seemed to be doing well.

"But he *doesn't* do well," Shrum insisted. "He's going down on all the indexes. Stan is absolutely right. People would like him to succeed. Their own lives are implicated in it."

"He's doing well on education," a reporter pointed out. "The ABC-Post poll this morning says that he has about 61 percent approval on education—a traditional Democratic issue. What does that tell you?"

"That tells me that is the one place where he came in as president and he tried to act as if it had been a really close election that he might not have won," said Shrum. "He sought a bipartisan way to deal with this. He worked with Senator Kennedy."

"You don't think his heart's in education?" said Sperling, playing devil's advocate. "It's all political, isn't it? It's just a device that he used?"

"No, I didn't say that," Shrum was backpedaling. "I'm not talking about his motivation. I'm talking about what he actually did. What he did, whatever his motivation, reflected the political reality coming out of the election."

"However it worked out politically; it's been a plus for him, though, hasn't it?" Sperling persisted.

"Sure," acknowledged Greenberg.

"Sure," acknowledged Shrum.

They had to hand it to Sperling. Eighty-six years old and the guy was still spry enough to cajole a grudging concession from the toughest Democratic strategists in the business. No wonder Sperling enjoyed making that short walk across Sixteenth Street from the *Christian Science Monitor* to the St. Regis.

"Stan, Stan," called a woman. "How do you think this is going to play out next year in the congressional elections? And do you think Clinton's going to play any role here in campaigning for people? What will he do?"

"Um, I have no idea," said the man who was unceremoniously fired from Clinton's inner circle. "I'll let James speak to that. I have no idea. I assume he'll continue to do fundraising for people. And I assume he'll write his book and pursue his life. And I'll let James speak to that.

"But look, we've got, what, fourteen months left until the elections," Greenberg said. "There isn't any reason to think that the budget situation's going to get better. Maybe the economy'll come surging back. But if you get another nine months certainly of either down or stagnant economy, I think you'll have fairly deep impressions that come out of this. And I think you have the possibility of a significant shift to the Democrats."

He added, "The disappearance of the surplus is powerful. It's symbolic. The country had a very strong sense of growing well-being over the eight years of the Clinton years. And they have a growing sense of not well-being now."

A woman said, "To a certain extent that's been the argument, right? I mean, the Democrats' argument has been to make the Republicans own this—and then stand back."

"I think they should," Greenberg said. "Look, this argument has a sequence to it and the starting point for it is: They own it. But ultimately I think the Democrats have to go further."

"A rollback of the tax cut?" the woman said.

"Ultimately," Greenberg agreed. "In the short term, it is better to get the contours of the debate set. This was their budget. It is their budget that produced this disappearing surplus. And it's their burden to therefore come back and offer an alternative budget."

Shrum said, "We should let the country hold Bush responsible for what he's done and hold Bush responsible for, in the short space of nine months, getting rid of the surplus, dipping into the Social Security trust fund, and ending up with no money left for a prescription drug benefit."

"Is there a price to be paid by either Democrats or Republicans if a prescription drug benefit is not enacted?" a reporter asked.

"Oh yeah, a big price, and I don't think it's to be paid by Democrats," Shrum said. "Voters are actually pretty smart. They understand that if Al Gore were president and you had the Democratic Senate, or the Senate you have now, and you had this House, with some moderate Republicans, you'd pass a prescription drug benefit. They can figure this out."

If Al Gore were president! That was the overriding thought that burned in Shrum's brain. Nine months had passed since the election had finally been decided, and Shrum was still insisting Gore had won. He simply couldn't let it go. Widely considered the most ruthless and aggressive media strategist in the Democratic Party, Shrum had been a major force in Gore's win-at-any-cost strategy, especially those thirty-six days of scorched-earth political warfare in Florida. As Gore's chief political strategist, Shrum was particularly galled by the outcome. Although most Americans had never heard of him, everyone in national politics now knew Bob Shrum as the guy who hadn't been able to capitalize on the strongest hand any pol could hope to be dealt—a White House incumbent, presiding over a period of unprecedented peace and prosperity, with the wind at his back, challenged by an inarticulate lightweight who couldn't even remember the names of world leaders. What more could Shrum have asked for? And yet he had failed to get Gore elected, plain and simple. Gore's humiliation was Shrum's humiliation, at least in the world that mattered to him most—Washington.

Shrum had come to Washington from Los Angeles in the 1960s to attend Georgetown University. That's where he first met Bill Clinton, who was three years behind him. It's also where Shrum sharpened his tongue to a razor's edge. He was named the top college debater in America. Shrum went on to graduate from Harvard Law School, although he never bothered to take the bar exam. Instead he plunged directly into what would become his life's work—trying to elect liberal Democrats. He wrote speeches for failed presidential candidates Ed Muskie and George McGovern in 1972. He joined Jimmy Carter's campaign in 1976, but quit after ten days because he found the candidate insufficiently liberal. In 1980, Shrum helped Ted Kennedy weaken Carter in the Democratic primaries. Although Kennedy ended up losing, his vaunted "dream shall never die" concession speech at the Democratic National Convention was one of Shrum's proudest achievements. He returned with Kennedy to Capitol Hill and served as his press secretary for the next four years. Although Shrum went back to his political consulting business in 1984, he never stopped writing Kennedy's important speeches. There was the all-purpose apology speech of 1991, after Kennedy went barhopping with a nephew who ended up being accused of raping a woman in Palm Beach. Shrum also drafted eulogies for Jacqueline Onassis in 1994 and John F. Kennedy Jr. in 1999. He penned scripts for the Kennedy

Center Honors and even the Emmy Awards. He wrote them out long-hand because he never learned to use a computer.

Along the way, the gregarious pol grew gloriously rich on a steady diet of deep-pocketed clients ranging from New York Mayor David Dinkins to Israeli Prime Minister Ehud Barak. Shrum had no compunction about turning his poison pen against fellow Democrats when it suited his purposes. In 1990, he produced an ad that practically branded Democrat Ann Richards of Texas a drug addict. Richards, who as state treasurer was seeking the Democratic gubernatorial nomination, had acknowledged struggling with alcohol in her past. Shrum twisted this courageous admission into something ugly.

"Did she use marijuana, or something worse, like cocaine?" his TV spot insinuated. "Not as a college kid, but as a forty-seven-year-old elected official sworn to uphold the law?"

Such were the ads that made Shrum a millionaire many times over. He bought a tony Georgetown house that became a salon for dazzling dinner parties. He invited all the A-list Democrats. In 1988, Shrum married Marylouise Oates, a former society columnist for the *Los Angeles Times*. That same year, he joined Richard Gephardt's presidential campaign and was largely responsible for its negative tone. Four years later, while working on Nebraska Senator Bob Kerrey's campaign in the Democratic primaries, Shrum even attacked his old schoolmate from Georgetown.

"Under Bill Clinton, Arkansas dumped more toxic waste into rivers and lakes per capita than any other industrial state," the ad intoned. When Clinton went on to vanquish Kerrey, however, Shrum switched sides and wrote the speech Clinton delivered at the Democratic National Convention. Having backed losers for two decades, Bob Shrum finally latched onto a winner. After the election, the new president began using Shrum to write his State of the Union addresses.

But Shrum's most famous speech was the one Clinton never delivered. In August 1998, after Clinton was forced to acknowledge his affair with Monica Lewinsky, Shrum penned a graceful, penitent speech that began, "No one who is not in my position can understand the remorse I feel today. I have fallen short of what you should expect from a president." Clinton rejected the speech as overly contrite and instead unleashed an angry screed against Independent Counsel Kenneth W. Starr. Both Democrats and Republicans immediately viewed this as a blunder. As if to proclaim "I told you so," Shrum framed the undelivered speech and hung it on the wall of his Wisconsin Avenue office near Georgetown.

Not that Shrum shied away from vitriolic attacks when he found them useful. In 1998, he won the "Most Brutally Effective Attack Spot" award from *Campaigns & Elections* magazine. This dubious honor was for a TV ad that accused Ellen R. Sauerbrey, the Republican candidate in Maryland's gubernatorial race, of amassing a "shameful record on civil rights." The "civil rights" measure Sauerbrey had supposedly opposed was actually a sexual harassment lawsuit bill that was too odious even for the state's notoriously liberal, Democrat-controlled Senate. Maryland Republicans and Democrats joined in condemning the ad. But the condemnation came too late. Sauerbrey was defeated.

Now the hulking, balding Shrum, fifty-seven, was using the same tactics against Bush, the presidential pretender who had exiled him to the political wilderness. Only instead of playing the civil rights card, Shrum was trying to scare senior citizens into believing the president was jeopardizing their Social Security payments and prescription drugs. As Shrum finished his breakfast in the Mount Vernon Room, he predicted political doom for Bush and the rest of the Republicans.

"They don't have an issue," he concluded. "They don't have an issue that the country can clearly comprehend."

When someone pointed out that Bush did have an energy plan, Greenberg proceeded to ridicule it.

"I heard that this administration was gonna go out and send everyone out in order to make their case on the energy bill," he said incredulously. "I mean, I don't know any Democrats who say, 'Oh my God, they're going to articulate their position on the energy bill.'"

This triggered a belly laugh from Shrum.

"The more they articulate their position on the energy bill," Greenberg said, "the happier I am."

A reporter helpfully asked why the Democrats weren't exploiting another Bush vulnerability—his image as a tool of big oil.

"At the beginning of summer, when gasoline prices were rising, Democrats vowed to make an issue of that, to relate Bush to all his friends in the oil companies," the scribe said. "And then of course prices began to fall and that kind of disappeared."

"It's in the bank," Greenberg said with satisfaction.

Several people laughed, but the reporter remained puzzled.

"It's in the bank?"

"Well, I mean, 53 percent of the American people think he's the president for the oil companies," Greenberg beamed. "There has been a searing impression of who he's for, and what he's willing to do—even at a time where the national interest requires a different course of action."

Carville then launched into a discussion of Bush's weak communication skills.

"Somethin' tells me that Bush ain't Clinton," he said with a laugh. "I mean, it's one a those sort of overmatched—where you have a strong power forward against a weak guard—and they don't match up."

"May I break in for just a moment, please?" Sperling persisted. "You know, I feel so sorry for this poor guy, George Bush."

"I know," Shrum said with a gleeful laugh.

"He's in terrible shape here," Sperling added with mild sarcasm. "Are you saying that this president is not formidable, politically, at this point?"

"He's not formidable, politically," Greenberg said.

"He's not formidable," Sperling repeated. "Is he vulnerable? What is the word? I mean, what is he? Is he a pushover? Is he a—"

"No," Shrum said. "In 1982, Reagan looked like he was in terrible shape after the congressional elections. But then he won in '84. I think there are two fundamental differences. One: He ain't Ronald Reagan, in terms of his capacity to move the country."

"Well, Ronald Reagan wasn't Ronald Reagan back then either, remember?" Sperling said.

"No, but Reagan was a tremendous communicator," Shrum said.

"Okay," Sperling allowed.

"And number two: Reagan came in at a time when people believed the country was not only weak overseas, but that there was a real economic crisis," Shrum said. "Bush came in, inherited this large surplus, inherited what people perceived to be a good economy. I think if it comes back, he gets some credit, or at least some of the animus goes away. But I don't think that at this point he is positioned to be seen as the president who forged our prosperity."

He added with a cough, "The unemployment rate's going up and the surplus is gone and health care costs are going up and people feel in their own lives a sense of economic threat."

"The truth of the matter is, Mr. Sperling, people basically like this president as a person, and they want him to succeed," Carville conceded. "But they have some pretty serious doubts that have not crept in—that are sort of there. I mean, you have almost half the country saying he's in over his head. You have over half the country saying he's more for the powerful."

Yet Carville, like Greenberg, lamented that most of America seemed unwilling to give up on Bush.

"They're not going to—as much as I may like it and wish for it— they're not going to pull away completely from him seven months into his administration," Carville said glumly.

"Right," said Shrum.

"Bush's likability is higher than Gore's," Carville pointed out. But he added, "I don't care if people like him or not, just so they don't vote for him and his party. That's all I care about."

This bit of down-home political wisdom sparked laughter throughout the room.

"You know, I certainly hope he doesn't succeed," Carville admitted. "I'm a partisan Democrat. But the average person wants him to succeed."

"Is that desire for him to succeed a permanent attitude or does it turn around?" a journalist said. "And what does it take to turn it around?"

"I think it's a permanent attitude toward the American presidency," Shrum said. "And then I think people render a judgment in elections."

He predicted voters would "try to move the country in a different direction, since they're not very happy with the direction it's moving in right now."

Carville went further, pronouncing the Bush presidency an abject failure on virtually all fronts.

"Where are they succeeding?" he demanded. "If you look at this administration, where are they succeeding? They're not succeeding in the economy. They're not succeeding in health care. They're certainly not succeeding abroad. I mean, if you look around— My line is: We're busted at home and distrusted around the world."

Carville was referring to distrust from European elites, who preferred Clinton's liberalism to Bush's conservatism. During two trips to Europe that summer, the president had been severely caricatured by continental editorial writers. Liberals on both sides of the Atlantic warned that Bush would spark a new arms race if he insisted on withdrawing from the 1972 Anti-Ballistic Missile Treaty with Moscow in order to build a missile defense shield, an idea they had mockingly dismissed as Star Wars when it was first proposed by Ronald Reagan. Bush was also derided as naive for gushing over Russian President Vladimir Putin, a former KGB agent, after their first meeting in June. "I looked the man in the eye—I found him to be very straightforward and trustworthy," he announced at a press conference. "I was able to get a sense of his soul."

The ABM Treaty wasn't the only international agreement Bush was threatening to trash. He also planned to withdraw from a treaty, signed by Clinton, that would subject American soldiers and diplomats to the International Criminal Court, a United Nations war crimes tribunal that was scheduled to begin operations in The Hague on July 1, 2002. Nor did the president have any use for the Kyoto Protocols, also signed by Clinton, aimed at reducing global warming. Carville and other Democrats regarded this reckless unilateralism as just another nail in Bush's political coffin. And in addition to the president's missteps on foreign and domestic affairs, there was always the possibility of some unforeseeable political calamity.

"What I learned during eight years with Clinton is: You always think that somethin's gonna blow you up one day," he said.

Somethin's gonna blow you up one day! That was the overarching lesson Carville had drawn from his time with Clinton. And that was the terrible fate he now wished upon President Bush. Not literally, of course. But he desperately wanted something to blow Bush up politically. So deep was his antipathy toward the new president that Carville openly, publicly wished him ill. Never mind that his own wife, Mary Matalin, was assistant to the president, which meant Bush's failure would become her own. The only thing that mattered was that Bush, through some perverse cosmic injustice, had somehow ascended to the presidency after losing the popular vote to Al Gore. Carville, of course, had backed Gore, although he was never put on the payroll as Greenberg and Shrum were. After all, it was no longer politically wise for an American presidential candidate to hire James Carville. Carville may have been the brilliant strategist who got Bill Clinton elected in 1992, but his subsequent fame and reputation as a partisan bomb thrower had effectively ended his days of doing what he loved best—running an American presidential campaign. The truth was that Carville had become too big, too rich, too famous for the game, and was therefore relegated to cheering from the sidelines. He did things like lend his signature to direct-mail letters that raised millions for the Democratic Party. He occasionally appeared on political talk shows to savage a Republican or defend a Democrat. But he could never again mastermind a behind-the-scenes "stealth" campaign, like that glorious, heart-stopping victory in 1992.

Carville, fifty-six, sometimes pined for those days of anonymity. When he signed on to Bill Clinton's campaign nine years before, he was a virtual unknown. Outside the tiny universe of political strategists, the only people who truly knew Chester James Carville Jr. were those in and around Carville, Louisiana, a one-stoplight town on the Mississippi named for his grandfather, the local postmaster. The eldest of eight children, the hard-partying Carville flunked out of Louisiana State University in 1966 and then assuaged his Catholic guilt by joining the Marines. Two years later he returned to LSU to finish his bachelor's degree and went on to earn a law degree. But life as a litigator in a Baton Rouge law firm was unfulfilling, so he called it quits after six years to devote himself to his true passion, politics. His bare-knuckled style earned him the nickname Ragin' Cajun, although he lost most of his campaigns. He hit bottom while trying to work his way into a position of influence on Gary Hart's 1984 campaign, the one in which it was revealed that the candidate's name had once been Hartpence and that he had a reputation as a womanizer. One raw, rainy night in Washington, Carville was walking down Massachusetts Avenue when his garment bag broke, spilling his clothes into a mud puddle. Overwhelmed by a sudden sense of hopelessness, he sank down to the curb and bawled like a baby. Some Ragin' Cajun. Inside his pocket was $36, his entire earthly fortune. Broke, dejected, and pushing forty, Carville borrowed $5,000 from a friend and went back to practicing law.

Two years later, Carville decided to take one last, desperate shot at politics. He signed on with former Pennsylvania auditor Bob Casey, whose trio of failed gubernatorial bids had earned him the nickname Three-Time Loss from Holy Cross. And it looked as if the fourth time was not going to be the charm either. So Carville leaked to a newspaper a tantalizing story that protected his candidate while trashing the opponent, former lieutenant governor William Scranton III. Carville told the publication that Casey had forbidden him to air a TV ad alleging past marijuana use by Scranton. "It was manipulation," Carville later said, laughing but admitting this was not his "finest hour." It worked. Casey pulled within eight points a week before election day. Carville then dug up an old college photo of a shaggy-looking Scranton and turned it into a TV spot, complete with psychedelic sitar music and a voice-over quoting Scranton advocating transcendental meditation in state government. It was enough to put the Three-Time Loss from Holy Cross into the governor's mansion. And it brought the Ragin' Cajun back from the dead. James Carville never forgot the value of attack politics.

All of which came in handy in 1992, when he took charge of Clinton's campaign. Carville was the one who directed Greenberg and the rest of the war room to repeatedly pull the candidate's fat out of the fire. When Clinton won, Carville sobbed during a speech to the campaign staff, which was captured in the Oscar-nominated documentary film *The War Room*. Matalin, who had been dating Carville for two years despite serving as political director of President Bush's campaign, blubbered, "You make me sick. I hate your guts." A year later they married.

Carville now set about the task of getting rich and famous. He wrote books, landed foreign clients, appeared on TV shows and in movies, and cut lucrative endorsement deals with Heineken, Alka-Seltzer, American Express, and Cotton Inc. He and Matalin gave speeches for $25,000 a throw and perfected their he-said-she-said schtick during periodic stints on *Meet the Press*. They bought a spectacular farmhouse out in Shenandoah County, Virginia, and a stylish townhouse in Washington. Carville barely broke a sweat in 1996, when Clinton breezed to reelection. But he was called back to urgent duty in 1998, when the Lewinsky scandal exploded, threatening Clinton's very presidency. Carville went on a rampage like never before, openly declaring "war" on mild-mannered Independent Counsel Kenneth W. Starr. He didn't let up until the Senate finally acquitted Clinton. That was what everyone ended up remembering about Carville, the fact that this bald-headed maniac had gone after Starr like a junk-yard dog. His own wife called him Serpenthead, although he preferred the moniker Corporal Cueball.

The all-out brawl over Clinton's impeachment made James Carville so famous that he could no longer walk down a street in America without being recognized. Carville came to view the impeachment battle as his "last hurrah," since he could never again be the consummate insider of a presidential campaign. Now he was just the opposite, the very public outrider who raised money, rallied the troops, and ranted on Sunday-morning talk shows. "In America, once you become a famous person, the only way you can earn a living is by being a famous person," he lamented to me. "You can't just, like, go back." Democrats began treating him as if he had the word "emeritus" after his name. They became exceedingly deferential to him. For a guy who made his bones as a brawler, all this politesse was downright unsettling. Even when Gore occasionally called him during the 2000 campaign, the sitting vice president would say things like, "We just want to be sure that you're happy." And the Republicans were even more polite to Carville when he showed up at the Republican National Convention to do TV commentary in 2000. The man who had been forced to sneak into the GOP's 1996 convention was now treated like a rock star. The adulation was nice, but deep down Carville longed for the days when politics was more of a contact sport.

The reporters had pretty much finished their breakfast by now and some were working on their second cups of coffee. But no one seemed to want to end this discussion of Bush's failed young presidency, least of all Carville. He pointed out that the front page of that day's *Washington Post* revealed more Bush weaknesses. One story complained there weren't enough fetal stem cells available for medical research, thanks to Bush's ruling out further harvesting of human cells from aborted babies. And Carville predicted Bush would face more trouble over arsenic levels in drinking water.

"All these things are a series of sort of info-cuts, if you will," he explained. "There's a certain accretion every time another story comes out."

He added, "Then you have the polls. And every time that you turn around, there's somebody that's throwing a new thing out there at these guys."

"Have any of you ever seen before polling data that shows 45 percent of the voters thinking the president is in over his head?" asked a reporter.

"No," Greenberg said bluntly, drawing laughter. He did not mention that he had conducted a separate poll three months earlier that showed 47 percent of Americans believed Bush was in over his head. There was no need to point out that this number was actually falling.

"Anything comparable to that?" the reporter said.

"No," Shrum said.

"I'm sure Jimmy Carter's numbers, if we asked in the late '70s, would have been tough numbers," Greenberg allowed.

"What do you make of that?" the reporter said.

"Well, Jimmy Carter wasn't president again," Greenberg said, setting off another round of laughter.

"We've got 45 think he's in over his head and 41 disapproves," Carville said. "What you make of it is: His margin of error—I mean the number of people that he can lose—is getting less and less and less.

"There's one thing Bush has never been able to do," he said. "The real skilled politicians are able to go take 10, 12 percent out of the other guy's pocket. The Reagan Democrats. And Clinton got the sort of suburban Republican women. I mean, they got all of their party and their ability was to draw a little bit from the other side.

"In the campaign of 2000, both candidates got exactly what they were supposed to get," Carville continued. "Not one got one single vote other than the votes they were supposed to get. And since Bush, if you look at—"

"Not a point," interjected Greenberg. "He has not gotten—"

"—he has not gotten a point—" echoed Carville.

"—a point above his vote," Greenberg said.

"—above his vote, where he started," Carville agreed. "And until he can do that, the Democrats are not gonna be scared. And this is a town that really operates—excuse me, a city; I hate calling it a town— this is a city that operates on fear. And the Democrats don't fear Bush—nor do Republicans.

"In President Clinton's first term, they didn't fear him either. But once the budget battle came, the Republicans became scared of him, because he was taking votes away from them. Then you had all of these negotiations that went his way.

"Bush has yet to instill any fear," Carville concluded. "He's yet to get one vote other than what he should be getting. And in fact some of those are startin' to have doubts. If he starts losing any of those voters, his political strength will be sapped bad."

"I think Bush is on the verge of instilling a different kind of fear in the congressional Republicans than James is referring to," Shrum said, getting the laughter rolling again.

"The myth is that this is a strong president; he is not," Carville said. "Bush has not done any better as president than he did as a candidate. He got what he was supposed to get—no more. And the measure of success in this business, again, is your ability to get a part of what you're not supposed to get. That's how you become a successful president. That's how you become a successful politician."

"Can I just ask you to sum up here?" a reporter began.

"This has to be the last question," interjected Sperling, mindful that the allotted hour for the breakfast had elapsed.

"You guys are really excited you got health care and the economy coming your way going into 2002 and 2004," the reporter said. "Is there some additional issue beyond that, that you see?"

"I don't know which ones Bush would latch on to," Shrum said. "I don't think he's gonna go out there and run on his environmental or energy policies."

"They'd have to run on their successful foreign policy," Carville said sarcastically as knowing laughter filled the room.

Democrats and the press considered Bush's foreign policy team a collection of hopelessly obsolete "retreads" cobbled together from previous Republican administrations. *New York Times* columnist Maureen Dowd wrote that Vice President Dick Cheney and Defense Secretary Donald Rumsfeld were "out of touch" and didn't "know anything about how the world works." She was especially harsh on Rumsfeld, whom she lampooned as "Rip Van Rummy." The *Washington Post* was already speculating about successors to the defense secretary. Even Secretary of State Colin Powell, a media darling, was being portrayed as ineffectual among the right-wing Bushies. On September 10, *Time* magazine's cover lamented, "Where Have You Gone, Colin Powell?"

As the laughter died down, Sperling brought the breakfast to a close.

"I think you've had your say today and it's been a good morning," he concluded. "We enjoyed having you fellas. And come again."

"Thank you, Mr. Sperling," Carville said.

"Thank you for doing this," Greenberg said. "We consider you the best releaser of our polls."

"I have lived through the sunny-side eggs to the scrambled eggs—that's how long I've been coming to this thing," said Shrum, provoking more good-natured laughter.

As he spoke, his cell phone began ringing. It had one of those ringers that played classical music instead of a conventional ring tone. This one was playing a tinny, electronic version of Mozart's Symphony No. 40: *Da-da-lee, da-da-lee, da-da-lee-dee; dee-da-lum, dee-da-lum, dee-da-lie....*

Sperling was oblivious to the ringing phone and kept right on talking to Shrum. He was assuring him he looked "about a third smaller" than other large men who had indulged in the fat-rich foods served at Sperling Breakfasts over the years.

"Oh yeah," Shrum chuckled with self-deprecating sarcasm. "I am a third smaller."

Shrum's phone kept playing the symphony's first movement and Sperling kept chattering on about heavyset old-timers who had attended these breakfasts, including "a poor fellow that's gone to his reward, I think."

"Yeah," Shrum said absently, trying to find a polite way to end this conversation so he could answer the phone.

"Yeah, real nice guy, he was," Sperling continued breezily. "I think he tried to get it figured out. Never could."

By this point the phone had been ringing so long that the twenty-second snippet of Mozart began to play a second time. *Da-da-lee, da-da-lee, da-da-lee-dee; dee-da-lum, dee-da-lum, dee-da-lie....* Still, Sperling was utterly unfazed.

"Yeah," said Shrum, who decided simply to press the button and answer the phone. "Let me—"

"So nice of you to come," Sperling said.

"Listen, it was great," Shrum managed, momentarily neglecting his caller.

"It's fun kicking things around like this," chattered Sperling, as if Shrum did not have a cell phone pressed to his ear.

"Thanks, yeah, we'll do it," Shrum said in the tone of a man being pulled away against his will.

"Let's do it again," Sperling said cheerily. "Let us know when you want to come in."

But Bob Shrum was no longer listening to Godfrey "Budge" Sperling. He was now listening to his assistant, back at the office, who had been given specific instructions not to call unless it was an absolute emergency. Shrum was so dumbfounded by the words he was now hearing that he repeated them aloud, for the benefit of everyone else in the Mount Vernon Room.

"A plane has just crashed into the World Trade Center."

The room froze. Everyone strained to listen in on Shrum's astonishing conversation.

"What kind of plane?" he said before again parroting his assistant's words for the benefit of the room. "A 737!"

Soon there were other cell phones ringing in the Mount Vernon Room. A reporter headed for the exit, followed by another. But most remained frozen in place as the terrible news trickled in.

Now Greenberg's phone was ringing. His assistant informed him that a second plane had hit the second tower. Shrum got the same news in a follow-up call from his own assistant. It looked like a coordinated attack by terrorists. It was nothing short of a catastrophe.

Before anyone else could leave the room, Carville was on his feet. The cynical strategist who had just described Washington as "a city that operates on fear" suddenly felt a stab of worry about his own wife, Mary Matalin, who was in the White House at this very moment, and their two young daughters, who were across town. The wizened oracle who had just finished articulating every president's secret fear—*somethin's gonna blow you up one day!*—now realized the terrible truth of his words. And even as these alarm bells clanged away inside Carville's shining skull, the wily pol already sensed—more quickly than anyone—the seismic shift that had just riven the political landscape.

"Disregard everything we just said!" commanded Corporal Cueball. *"This changes everything!"*

Chapter Three

Bifurcation

"A SECOND PLANE HIT *the second tower. America is under attack.*"

The whispered words instantly bifurcated the presidency of George W. Bush. The old phase—those 234 days of stem cell debates, media recounts, arsenic flaps—was suddenly, irretrievably over. And now there was this new phase, which began with Card's impossible words: *America is under attack!*

Although he was facing the students, Bush was no longer focusing on them in the slightest. He was too busy struggling to process the meaning of this monstrous new reality. America hadn't been attacked since Pearl Harbor, before Bush was born. Its mainland hadn't been attacked since 1812, when James Madison was president. And now here he was, George W. Bush, the forty-third president of the United States, sitting in a second-grade classroom in sunny Sarasota, on an ordinary September morning, while the nation he had sworn to protect and defend was *under attack* a thousand miles away.

"And I looked at him, and that's all he said," Bush told me later. "Then he left. There was no time for discussion or anything. And I can't remember anything the lady was saying from that point on. I might have been looking at her, but I wasn't hearing. And my mind was registering what it meant to hear 'America is under attack,' and to be the commander in chief of the country at that moment."

Card straightened up and backed away after delivering the crushing news. An expression of grim sobriety spread across the president's face. He raised his chin and nodded almost imperceptibly to signal that he got the message. His eyes darted nervously around the room, as if he didn't know quite where to focus them. To his left, at the back of the room, a young staffer murmured furtively into a microphone tucked up his sleeve and then whispered to White House Press Secretary Ari Fleischer. The presidential spokesman grimaced as he punched a button and read a message on his pager. Bush risked a glance at the journalists, who were devouring him with their ravenous lenses. He knew they were not transmitting images of him in real time, since this event had not been set up as a live feed. But they were making a tape of Bush that would be dumped onto TV as soon as the event ended. Any presidential slipup would be delayed by only a few minutes before being dissected by the entire world. He rolled eyes to his right, where Card took up a position with the other dignitaries. He was standing next to Florida Lieutenant Governor Frank Brogan, who evidently hadn't got the word, because he still had a big grin on his face. Finding all of these focal points unsatisfying, the president finally lowered his gaze to the gray industrial carpet. But the distress now showed on his mouth as well. He licked his upper lip, gnawed on his lower, and then pursed them both together. Unlike Card's poker face, the president's countenance always betrayed his inner emotions.

"At the count of three," Daniels instructed her students, blissfully unaware of the tragedy. "Everyone should be on page 163. If the yellow paper's going to bother you, drop it."

Bush wondered whether he should excuse himself and retreat to the holding room, where he might be able to find out what the hell was going on. But what kind of message would that send—the president abruptly getting up and walking out on a bunch of inner-city second-graders at their moment in the national limelight? Bush might look rattled, or worse, panicked. The last thing the nation needed at this moment was a panicked president. Such an image might even play into the hands of the attackers. No, better to remain calm and sit tight for now. Bush sensed that his demeanor would be almost as important as his actions in these first crucial moments. "The real measure of a person is how he responds to bad news," he had written in his memoirs.

"Everybody touch the title of your story," Daniels was saying. "Fingers under the title. Get ready to read the title — the — fast — way."

She paused while a straggler found the correct page. The president, who hadn't bothered to pick up his own book, seemed to be staring at a point in space several light years away.

"We're waiting for one member," Daniels said.

Bush abruptly looked at the teacher to see whether she was referring to him. When he saw that her gaze was fixed instead on a girl in the front row, the president swiveled his head in the direction of the girl, as if relieved that he hadn't been the one to get caught holding up the reading drill. Then he quickly slipped back into his reverie and gnawed some more on his lower lip.

"Thank you," Daniels told the girl. "Fingers under the title of the story. Get ready."

"The — Pet — Goat," the children recited as their teacher thumped her pen on a book to keep time with each syllable.

"Yes, 'The Pet Goat,'" Daniels said. "Fingers under the first word of the story. Get ready to read the story the fast way. Get ready."

Bush absently picked up his book from the pink easel next to him. He glanced at the cover, which showed a cuddly dragon surrounded by butterflies. Turning to the bookmarked page, he tried to follow along with the class.

"A — girl — got — a — pet — goat," the children said.

"Go on," instructed Daniels, thumping away with her pen.

"She — liked — to — go — running — with — her — pet — goat."

"Go on."

As the children plowed through the story, Bush found it impossible to keep his eyes on the page. He kept gazing upward, lost in a tumult of urgent thoughts. So the first plane crash had not been an accident after all. The second crash had proven that much. But what else did it prove? Card hadn't given him a hell of a lot of information, had he? *A second plane hit the second tower!* Such an economy of words. That was just like Andy. But what kind of plane? Another small, twin-engine job? Who were the pilots? Why had they done it? How many Americans had they killed?

"But — the — goat — did — some — things — that — made — the — girl's — dad — mad."

"Let's clean that up," Daniels said.

Bush zoned back in for a moment and noticed someone moving at the back of the room. It was Fleischer, who was maneuvering into a position that allowed him to catch the president's attention without alerting the press. He was holding up a legal pad and flashing it in Bush's direction. There were big block letters scrawled on the card-board backing of the tablet. Fleischer was sending him a message! But what did it say? Bush tried not to make it obvious that he was reading this impromptu cue card. He didn't have his glasses on, but could make out the lettering: "DON'T SAY ANYTHING YET." Fleischer didn't want him talking to the press about the World Trade Center. Now that a second plane had crashed, the remarks Bush had drafted about directing the full resources of the federal government to the accident site would be woefully inadequate. After all, it was no longer an accident. The planes had slammed into the World Trade Center *on purpose*.

"But — the — goat — did — some — things — that — made — the — girl's — dad — mad."

"Go on."

"The — goat — ate — things."

"Go on."

Bush looked at the teacher and managed a wan smile. He redoubled his efforts to appear at least as though he were concentrating on the lesson. But it was no use. The president's mind raced with more questions. How could this have happened? Who could have perpetrated such a diabolical crime? No, this was more than a crime. This was *war*, plain and simple. Someone had suddenly declared war against the United States of America, the mightiest nation on earth.

"Victory clicked into my mind," Bush told me. "The one thing that became certain is that we wouldn't let this stand. I mean, there was no question in my mind that we'd respond. I wasn't sure who the attacker was. But if somebody is going to attack America, I knew that my most immediate job was to protect America by finding him and getting them."

"The — girl — made — him — stop — eating — cans — and — canes — and — caps — and — capes."

"Good job," Daniels said. "Turn your page."

"Really good readers," said Bush, zoning back in for a moment. "Whew! These must be *sixth*-graders."

The second-grade teacher laughed politely at this bit of presidential flattery.

"Fingers under the first word," she said. "Let's go."

"But — one — day — a — car — robber — came — to — the — girl's — house."

"Go on."

"He — saw — a — big — red — car — near — the — house — and — said, — 'I — will — steal — that — car.'"

"Go on."

Would this reading drill never end? Bush desperately craved information about the attacks. Unlike the journalists and presidential aides at the back of the room, he carried no pager or cell phone or other electronic device to provide up-to-the-minute news bulletins. There hadn't even been a television in the holding room, so Bush had no mental picture of the disaster.

"I couldn't envision it," he told me. "I could not envision what it meant to see an airplane fly into a building. Because what you can envision is the aftermath, and you can see in your mind's eye. But I wasn't thinking about what it looked like. I was thinking about what the heck we were going to do. I'm an action-oriented guy. And I am thinking to myself: What is it I need to do?"

"He — ran — to — the — car — and — started — to — open — the — door."

"Go on."

"The — girl — and — the — goat — were — playing — in — the — back — yard."

"Go on."

"They — did — not — see — the — car — robber."

Finally, the children reached the last line: "More — to — come."

"What does that mean?" said Bush, forcing himself to focus on the children now that their reading drill was over. "'More to come'?"

Nearly all the children raised their hands. Bush pointed to a black girl whose braided hair was tied up in a ribbon adorned with blue-and-white balls. She explained that something else was going to happen.

"That's exactly right," said the president, who dearly hoped this was not some ominous prophecy.

Now that the lesson was over, Bush would finally be able to return to the holding room and get to work. But there was no sense in rushing his exit. The press might interpret haste as distress. What was the line the *New York Times* had used that very morning? *"There is a whiff of panic in the air."* Bush was not about to lend credence to that particular image. He decided to remain seated, as if he were in no hurry whatsoever to leave the second-grade classroom of Sandra Kay Daniels.

"Hoo!" the president exclaimed. "These are great readers."

"Yes, they are," cooed Daniels, no longer the drill sergeant.

"*Very* impressive," Bush said. "Thank you all so very much for showing me your reading skills. I'll bet they practice, too. Don't you?"

"Oh yes," Daniels said. "That's a requirement—homework, reading homework."

"Reading more than they watch TV?" asked Bush, now openly stretching out the moment. The notoriously punctual president who just minutes earlier had been prodding Daniels to get down to brass tacks was now lollygagging as if he didn't want the session to end.

"Oh yes," Daniels assured him. "Oh yes."

"Anybody do that?" Bush said dreamily to the children. "Read more than you watch TV?"

The students raised their hands, some of them giggling sheepishly. The only children in America who read more than they watched TV.

"Oh, that's great," purred Bush, smiling as if he didn't have a care in the world. "Very good. Very important to practice."

Turning to Daniels in the most relaxed manner imaginable, he added, "Thanks for having me."

"Thank you for coming," Daniels said.

"I'm very impressed with how you read this book," Bush said breezily to the children, closing the text and placing it back on the easel. He continued to linger in his seat.

"Boys and girls, close your readers," Daniels said. "Place them under your chairs."

"And thank you so much for doing a great job this morning," Tosé-Rigell said to the children as she approached Bush. The dawdler in chief did not even get up.

"Thank you, press," announced White House press wrangler Gordon Johndroe, who was responsible for herding the pool away from the president at the conclusion of such events. "If you could step out the door we came in, please."

Ignoring Johndroe, a reporter called out, "Mr. President, are you aware of reports of the plane crash in New York? And is there anything—"

"I'll talk about it later," said Bush, rising to his feet and holding up his right hand in the "back off" gesture. He stepped forward and shook hands with Daniels, slipping his left hand behind her in another photo-op pose. He was taking his good old time.

"Thank you all!" Johndroe barked from the back of the room, cutting off further questions. "We can step out the door we came in."

Bush lingered until the press was gone. Then he turned to Tosé-Rigell, who was waiting to take him to the library for his speech on education. He pulled her aside for the first private conversation in this new phase of his presidency.

"I'm so sorry," he said. "But a tragedy has occurred."

The president told her of the second plane crash and explained that there would be no speech on education. Instead, he would need to use her school as the site of his first postattack remarks to the nation.

"I'm going to have to address some things," he said. "I really wish it would have been a different set of circumstances."

"I fully understand," Tosé-Rigell said. She told him how frantic she gets when one of her students doesn't arrive home immediately after school. She likened the people in the World Trade Center, many of whom must be missing at this very moment, to students for whom the president was responsible.

As Tosé-Rigell conversed with Bush, she sensed that a transformation had taken place. The man she had viewed as a phony just minutes earlier was now calmly apologizing for the fact that his planned education speech at her school would have to be scrapped because, after all, *America is under attack*. She was astonished by his heartfelt sincerity, especially since Bush hadn't had time privately to gather his wits.

"That's not something that you can fake," she told me later. "I'm telling you, I was very impressed. I don't know what spurred him on. I don't know if he tapped into his faith. I don't know if there were people around the country praying for him.

"But at that moment in time, he was very, very composed," she said. "All I can say is he looked very presidential."

Thus did Gwendolyn Tosé-Rigell, an African-American principal of an inner-city school, a Democrat who had voted for Al Gore, become the first of many people across America and around the world to conclude that George W. Bush was somehow profoundly changed by the terrible events of September 11.

"From that point on," she said, "I was a convert."

When Bush returned to the holding room, he found it bustling with activity. A television on a cart had been rolled in and hooked up, providing the president with his first look at actual footage of the stricken World Trade Center. Sitting at a table with his ear pressed to a secure telephone, Bush craned around and watched the sickening images from clear across the room. Live shots of the smoking towers were interspersed with horrifying replays of the second plane slamming into the structure and exploding into a colossal orange fireball. The first plane had hit at 8:46 A.M., during Bush's ride across the John Ringling Causeway. The second plane had hit at 9:03, a single minute after the president stepped inside the classroom. Both appeared to be large jetliners, not small twin-engine planes. While there was no footage of the first crash, at least not yet, the second had been captured from multiple angles. One sickening piece of videotape featured a head-on shot—the twin-engine jetliner closing in on the south tower and then disappearing behind the 110-story building just before impact. There was a stomach-dropping moment of lag time and then flames exploded from the front and side of the building, swelling and merging into a gigantic sphere, twenty stories high, that engulfed the tower and rolled upward as chunks of fiery debris rained down on smaller buildings below. The mushrooming fireball blackened as it ascended the tower and was finally subsumed by the plume from the north tower. God only knew how many human beings had been incinerated in that blink of an eye.

"I told Ari to take notes," Bush told me. "I wanted Ari to have a full understanding of what he saw and my reactions to that. I recognized that a lot of this was going to end up being such a blur that I wouldn't have an accurate accounting."

Bush talked first with the vice president, who was back at the White House. Cheney had actually watched the second plane hit on live television from his West Wing office. He was already huddling with Rice to talk about mobilizing an antiterrorism task force. Also in Cheney's office were his chief of staff, Lewis "Scooter" Libby, and vice presidential advisor Mary Matalin, the wife of James Carville.

"First of all, we had to figure out what we were going to do and where we were going to make decisions from," Bush told me. "And the Secret Service and the Mil Aide was in the process of getting information about where the president ought to go. One thing for certain, I needed to get out of where I was."

He added, "I didn't spend that much time about my own safety because I knew others were worried about that. What I was interested in is making sure that the response mechanism that was under my control was sharp and ready to go. And that meant defense, for starters."

But he also realized he would have to make a public statement. Bush tried to flesh out the scant information that was available in those first frantic minutes. He and Cheney agreed that terrorists were probably behind the attacks, and the president decided to say so to the nation. He began to scribble notes with the Sharpie fine-point marker he always carried in the inside breast pocket of his suit for the purpose of signing autographs.

The president also called FBI Director Robert Mueller, who had been on the job all of six days, because the agency had investigated previous terrorist strikes against American targets, on U.S. soil and overseas. These included the 1993 bombing of the World Trade Center, the 1998 bombing of American embassies in Kenya and Tanzania, and the 2000 bombing of the USS *Cole* in Yemen, which killed seventeen sailors. The suspected culprit in all these cases was Osama bin Laden, the Saudi-born Islamic fundamentalist who headed the al Qaeda terrorist network and was protected by Afghanistan's radical

Taliban regime. The FBI already suspected bin Laden in today's attack. Just four days before, the State Department had issued a worldwide terrorism caution to American citizens traveling abroad, as well as to U.S. government facilities—although the World Trade Center had not been singled out. Bush also learned that the jetliners were commercial American aircraft, at least one of which had apparently been hijacked out of Boston. After talking with Mueller, the president consulted with New York Governor George Pataki. Then he hung up and turned to his top aides—Rove, Card, Fleischer, and White House Communication Director Dan Bartlett.

"We're at war," Bush announced.

He jettisoned the education speech he had been scheduled to deliver. Americans needed to hear directly from their president about the tragedy. The press was already waiting for him in the school's library, where two hundred students, parents, school officials, and local dignitaries had been gathered for hours.

Fleischer and Bartlett hastily drafted a statement, but Bush wanted to change it and put it into his own words. Using his Sharpie, he scribbled three sheets of notes on crinkly white paper. He gathered them up, got to his feet, and headed for the library.

"I remember I had to convince myself to be as calm and resolute as possible, because I knew people were watching," the president told me later.

"I can be an emotional guy. And I was worried, emotional, about loss of life, because the magnitude of what had happened had come home. And at the same time, I knew I needed to send a sense of, you know, calm in the face of what could be panic. And I think I was able to achieve that.

"I can remember having to be conscious, conscious of how—"

"Of your demeanor, because you didn't want to alarm anybody?" I said.

"It's the first time I've really— Usually when I get up at these things, at these big events, I just kind of let 'er go and hope for the best. This moment, I was conscious of what was going to happen, because I was feeling emotions inside me," he explained.

"I was not doubtful," the president added. "I was firm in what I knew we needed to do."

Even before Bush walked into the library, many of the people there knew about the terrorist strikes. The larger White House press corps, which had arrived around 8:30 A.M., had been alerted by cell phones and pagers about the first plane crash. Reporters left their seats and discovered a side room that contained several televisions. Some saw live coverage of the second crash. Others crowded in moments later and watched the replay over and over, as if expecting it somehow to turn out differently.

At length, they drifted back to their seats and waited for the president. A sound system blared "Dirty Work," a 1972 song by Steely Dan.

> . . . *I'm a fool to do your dirty work, oh yeah,*
> *I don't wanna do your dirty work, no more. . . .*

The reporters whispered updates to some of the parents and dignitaries, and news spread through the crowd. But some people positioned close to the presidential podium remained unaware of the tragedy and a few continued to laugh with nervous excitement.

> . . . *Like the castle in its corner in a medieval game,*
> *I foresee terrible trouble, and I stay here just the same.*

I'm a fool to do your dirty work, oh yeah,
I don't wanna do your dirty work, no more....

The music stopped just before 9:30. Bush emerged from behind a blue curtain and strode ten paces to the podium, clutching the sheaf of hand-scrawled notes in his left hand. The audience broke into applause and rose to its feet, prompting shouts of "Down in front!" from the cameramen at the back of the room. The president spread his notes on the podium and took a deep breath, exhaling through his mouth with enough force to roll his lower lip outward. He gestured for the audience to sit down. His expression was grave, tense, almost pained.

"Thank you," he said before the applause subsided. "Ladies and gentlemen, this is a—difficult moment for America."

Bush unfolded his hands and straightened the papers on the podium before folding his hands again and looking back up at the crowd.

"I, um, unfortunately will be going back to Washington after my remarks. Secretary Rod Paige and Lieutenant Governor"—Bush cleared his throat after this awkward formulation—"will take the podium and discuss education.

"I do want to thank the folks here at, uh," Bush glanced at his notes, "at, uh, Booker Elementary School for their hospitality.

"Today, we've had a national tragedy," the president said.

At that moment, a balding man in the audience stood up to snap a picture, obscuring the view of some press people behind him. One of the cameramen hissed *"Sir,"* which caused Bush momentarily to glance in that direction. Even during the gravest presidential crisis imaginable, the press couldn't keep still.

"Two airplanes have crashed into the World Trade Center in an apparent terrorist attack on our country," Bush plowed on.

A smattering of gasps and murmurs rippled through the crowd. People cut worried glances at one another. The first page of notes rustled as the president set it to one side.

"I have spoken to the vice president, to the governor of New York, to the director of the FBI. And I've ordered that the full resources of the federal government go to help the victims and their families and the—and to conduct a full-scale investigation to hunt down and to find those folks who committed this act."

Those folks! Bush was describing the monsters who had perpetrated the most heinous crime against America in sixty years as *folks*, as if they were down-home, salt-of-the-earth types who swapped stories around the old front porch. He tried to set aside his second sheet of notes, but it caught on the corner of the first sheet and made another rustling sound.

"Terrorism against our nation will not stand," he said.

The choice of words instantly recalled his father's threat, issued more than a decade earlier, that Saddam Hussein's invasion of Kuwait "will not stand." The phrase had become so identified with the elder Bush that comedian Dana Carvey had used it to lampoon the old man on *Saturday Night Live*. Although the forty-first president had made good on his threat against Saddam, he went on to lose the 1992 election. Thus, the son's reliance on the father's rhetoric at this moment of maximum peril was vaguely unsettling.

"And now if you'd join me in a moment of silence."

Bush bowed his head and tightly closed his eyes. After five seconds, he looked up and unfolded his hands.

"May God bless the victims, their families, and America," he said as he tried to set aside the third sheet of notes. It got stuck on the second sheet, producing yet another round of rustling. "Thank you very much."

There was a hint of emotional strain in his final words as the president turned to go. He took a half step away from the podium, but stopped to finish gathering up his crinkly papers, which seemed stubbornly to resist his fingers. Bush headed for the exit, not stopping as he shook Lieutenant Governor Brogan's outstretched hand. With his back to the cameras, he waved to some of the clapping people who had been standing behind him, along the wall, and paused to shake hands with four women before disappearing behind the blue curtain. He ignored the shrill call of a CNN producer: "Sir, anything else you can tell us about the attack today?"

Outside, the president headed for his limousine, which barreled onto Martin Luther King Jr. Way at 9:34. Back in the ghetto again, Bush's limousine turned toward the airport along North Washington Boulevard. Presidential motorcades almost always move along at clips that would be considered reckless if the streets weren't closed, but this one went even faster. Bush was hurtling alongside a set of railroad tracks at 80 mph, or twice the speed of his ride from the Colony. Everything outside was a blur. Vacant fields. Patches of trees. Madam Mitchell's Psychic Palm & Card Reader. A business called The Hook Up, where enormous yellow letters extended above the roofline to spell out "LOUD CAR STEREOS." Bush noticed people smiling and waving at the sides of the road, oblivious to the tragedy that had befallen the nation.

He worked the phones as the limo careened left onto University Parkway. The limo passed the Sarasota Kennel Club, a fancy name for the dog track, and sped by the main entrance to Sarasota-Bradenton International Airport, a fancy name for the local airstrip, which had no direct flights to or from a single international destination. It hauled ass north on Route 41, passing the gaudy Sarasota Classic Car

Museum, where several hot rods were parked right on the roof, and the grandiose John & Mabel Ringling Museum of Art. Finally, the motorcade veered down tiny General Spatz Road, ignoring a sign that declared "No Airport Access." It blew through a small, unmarked gate in a chain-link fence and raced across the tarmac. The caravan cut directly in front of Air Force One's nose and then swung around the right wing, around the tail, and behind the left wing. Bush emerged from the limousine at 9:43 A.M., moments after being told a third jetliner had just slammed into the sacrosanct symbol of America's military might, the Pentagon.

While the president ascended the stairs to Air Force One aft of the left wing, the reporters headed for the rear entrance to the plane. But Secret Service agents stopped them and ordered them to drop their gear for a security sweep. Although everyone in the presidential motorcade had already been swept back at the school, the Secret Service was taking no chances. Even staffers who wore special lapel pins denoting their status as White House employees had their belongings checked by bomb-sniffing dogs. The mood was extraordinarily tense.

"If you're not essential, you're not getting on the airplane!" a military aide snapped to no one in particular at the foot of the rear entrance. "We gotta hurry up and get out of here. Let's go!"

Bush headed directly to his private cabin near the front of the plane, a small chamber with cream-colored curtains pulled back to reveal a bank of airline windows, one of which was adorned with the presidential seal. He peeled off his suit jacket and slid behind a polished wooden desk that was set at an angle in the middle of the cabin. He settled into a tan leather reclinable chair, the tall back of which was draped with his presidential flight jacket. The words "Air Force One" were embroidered over the heart. On top of the desk was a secure telephone, a leather-trimmed blotter, a legal pad, a couple of Sharpie markers, and several plastic bottles of water in cup holders. A plate containing grapes, a banana, and other fruit was perched on a window ledge to his left. There was also a television mounted in a dark wooden panel above a couch opposite his desk.

The president's first act was to order additional protection for his nineteen-year-old twin daughters—Barbara at Yale and Jenna at the University of Texas—as well as his wife, who was on Capitol Hill. Instead of testifying about education, Laura Bush had used her brief appearance before Kennedy's committee to issue a national appeal for calm in the midst of this unprecedented crisis. Before she was whisked away to a secure location, Kennedy embraced the First Lady in a show of support the president would not soon forget.

"I was worried for my wife," he told me, "until I called her and heard her voice."

More than anything, Bush wanted to get back to Washington. In the past he often derided the city as a self-important echo chamber where politicians lost touch with ordinary citizens. But now with America under attack, the president fairly ached to get back inside the Beltway.

And yet he knew the capital was anything but safe. He heard more details about the third jetliner scoring a direct hit on the Pentagon, the seemingly impregnable fortress of the world's sole superpower. If the terrorists could strike debilitating blows to the hallowed icons of America's military and financial prowess, where else would they strike? Before Bush had time to ponder this question, he was provided with the chilling answer—the *White House!* It was being evacuated at that very moment. Members of his own staff were streaming out of the West Wing, running down the asphalt driveway for their very lives. Secret Service agents yelled at women to remove their high heels in order to run more quickly. Apparently a fourth jetliner was headed for 1600 Pennsylvania Avenue, the place where the president spent his workdays and laid his head down to sleep at night, the holiest of holies among America's venerated symbols of democracy. Secret Service agents had already hustled Cheney into a bombproof bunker far below the West Wing. Deputy press wrangler Reed Dickens was chasing journalists out, including Ron Fournier of the Associated Press, who stubbornly insisted on being the last to leave.

The president got on the phone with Cheney, whom he had nicknamed "Vice," and instructed him to brief congressional leaders. But Capitol Hill was also being evacuated, along with the Supreme Court. The terrorists had managed to spook all three branches of the federal government.

"Sounds like we have a minor war going on here," Bush told the vice president. "I heard about the Pentagon."

In the bunker with Cheney was Transportation Secretary Norman Mineta, who had already ordered all commercial aircraft immediately grounded. But there were still thousands of planes in the air, including a domestic flight and two international flights that were unaccounted for. As far as the administration was concerned, these three planes constituted another potentially lethal wave of airborne missiles.

After his call to Cheney, Bush turned to the men gathered around his desk—Card, Rove, Fleischer, and the military aide who carried the nuclear football, Lieutenant Colonel Tom Gould. He made it clear this was no time to go wobbly, in Margaret Thatcher's famous phrase. At this moment of maximum peril, the president needed men of action.

"That's what we're paid for, boys," Bush said. "We're gonna take care of this. When we find out who did this, they're not gonna like me as president. Somebody's going to pay."

Air Force One took off at 9:57 A.M. and began climbing to the unusually high altitude of 45,000 feet. Soon the president was back on the phone with Cheney, who posed a question that would have been unthinkable an hour earlier. Fighter jets were being scrambled and the pilots wanted to know the rules of the road. If they encountered another hijacked plane that refused to be deterred from a suicide attack, should they shoot it down? They needed an explicit order from their commander in chief.

So this is what it had come to. A scant three hours earlier, Bush had been discussing the Little League game of Dick Keil's son and the fact that Barney couldn't take part in presidential jogs. *Such trivial concerns!* And now he was being asked to make the most momentous decision of his life: whether U.S. fighter jets had the right to shoot down civilian airliners that were packed with innocent men, women, and children. Bush talked it over with Cheney. If he didn't give the order, another plane might slam into a building, killing countless people on the ground. On the other hand, if he did give the order, he might be signing the death warrant for hundreds of civilians aboard a commercial aircraft. Of course, they would die anyway if their plane slammed into a crowded building. But if the jetliner were shot down over an uninhabited area, at least no one on the ground would be killed. Cheney was waiting for an answer. Did the pilots have permission to shoot down jetliners or not?

"You bet," Bush told the vice president. The president told me later that this wasn't a difficult decision to make, "once I realized there was a protocol...because again, I now realized we're under attack. This is a war. And it took me no time to realize it was a war."

The president then explained the shoot-down order to Donald Rumsfeld, who was at the still-burning Pentagon. The defense secretary had predicted that very morning, at an 8 A.M. breakfast meeting, that within a matter of months, a calamity would shock the nation into realizing the need for a strong military. While he was still speaking, someone walked in and handed him a note that said a plane had just struck the World Trade Center. The man derided by Maureen Dowd as not knowing "anything about how the world works" adjourned the meeting and rushed to his office for a CIA briefing. Fifteen minutes later, he felt the Pentagon shake all around him. "Rip Van Rummy" hustled through a smoke-filled corridor, down a stairwell, and outside, where he saw his own employees lying on the grass with their clothes blown off, their bodies covered with burns. The bespectacled sixty-nine-year-old "retread" from the Ford administration helped load them onto stretchers and ordered others to hold IVs while the wounded were carried to ambulances. Then he returned to his office, only to find it filling with smoke. So he moved to the war room in an underground bunker known as the National Military Command Center. One of his first acts was to send up a specially outfitted 747 that could function as a "survivable" airborne command post in the event that ground facilities were destroyed. With the Pentagon itself going up in flames, it seemed like a prudent step. Rumsfeld and his top brass also dispatched fighter jets to patrol Washington and New York, as well as AWACS radar planes to monitor the East and West Coasts. An "escort package" of F-16s, F-15s, and AWACS was scrambled to protect Air Force One.

After two more conversations with Cheney and a briefing from a CIA official, the president instructed Rumsfeld to order all U.S. military bases, domestic and on foreign soil, to raise their threat alert status from normal, which is the lowest of five levels, to Delta, the highest. At 10:20 A.M., Bush also elevated the Defense Readiness Condition (DefCon) from Four to Three, the highest level in twenty-eight years. (The scale ranges from DefCon Five, which signifies peacetime, to DefCon One, for all-out war.) During the Cold War, such a move would automatically be matched by the Soviets. But Russian President Vladimir Putin figured the last thing Bush needed to worry about at this moment was heightened tension in Moscow. So he quickly notified Rice that he was ordering Russian troops to stand down instead. It was Russia's way of proclaiming itself an ally of the United States in this frightening new war.

On the second floor of Air Force One, up in the bulbous nose of the 747, Air Force officers running the communications center dialed through local television signals and fed them into the plane's numerous TV sets. The grainy pictures faded in and out as the plane passed from one local TV market to another. At one point everyone on the plane was watching KXAS, the NBC affiliate in Dallas/Fort Worth, where White House counselor Karen Hughes had spent seven years as a reporter. All the stations kept showing replays of a calamity that had occurred two minutes after Air Force One had taken off—the collapse of the south tower of the World Trade Center, the one that Bush and the rest of the nation had seen struck by the second plane. It was an astonishing sight. The tallest skyscraper in New York had simply imploded. One moment it was standing there, 110 stories tall, and the next it simply collapsed to the ground in spectacular slow motion. As one floor flattened upon another, an avalanche of dust and debris billowed out from all sides, cascading outward in a widening cloud of black and gray that enveloped smaller buildings for blocks in every direction. It was like a mushroom cloud in reverse, with the cap of the mushroom descending as it broadened, reaching maximum width as it hit the floor of Manhattan and fanned across the city's concrete canyons, finally curling skyward as it slammed against the sides of countless structures. The mushroom's smoky gray stalk hung in place like some ghostly shroud, as if it might still be concealing the tower itself. But within moments this phantom tower melded into the all-encompassing cloud of smoke that now choked the city.

As Air Force One hurtled north across Florida, its TV screens were filled with apocalyptic images of shell-shocked New Yorkers running for their very lives from onrushing walls of ash and smoke that loomed fifty stories tall and reached down to choke the very subways. Men and women in suits and skirts staggered down streets covered from head to foot in gray ash. The stuff was caked on their clothes, hair, and skin. Looking as though they were encased in some strangely flexible concrete, they clutched handkerchiefs and hats over their mouths and noses in futile attempts to filter out the oppressive filth. Some paused to tell reporters of unspeakable horrors they had just witnessed. Several people had looked up in time to see one of the planes crash into the towers. Others saw office workers jumping from the upper floors of the Twin Towers to escape the stupendous heat and flames. Still others had been inside the towers and managed to hustle down seventy or eighty flights of stairs as the buildings heaved and groaned all around them.

The scenes in Washington were almost as horrific. Gigantic plumes of smoke billowed from the Pentagon. Most of the 22,000 employees were being evacuated. Uniformed military officers were sprinting down Interstate 395, which had been closed to vehicular traffic. Civilian office workers joined in the mad rush away from the flaming fortress. Reporters described how the jetliner had staved in the south side of the structure. The plane had ripped a hole 150 feet wide, collapsing five stories and sending flames spreading toward the center of the building, which consisted of five concentric rings. The evacuations and road closings there and across the Potomac were creating a traffic jam unparalleled in a city long inured to gridlock. U.S. fighter jets appeared and began to patrol the nation's emptying capital.

At 10:28 A.M., the televisions aboard Air Force One showed live images of a scene that left everyone on board, including the president, aghast. The north tower of the World Trade Center, the one with the TV antenna sticking straight up from the roof like a giant toothpick, collapsed under its own weight. The antenna remained strangely erect and anchored to the roof as it rode the flaming pancakes down toward the street. Great fountains of debris spewed outward from all sides, creating a second reverse mushroom cloud as it hit Manhattan's floor. The stalk became another phantom tower that hung in the air like a magician's smoke that shrouds the disappearance of a sequined assistant.

Although Air Force One was over the coast of Georgia, it was picking up a surprisingly strong signal from KXLT, the Fox affiliate in Rochester, Minnesota. News anchor Jon Scott, whose commentary on the disaster for the past ninety minutes had been measured and dignified, chose to let the pictures speak for themselves when the second tower disintegrated. After several long moments of solemn silence, he said simply, "America, offer a prayer."

Bush could barely believe his eyes. All of lower Manhattan was utterly subsumed by a gargantuan cloud of smoke and ash that now rose a full mile into the sky, obscuring even the tallest buildings. The sheer volume of particulates overflowed the city streets and spilled out into New York Harbor, drifting south in a toxic haze that stretched for miles into Upper New York Bay and dwarfed the Statue of Liberty.

The cloud was still rising at 10:32 A.M., when Cheney phoned Bush again to alert him that a call had come into the White House switchboard, warning that the next target was Air Force One. The caller even knew the plane's secret code name, which was Angel. With the phone still pressed to his ear, Bush turned to Gould, the carrier of the nuclear football, and said, "Angel is next."

Was nothing safe? Air Force One was supposed to be the most secure and technologically sophisticated aircraft in the world. Packed with antimissile devices, encrypted phone lines, and enough armor to withstand a small nuclear blast, it had a perfect safety record. And now these terrorists, who had proven themselves capable of attacking the Pentagon and World Trade Center with breathtaking savagery, were brazenly coming for the president's personal airplane. "Who *are* those guys?!" The line from the film *Butch Cassidy and the Sundance Kid*—in which the outlaws are increasingly unnerved and astonished by the prowess of their pursuers—seemed terribly apt right now. Suddenly it was perfectly feasible that these terrorists could strike Air Force One, which, except for the White House, was the most potent and recognizable symbol of the American presidency. To make matters worse, the "escort package" of fighter jets and AWACS had not yet arrived to protect Air Force One. And there were still three stray planes out there that, as far as Bush knew, might be under the control of hijackers.

The president told Cheney, "We're gonna find out who did this, and we're gonna kick their ass."

But the vice president kept piling on the bad news. There was a report of a car bomb at the Lincoln Memorial and another at the State Department. There were indications that an unidentified plane was five miles from Washington and closing fast. Cheney had already reassured a jittery military that it was authorized to shoot down the plane if it failed to obey radio and visual orders.

"There is a fog of war," Bush told me. "At this point, the information was sketchy, and the facts were just flying at us. You know:

Attack on the State Department. Plane aimed for the White House. Crash. We actually had a threat, potential threat on the ranch. I mean, we were hearing all kinds of things."

Although Air Force One was still headed for Washington, Bush and his aides began to discuss the possibility of changing destinations. After all, if the terrorists had targeted the president's plane, they would certainly be expecting him to continue his flight to Andrews Air Force Base in Maryland.

"What about Camp David?" Bush suggested. The presidential retreat in the Catoctin Mountains of Maryland was fifty miles from the White House. Cheney thought that was too close. He favored sending Bush to a military base, such as STRATCOM, the underground Strategic Command bunker at Offutt Air Force Base in Nebraska.

Meanwhile, there was a bit of good news: The president's wife and daughters had been successfully moved to safe locations. In a moment of lightheartedness, Bush even inquired about his beloved Scottish terrier.

"And Barney?" the president said.

"He's nipping at the heels of Osama bin Laden now," Card deadpanned.

At 10:37, Card relayed a report that a plane had crashed near Camp David. But Rove said the real crash site was south of Pittsburgh. The plane had gone down at 10:10 A.M., thirteen minutes after Air Force One had taken off. Bush checked in with the Secret Service for another update on the safety of his family. Then he and Card assessed the intelligence they had gathered so far.

"Smells like Osama bin Laden to me," Card said.

At 10:41 A.M., Cheney called again with a recommendation that did not surprise Bush. Both the vice president and Rice said Washington was no longer safe enough for his return. There was no sense in coming home if that meant accommodating the terrorists' desire to decapitate the government. Bush couldn't think of a good argument to the contrary, so he gave the order to divert the plane, which was off the coast of South Carolina and had already completed half of its 900-mile journey to Washington. Suddenly it veered west, but not toward Offutt Air Force Base, which was over 1,000 miles away. Instead, Air Force One headed for Barksdale Air Force Base near Shreveport, Louisiana, which was just 800 miles away. The plane still had over 50,000 gallons of fuel—enough to fly nonstop to New Zealand—and could remain aloft even longer, because it could be refueled in midflight. But Bush wanted to address the nation as soon as possible and, thanks to the plane's ability to travel at 700 mph, Barksdale was just over an hour away. The president instructed Fleischer to draft a statement. The spokesman immediately began filling his legal pad with remarks, which were edited by Karen Hughes during a subsequent phone call.

As Air Force One passed over Mississippi, its passengers noticed that an F-16 fighter jet had taken up a position just off the tip of the left wing. Bush walked into a window-lined hallway outside his cabin, placed his hands on his knees, and stooped at the waist to get a good look at the mosquito-like jet gleaming in the brilliant blue sky. It was so close you could make out the profile of the pilot's face. Meanwhile, two more fighters appeared off the plane's right wingtip.

"I'll never forget looking out the airplane and seeing the F-16s on our wing," he told me. "I was very worried about the nation. I wasn't sure what was going to happen next. We just didn't know."

On TV, the news anchors were by now wondering aloud about the president's location. After all, it had been nearly two hours since Bush had addressed the nation. During that time, a jetliner had slammed into the Pentagon, killing hundreds, and another had plowed into a field in Pennsylvania. Both towers of the World Trade Center had collapsed and the White House had been evacuated. And yet no one even knew where Bush was. Fox News Channel anchor Brit Hume broached the subject as delicately as possible.

"This may be a nation at this moment that needs to hear from its government," he said at 11:28 A.M. "The Secret Service is not saying exactly where the president of the United States is."

The bottom of the TV screen bore the words: "FOX NEWS ALERT— SECRET SERVICE WILL NOT CONFIRM PRESIDENT BUSH'S LOCATION."

This presented a dilemma to the thirteen journalists on Air Force One, who were relegated to the back of the plane, behind the cabins reserved for the president, senior staff, guests, and Secret Service. Bush and his advisors knew the increasingly restless reporters would want some basic information, starting with their mysterious destination. But if the press learned that Air Force One was headed for Barksdale Air Force Base in northwest Louisiana, then so would the terrorists, who were no doubt monitoring the media. The reporters, who would be able to figure out their location as soon as they landed, would undoubtedly use their cell phones to alert the world. So Ari Fleischer was dispatched to the back of the plane with specific instructions to muzzle the press. He told the journalists they could only report that they were in "an unidentified location in the United States." They were even barred from using their cell phones, since the devices might emit signals that could somehow be tracked by terrorists.

But such secrecy had a political price. At 11:56 A.M., Hume gingerly pointed out that it had now been nearly two and a half hours since Bush addressed the nation. The newsman suggested that "with

Americans in the streets and government buildings on fire," the country wanted to see its president back in the White House.

"There's a very great likelihood that the Bush administration will want to have him here and in familiar surroundings, and seen in familiar surroundings, as soon as possible, in an effort to calm the nation," Hume said. "Except for the remarks that we heard from President Bush earlier this morning, just before he took off from down in Florida to come back here, this is a nation that has not heard publicly from its government."

He added that he imagined "the president is headed in this direction" and might soon land at Andrews Air Force Base.

But Bush had landed at Barksdale eleven minutes earlier. He was lingering on the plane to gather more intelligence. Since there was no mobile gangway on the tarmac, the president would be unable to emerge from his customary door in the top half of Air Force One. So he worked the phones while the flight crew opened a hatch near the belly of the plane and lowered a set of retractable stairs. Just before noon, the president emerged under a clear, hot sky, although it was not as humid as Florida and there was a slight breeze.

As Bush descended, he could tell right away how drastically things on the ground had changed while he had been in the air. For starters, the tarmac was teeming with camouflaged soldiers in full battle gear, brandishing M-16s as they scrambled to set up a perimeter around Air Force One.

"Hey, hey! Get to that wingtip!" a superior shouted to an underling. "Move to that wingtip NOW!"

Instead of the usual line of politicians and dignitaries at the foot of the stairs, Bush encountered a Secret Service agent and two Air Force officers. He saluted and then noticed his usual motorcade was nowhere to be found. Normally, when the president steps off Air Force One, he gets into his armored limousine, which is flown in ahead of time on a military transport plane. But there had been no time to get the car here. Nor was there time to assemble the usual caravan of black Chevy Suburbans and white passenger vans for the Secret Service, White House staff, and press. So Bush got into a dark blue Dodge Caravan with a small, wing-shaped antenna protruding from the rear of the roof. Card climbed in the other side, but his colleagues, including Rove and Bartlett, had to squeeze onto an Air Force minibus with the press. A soldier manned a machine gun turret atop a green Humvee.

"I was much more observant in Barksdale," Bush told me. "I'll never forget getting in a car and going about 150 miles an hour. I thought the most dangerous part of the whole day was driving across the tarmac, these guys with guns strapped on them."

This bizarre little motorcade sped to the General Dougherty Conference Center, a two-story building painted the color of cream, with brown trim. It had a red tile roof and stood next to a crepe myrtle tree with vivid red blossoms. A car blocked the driveway and several armed soldiers stood sentinel as Bush and his aides walked inside at the stroke of noon. The president entered a conference room, picked up a telephone, and began talking with Cheney again.

"I see four aircraft are lost," he remarked. There were still two international flights unaccounted for and Bush considered them potential missiles.

At 12:11 P.M., Bush emerged from the building and got back into the motorcade, which proceeded to building 245. A sign out front said, "Headquarters—Eighth Air Force." Inside, there was a door taped with a sheet of paper that said "DefCon Delta" in large black type.

Past this door the president went upstairs to an office that had a secure phone line. Soon he was talking again with Cheney. By now the press was clamoring for the president to address the nation publicly with reassuring words. The president was in complete agreement.

"I think it's important for people to see the government is functioning, because the TV shows our nation has been blasted and bombed," Bush said to his aides. "The government is not chaotic. It's functioning smoothly."

He added, "We're gonna get the bastards."

When Bush selected Cheney as his running mate thirteen months earlier, Democrats and the press chortled that his father had actually made the choice for him. Cheney, who had served as the elder Bush's defense secretary and overseen the Gulf War, was ridiculed as yet another "retread" whose selection was nothing more than a transparent attempt to lend some gravitas to Bush, a hopeless lightweight. But in those first hours after the terrorist attacks, the unflappable Cheney proved invaluable to Bush, who turned to this seasoned, sober sage more than he turned to anyone else.

"You're doing great," he told the vice president. "I'll stay in touch with you."

Trying to bring some sense to the events, he added, "It's the new war. It's the faceless coward that attacks." As he hung up, he made a mental note to repeat that line to the nation when he finally made it back to the White House.

Bush then headed for a conference room to deliver the remarks that Fleischer had drafted and Hughes had edited. Preceding the president down the hallway were two Secret Service officers, Bartlett, Rove, an Air Force officer, Fleischer, Card, and four more Secret Service officers. A couple of soldiers in green fatigues stood guard just outside a pair of polished wooden doors with brass hinges. Several aides and Secret Service agents remained in the hallway. Bush strode into the room at 12:36 P.M., his jacket unbuttoned, his right hand clutching a neat stack of white papers. A flurry of flashes erupted and the president blinked four or five times in rapid succession. He placed his papers on a polished wooden lectern flanked by two American flags. He exhaled audibly through his mouth as he buttoned his jacket. He cast a wary glance to his right and paused several seconds to make sure the cameras were ready for him. It had been three hours and six minutes since he had addressed the nation and he knew it would be even longer before America would hear what he was about to say. This was not a live feed so his remarks would be viewed on tape delay.

Months later, when asked by a troubled teenager how he felt when he first heard the news on September 11, Bush replied, "I was angry, and I wept." He did not say exactly when he wept, but when the president walked into that conference room at Barksdale Air Force Base, reporters noticed that his eyes were rimmed in red.

"Freedom itself was attacked this morning by a faceless coward," Bush began.

"Eric," said the cameraman. Incredibly, he was again scolding Eric the soundman for holding his boom microphone too low.

"And freedom will be defended," continued the president, unfazed.

"*Eric!*" the cameraman said.

"I want to reassure the American people that full—the full resources of the federal government are working to assist local authorities to save lives and to help the victims of these attacks."

It was the sort of minor stumble no one would have noticed under normal circumstances. But reporters had waited so long for the president to speak that they would dissect his words with unusual harshness and note this innocuous flub.

"Make no mistake," he continued. "The United States will hunt down and punish those responsible for these cowardly acts.

"I've been in regular contact with the vice president," Bush said as a beeper went off somewhere in the room, "secretary of defense, the national security team, and my cabinet.

"We have taken all appropriate"—he mispronounced the last syllable as "ate"—"appropriate security precautions to protect the American people."

"Our military at home and around the world is on high alert status," Bush said, giving "high" the southern pronunciation "hah." "And we have taken the necessary security precautions to continue the functions of your government."

Your government. It was an odd choice of words, as though Bush himself were exempt from the government he headed.

"We have been in touch with the leaders of Congress and with world leaders to assure them that we will do what is—whatever is necessary to protect America and Americans."

Another minor flub, but now the press had its trifecta.

"I ask the American people to join me in saying a thanks for all the folks who have been fighting hard to rescue our fellow citizens and to join me in saying a prayer for the victims and their families."

Bush said this without looking at his notes. He glanced one last time at the podium and then concluded his remarks with a touch of defiance.

"The resolve of our great nation is being tested. But make no mistake," he warned, shaking his head. "We will show the world that we will pass this test. God bless."

He started to step away from the podium and then remembered his remarks, which he picked up with his right hand and shifted to his left as he strode from the room, bending the pages lengthwise along the way.

Bob Woodward of the *Washington Post* would later write, "It was not a reassuring picture. He spoke haltingly, mispronouncing several words as he looked down at his notes." Howard Fineman of *Newsweek* would go on TV to declare this speech "the low point" in the president's war on terrorism.

But in fairness, the president's voice did not crack or quaver. For a man who had long poked fun at his own tendency to mangle the English language, he did not fracture his syntax any more than usual. For a leader who had great difficulty concealing his emotions, he did not choke up. Besides, once he was away from the cameras, he was markedly more animated.

"I can't wait to find out who did it," Bush privately told the base commander two minutes after his remarks. "It's going to take a while. And we're not gonna have a little slap-on-the-wrist crap."

Fifteen minutes later, he was on the phone to Senator Charles Schumer, New York Democrat.

"It's a sad day for America," Bush was saying. "Condolences go to everyone in New York. The government is functioning. We'll come together. God bless."

Then Bush talked again with Rumsfeld, who informed him it was an American Airlines jet that hit the Pentagon. The president decided this was the time to make it clear to "Rummy" that there would be a counterattack and that the military would not be hamstrung by politics the way it had been in Vietnam.

"It's a day of national tragedy and we'll clean up the mess," the president said. "And then the ball will be in your court and Dick Myers's court to respond."

He was referring to General Richard Myers, the incoming head of the Joint Chiefs of Staff. Bush knew that U.S. soldiers, sailors, marines, and airmen all over the globe would be looking to the commander in chief for some clear direction at this historic moment. He figured there was no sense in making them wait.

Just after 1 P.M., the president received an intelligence report from the base commander that a high-speed object was headed for his ranch in Crawford, Texas. Bush ordered an underling to notify everyone at the ranch, although it turned out to be another false alarm.

Meanwhile, a military public relations officer took the president's taped remarks outside the base gate to a TV satellite truck, where a technician popped the cassette into a deck and hit the "play" button to broadcast the speech to the world. It was 1:04 P.M. and Bush's location was still a mystery. TV anchors took note of the continued secrecy and emphasized that the president's remarks were taped, not live. The implication was that the White House had purposely delayed the airing of the tape in order to get a head start on the president's next secret destination. But in reality, the tape delay had been a function of mere logistics—there were no cables available at Barksdale for a live feed on such short notice. In fact, Bush remained at Barksdale more than half an hour after his taped speech was aired.

"You see the president touching down at an Air Force base, at an unknown—or at least previously unknown—location, dropping off a videotape, having taped a statement there, and moving on," said Hume, who correctly surmised it was the Secret Service, not Bush, who resisted returning to Washington.

"At times like these, the security becomes very tight and security officials exercise maximum authority and get control of the situation," he added. "So I think we're probably in for some more mystery about the whereabouts of the president of the United States for some time now."

Bush was again guarded by a camouflaged Humvee on the way back to Air Force One, which was still surrounded by soldiers facing outward, their guns drawn. A pack of military dogs was patrolling the tarmac.

When the president got back on Air Force One, there were fewer people on board than when he had disembarked a little over an hour earlier. In an effort to reduce the "footprint" of the presidential entourage, all nonessential passengers were told to stay put at Barksdale. This included a congressman, numerous White House staffers, and eight of the thirteen original journalists. The president's top aides had briefly considered dumping all the journalists but concluded that the tragic events of this day were too historic for a total news blackout. Still, there were some heated words on the tarmac from members of the Fourth Estate who did not appreciate being dumped in the middle of the biggest story of their careers. On the other hand, some of those who were chosen to continue traveling with the president feared for their own safety, although they didn't dare say so. One White House staffer who worked closely with the press, stenographer Ellen Eckert, was only too happy to be left behind. But at the last moment, Bush aides decided there might be a need for a stenographer. Indeed, it was entirely possible the president would make another public utterance, which would need to be recorded and transcribed by a White House steno. So Gordon Johndroe yelled across the tarmac to Eckert, who reluctantly boarded the plane.

As soon as Bush settled in behind his desk on Air Force One, he returned to the task at hand—figuring out a plan of action to respond to the terrorists.

"This administration will spend whatever's necessary to find, hunt down, and destroy whoever did this," he assured his aides.

Before the plane departed, he got on the phone again with Cheney to express his growing frustration at not being able to return to Washington. The president was reluctantly headed for Offutt Air Force Base in Nebraska, which had secure teleconferencing equipment that would allow him to conduct a 4:00 P.M. meeting of his National Security Council.

"I can assure you I'd like to come home now," he said. "Tonight would be great."

At 1:25, Bush turned to Card and the head of the Secret Service detail.

"I want to go back home ASAP," the president said. "I don't want whoever this is holding me outside of Washington."

"Our people say it's too unsteady still," said the Secret Service agent.

Bush sighed. "Cheney says it's not safe yet, as well."

"The right thing is to let the dust settle," counseled Card.

Bush acquiesced. He later told me this was the right decision, especially amid countless "fog of war" threats to Washington.

"History looks pretty clear. But at the moment, it's not clear," the president reflected. "The best thing to do is exercise caution and to get the president to a position where he can be in communications with his team. And you don't have to be looking at each other to be in communication. You just have got to be in communication."

Indeed, at 2:25 P.M., he was on a conference call with New York Governor George Pataki and New York City Mayor Rudy Giuliani, who had been temporarily trapped in one of the buildings near the attack site.

"Our sympathies are with you and the people of New York," Bush said. "I know your heart is broken and your city is stinging. Anything we can do to help, you let me know."

Even as Bush cautioned that "there's some possibility of a second wave," he tried to buck up the two leaders, especially Pataki.

"I've seen you on TV, George, and you've handled yourself very well," he said.

At one point a photographer for the Associated Press, Doug Mills, stepped inside the president's cabin and began discreetly snapping photos of Bush and Card in their shirtsleeves, conversing across the desk. The two men ignored Mills, who got his photos and withdrew.

At 2:58, the president again groused about his inability to return home.

"We need to get back to Washington," he told the Secret Service agent. "We don't need some tinhorn terrorist to scare us off. The American people want to know where their dang president is."

But first he had a National Security Council meeting to conduct. As Air Force One made its final approach to Offutt Air Force Base, Fleischer reappeared in the press cabin. The journalists figured he would again forbid them to reveal their location. But just then, a local Nebraska news affiliate broke into the national coverage it had been feeding viewers in order to show live pictures of Air Force One descending from the sky. It's not as if the plane was difficult to identify, even from a distance. With a wingspan of nearly 200 feet and a length of 230 feet, the massive aircraft had huge letters on the side proclaiming "UNITED STATES OF AMERICA." Its paint job alone—periwinkle blue on top and robin's egg blue down below—made the plane an instantly recognizable American icon. Even before the six-story-high behemoth touched down, the Nebraska journalists—who had instinctively gathered outside the gates of the local air base at this time of national crisis—were reporting Bush's arrival at Offutt. They had made no agreement with the White House to keep the president's location a secret. As a result, the national journalists on the plane figured all bets were off. They directed Fleischer's attention to the TV screen in the press cabin, which was showing live images of Air Force One's descent. The cat was already out of the bag.

Once again there was no mobile gangway, so the lower hatch was opened and the retractable stairs lowered. The president's aides got off the plane first. Only when the stairs were cleared did Bush appear in the opening and descend the fourteen steps, followed closely by a Secret Service agent. Two more Secret Service agents were at the foot of the stairs, along with a pair of Air Force officers. Bush snapped two salutes and waved to an aide as he stepped to the motorcade. Although his limousine was still missing, at least he didn't have to get into a minivan or Humvee. Instead, the president climbed into the back seat of a black sedan and noticed that a fairly respectable motorcade had been thrown together. There was a police car out front, followed by a decoy sedan and the president's car. Then came the dark SUV for the Secret Service, followed by a car, a minibus and a minivan for staff, and a final van for the press. There was an orderliness to the motorcade that suggested the situation was beginning to calm, that the first hint of normalcy had returned.

The motorcade proceeded at a sober pace, making wide, deliberate turns instead of cutting across the painted lines at breakneck speed in order to save time. At each intersection of the sprawling military base, soldiers in full battle gear stood sentinel along the side streets, their weapons drawn. The motorcade turned down a driveway in front of the main building, where sprinklers were watering a big front lawn that featured a white dummy missile emblazoned with the words "AIR FORCE." Bush's sedan passed a checkpoint manned by a helmeted, saluting soldier and stopped in front of the building near a sign that said "UNITED STATES STRATEGIC COMMAND." The president emerged, but instead of heading inside the large office complex, he took a few steps across the grass to a squat brick shack no more than ten feet tall. A soldier in a flak jacket opened a windowless steel door. On the door was a sign that read, "WARNING: Restricted Area." Bush and his entourage walked inside and descended to a subterranean bunker. When they got to the secure conference room, the president took the middle seat at a white hexagonal table containing several pitchers of water. A military officer sat to his right and Card sat to his left. On the wall facing Bush were two large video screens. The one on the left showed a mirror image of him and Card. The screen on the right was divided into four smaller panels, each of which showed National Security Council members sitting at tables in various Washington bunkers. These included Cheney, Rumsfeld, FBI director Robert Mueller, and George Tenet, the director of Central Intelligence. One of Tenet's first acts had been to dispatch several CIA employees to pull his son out of Gonzaga College High School near the Capitol, an act that unnerved fellow students and teachers who had just decided against evacuation.

Behind the president were three elevated rows of chairs that remained empty, because most of his aides were not allowed inside. So he and Card were pretty much alone as they listened to mounting evidence that the attacks had been masterminded by Osama bin Laden, head of the al Qaeda terrorist network. For starters, several al Qaeda members had been among the passengers on the jetliner that hit the Pentagon, according to a cursory review of the plane's manifest. Secondly, intelligence operatives had intercepted phone calls among other al Qaeda operatives who were already congratulating themselves on the day's carnage.

By now more than five hours had passed since a plane had crashed. The jetliner that had ditched on a farm field in Pennsylvania had apparently been destined for the Washington area, although it remained unclear whether its target was the White House, the Capitol, or Camp David. All other commercial planes were on the ground and accounted for, although there was still plenty of worry that some other type of attack might occur. The Secret Service continued to insist that Washington was too dangerous for the president's return. Officials even made arrangements for Bush and his entourage to spend the night in the underground bunker. But the president had other ideas.

"We're going home," he said to his staff as he stepped into the hallway at 4:15 P.M., having concluded the meeting.

As Air Force One roared into a brilliant blue sky with its escort of fighter jets at 4:36 P.M., Bush reached his wife at her "secure location."

"I'm coming home," he told her. "See you at the White House.

"I love you," he added. "Go on home."

By this point the president felt comfortable enough to joke about the level of safety they could expect at home.

"If I'm in the White House and there's a plane coming my way, all I can say is I hope I read my Bible that day," joshed the president, a devout Christian.

One of the many shocks Bush received was the news that Barbara Olson had been one of the passengers on the plane that slammed into the Pentagon. Olson was a conservative author and commentator whose husband, Ted Olson, had won the historic *Bush* v. *Gore* case before the U.S. Supreme Court, which effectively ended the Florida recount wars. Bush nominated Olson to be U.S. solicitor general and Barbara played a key behind-the-scenes role in defending her husband against attacks by Senate Democrats during his confirmation hearings. Her second book, *The Final Days: The Last, Desperate Abuses of Power by the Clinton White House*, had just been sent to the printers.

At 4:55 P.M., Bush called Ted to offer his condolences. It turned out that Barbara had originally booked a September 10 flight but had rescheduled it for a day later so that she could have breakfast with her husband before departing on September 11, his birthday.

Ten minutes later, the president was on the phone to Karen Hughes to discuss plans for what the entire nation seemed to crave, a televised address from the Oval Office. As he articulated his thoughts, she scribbled notes that would be shaped into a speech.

"We'll find these people and they will suffer the consequences of taking on this nation," he vowed. "We will do what it takes. Everybody must understand: This will not stand."

The phrase "will not stand" did not make it into the speech, perhaps because the White House did not want to give ammunition to Democrats who had previously speculated Bush was getting too much advice from his father.

The president told Hughes he was grateful for the messages he had been hearing from world leaders. "The world is uniting against terrorism," he said. "No one is going to diminish the spirit of this great country."

As Air Force One traversed the Midwest, Bush got up and wandered the plane in his shirtsleeves. He paused in each cabin to say hello and chat with the passengers, hoping his presence would reassure them. For example, the Secret Service agents were deeply worried about their colleagues in New York, whose field office had been in the World Trade Center. Even when it became apparent that all but one employee of the New York office had survived, nerves remained raw among the agents aboard Air Force One. After all, they were guarding the president on a day when ruthless and cunning terrorists were obviously trying to kill him. So Bush lingered in the Secret Service cabin, trying to put the agents' minds at ease and even kidding with them a bit. While speaking to one of the agents, he jerked his thumb toward another in a playful, exaggerated gesture and pulled a funny face.

Bush then leaned into the press cabin, where stenographer Ellen Eckert had joined the five journalists and was sitting in the front row. With no work to do, Eckert had worried herself to a frazzle and was surprised to see the president, who hardly ever ventured back into the press cabin.

"Hey, sir," she said.

"Hey," Bush said. "How you doing?"

"Fine," she replied. "Uh, were you able to reach Mrs. Bush?"

The president walked up to Eckert and put his arm around her shoulder.

"I just talked to her," he said, patting the stenographer. "Thanks for asking."

As Eckert's eyes filled with tears, something unusual happened. Normally, when a president ventures back to the press cabin of Air Force One, reporters crowd around and aggressively grill him about the issues of the day until an aide, who is always present on such visits, cuts off questions and shepherds the commander in chief back to the safety of the front of the plane. This visit was dramatically different. For starters, Bush was alone. He had purposely refrained from telling his press wrangler, Gordon Johndroe, that he was visiting the journalists. But as it turned out, Bush didn't need Johndroe's protection. The reporters didn't even venture into the aisle, although some stood up and leaned on the headrests in front of them. Instead of interrogating the president about the cataclysmic developments of the day, they wanted to know how he was holding up.

"How are your spirits, sir?" asked photographer Doug Mills of the Associated Press.

As Bush began to answer, he noticed that cameraman George Christian of CBS was filming him. The president held up his hand and shook his head to signify he did not want this conversation recorded. Christian swung the camera away and turned it off.

Bush tried to reassure the journalists that everything was going to be all right.

"We're gonna get those bastards," he vowed. "No thug is gonna bring our country down."

He noticed that White House correspondent Sonya Ross of the AP was typing this quote into her laptop computer.

"Hey," he said with a glare. "That's off the record."

Ross agreed and the president decided it was time to go.

"I gotta get back to work," he said.

Instead of using this last opportunity to fire off questions, as the journalists had done after Bush's jog that morning, they said things like, "Keep your chin up," "We're thinking of you," and even, "We're praying."

Bush headed back toward the front of the plane, pausing in the senior staff cabin to talk with Johndroe.

"I just went back to the press cabin," the president remarked casually. Bush could see that Johndroe was horrified.

"I didn't say anything," Bush assured him. "I just said hello to them, told them I spoke to Mrs. Bush."

Bush could tell Johndroe was barely holding his emotions in check. He had gotten to know the young aide fairly well during the presidential campaign, when Johndroe made a habit of accompanying Bush on early-morning radio interviews. Now the president decided his stressed-out loyalist needed a little levity. He remembered that NBC had been granted permission to follow Bush around for an entire day in the near future. The network had been planning a special on the event for months.

"I think we're gonna be too busy to do that 'Day in the Life' next week," Bush deadpanned.

"Yes, sir," said Johndroe with a weak smile. "I don't think there's any point in doing that."

As the plane neared Andrews Air Force Base around 6:30 P.M., the Secret Service said it might be safer for Bush to complete the final leg of his journey to the White House via motorcade, not helicopter. But Bush figured the Secret Service wouldn't even be talking about the helicopter as an option if it weren't safe.

"I'm landing on the South Lawn in Marine One," he said. "People want to see me land on the South Lawn at the White House and go into the Oval Office, okay?"

Long shadows were stretching across the tarmac at Andrews when the president finally emerged, this time from the periwinkle top of the plane. With no Secret Service agent behind him, Bush descended the twenty-five red-carpeted stairs of the portable gangway with his left hand sliding along the chrome railing. At the bottom, he gave a salute and a handshake to a man in green camouflage fatigues and a black baseball cap. Dispensing with his customary wave to the press, who always gathered under the left wing to witness his disembarkment, Bush turned right and walked fifty paces to Marine One. Once airborne, the chopper flew close to the Pentagon so the president could get an eyeful of the damage. Smoke still billowed from the giant structure, which had a gash five stories high and 150 feet wide.

"The mightiest building in the world is on fire," he muttered as he stared out a window on the chopper's left side. "That's the twenty-first-century war you've just witnessed."

The green-and-white helicopter crossed the Potomac River and the Tidal Basin before swinging back around the Washington Monument. The sun was still illuminating the tops of the stately old trees surrounding the South Lawn as Marine One descended to the gloom of the grass itself at 6:54 P.M. When the massive rotors stopped spinning, Bush snapped a salute to a ramrod-straight marine at the door and headed for the Oval Office. He never thought he would be so relieved to see the White House again. He scanned the magnificent curve of the South Portico, with its stately columns framed by the gnarled magnolia tree planted by President Jackson. He gazed at the Rose Garden, still vibrant with late-summer blooms of white and pink. He crossed the running track and driveway, along which were stacked hundreds of picnic tables for use at a social event on the South Lawn. He cut up a sidewalk, passing the metal statue of a deer half hidden in the shrubs. He stepped to the stone patio just outside the Oval Office, where he was greeted by two of his closest advisors, Karen Hughes and White House Counsel Alberto Gonzales.

It had been thirty-three hours since Bush had departed the White House for what was supposed to have been a humdrum education trip. It had been less than ten hours since Card's whispered words had bifurcated his presidency. Some Democrats and journalists would all but accuse Bush of cowardice for not returning sooner, especially when it turned out that the caller who phoned in the threat against Air Force One had not used the code word "Angel" after all. The word was uttered by a White House staffer and then somehow incorporated into the threat report that was passed up the chain of command.

"I don't buy the notion Air Force One was a target," said Representative Martin Meehan, Massachusetts Democrat. "That's just PR, that's just spin."

Paul Begala, who had been Clinton's White House counselor, was even more blunt.

"He didn't come home for ten hours, ten hours when all the planes were accounted for," he said on CNN. "And he gave us some cock-and-bull story about Air Force One being under attack."

Begala ridiculed anyone who would "believe that story about Air Force One, because I didn't."

That evening, in the newsroom of the *Washington Post*, political reporter Dan Balz wrote, "Bush's decidedly low profile through much of the day was jarring even to some of his allies and raised questions about whether he should have done more to help reassure the country."

Maureen Dowd mocked a photo of Bush speaking by telephone to Cheney during those frantic hours aboard Air Force One. The columnist mused in the *New York Times* that Bush was "nervously inquiring of his adult supervisor, 'Hey, Dick, is it safe to come home yet?'" She added contemptuously, "This 'heroic' image captures the shaky hours before the president found his footing and his mission in life, a day of blank fear when Washington received no guidance from its leaders."

Such criticism angered Cheney, Hughes, and Fleischer, although the president himself never said anything, at least not publicly. Bush later told me he refused to let most of the criticism get to him, although some of the harsher comments did sting a bit.

"It was a momentary bother," he said, that critics were "somehow questioning my courage in the face of danger." He shrugged these critics off as "elites, these kind of professor types that love to read their names in the newspapers. I can't remember the exact quotes or who they were now—it's just faded. They're obscure people."

He added, "Most of those quotes weren't able to escape through my defensive systems; I wouldn't let them in."

Bush said he was confident that his decision to stay away from Washington for a while would be viewed historically as correct.

"I knew full well that I had made the absolutely right decision and history would record that. When the president is under threat, one thing for the good of the country is you want to remove the president from the immediate threat. There's nothing worse for a country having been attacked than a destabilized presidency. It would make matters a lot worse."

He added: "I knew we were going to get back there. It was just a matter of making sure."

Once he did get back, Bush immediately began working on his speech in a private study off the Oval Office. This was where the president decided to equate terrorists with those who harbor them, a policy that would come to be known as the Bush Doctrine.

After checking in on his wife and freshening up in the residence, Bush walked into the Oval Office. He sat at a desk made in 1880 from the timbers of the HMS *Resolute* and used by a long line of presidents, including FDR, Kennedy, and Reagan. At last in the setting that he and the nation craved, Bush began his speech at 8:30 P.M.

"Good evening. Today, our fellow citizens, our way of life, our very freedom came under attack in a series of deliberate and deadly terrorist acts. The victims were in airplanes or in their offices: secretaries, businessmen and -women, military and federal workers, moms and dads, friends and neighbors.

"Thousands of lives were suddenly ended by evil, despicable acts of terror. The pictures of airplanes flying into buildings, fires burning, \

huge structures collapsing have filled us with disbelief, terrible sadness, and a quiet, unyielding anger.

"These acts of mass murder were intended to frighten our nation into chaos and retreat. But they have failed. Our country is strong. A great people has been moved to defend a great nation.

"Terrorist attacks can shake the foundations of our biggest buildings, but they cannot touch the foundation of America. These acts shatter steel, but they cannot dent the steel of American resolve.

"America was targeted for attack because we're the brightest beacon for freedom and opportunity in the world. Today, our nation saw evil, the very worst of human nature, and we responded with the best of America, with the daring of our rescue workers, with the caring for strangers and neighbors who came to give blood and help in any way they could.

"Immediately following the first attack, I implemented our government's emergency response plans. Our military is powerful, and it's prepared. Our emergency teams are working in New York City and Washington, D.C., to help with local rescue efforts.

"Our first priority is to get help to those who have been injured and to take every precaution to protect our citizens at home and around the world from further attacks.

"The functions of our government continue without interruption. Federal agencies in Washington which had to be evacuated today are reopening for essential personnel tonight and will be open for business tomorrow. Our financial institutions remain strong, and the American economy will be open for business as well.

"The search is under way for those who are behind these evil acts. I've directed the full resources of our intelligence and law enforcement communities to find those responsible and bring them to justice. We will make no distinction between the terrorists who committed these acts and those who harbor them.

"I appreciate so very much the members of Congress who have joined me in strongly condemning these attacks. And on behalf of the American people, I thank the many world leaders who have called to offer their condolences and assistance.

"America and our friends and allies join with all those who want peace and security in the world and we stand together to win the war against terrorism.

"Tonight I ask for your prayers for all those who grieve, for the children whose worlds have been shattered, for all whose sense of safety and security has been threatened. And I pray they will be comforted by a power greater than any of us, spoken through the ages in Psalm 23: 'Even though I walk through the valley of the shadow of death, I fear no evil, for you are with me.'

"This is a day when all Americans from every walk of life unite in our resolve for justice and peace. America has stood down enemies before, and we will do so this time.

"None of us will ever forget this day. Yet we go forward to defend freedom and all that is good and just in our world.

"Thank you, good night, and God bless America."

The cameras had barely been switched off when Bush was up and making a beeline for the underground bunker known as the Presidential Emergency Operations Center (PEOC). It was getting late and he wanted to conduct another meeting of the National Security Council.

As he passed Johndroe, the young aide said, "Good job, Mr. President." At first Bush was too preoccupied to respond, but then he said, "Thank you, Gordon," and disappeared into the bunker.

Right away he noticed that the Secret Service agents—the hardcore ones who patrolled the White House grounds armed to the teeth and dressed in black from their baseball caps to their military boots—had unsheathed their long weapons. Bush didn't even know what kind of guns they were, but they looked extraordinarily lethal. One was leaning up against a wall next to an agent just outside the meeting room. These guys took out their big guns only under dire circumstances, as when an intruder jumped the fence on the South Lawn seven months earlier and was promptly shot.

"We get back there and had the big National Security Council, which went very well," Bush told me. "That's when we first got the indication—remember now, we're about six hours, or about eight hours or whatever it is, after the attack—we've identified, we think it's al Qaeda. Mueller has been on the job now for six days or seven days. And he's in there, and they think it's al Qaeda, and we start to develop our plans to get them.

"I mean, there wasn't any hesitation. We're starting the process of coalition-building and how to get 'em."

By the time Bush finished his NSC meeting and then met with a smaller group of aides—including Powell, who had raced back from Peru—it was after 10 P.M. Having begun his day with a high-speed, four-mile jog nearly sixteen hours earlier, having traveled thousands of miles in a nightmarish hopscotch of the nation, having given three televised addresses on the most tragic events in a generation, the president was exhausted. He was usually in bed by this time anyway, so he decide to head up toward the residence.

"I'm tired," Bush told me. "Of course, everybody's tired. And Laura's been down there for a while with the vice president and Mrs. Cheney and others."

But as he turned to leave the bunker, the president was buttonholed by a Secret Service agent.

"You'll be sleeping down here tonight," the agent said.

Bush had already eyed the bunker's ancient couch, which folded out into a bed, and concluded it would be excruciatingly uncomfortable.

"First of all, the bed looked unappetizing. Secondly, it was a little stale in there. And I needed sleep. And I knew that from this point forward, my life had been changed, as had the country's life been changed, and I needed to be clearheaded the next day, which meant I needed as much sleep as I could get.

"And the best way to get sleep is in your bed," he added. "Your own pillow, your own bed, your own little kind of body indentations in your—anyway. So I said no. And he tried to argue with me. I said, 'No, I'm not going to.'"

The agent acquiesced, but only after warning that if new threats materialized, he would have to roust the president. So Bush went up to his bedroom in the White House residence. He dictated some thoughts into his diary and discussed the day's stunning events with his wife.

"Laura takes her 'tacts off and we're in bed," he told me. "I've got Barney the dog, and Spot. And I'll be darned if twenty minutes later, I hear this guy: 'Mr. President, Mr. President! Incoming plane! We could be under attack! Come on! Right now!'

"So we get out of bed. I put on some running shorts and Laura put on her robe—and no contacts. And she's holding on to me, and I got Barney, and Spot's following. And we hustle down. We go running through, and all. And you know, my brother Neil is standing there, and he's headed down. And the butlers and the ushers. Anyway, everybody's heading down. We run into Condi and Andy. We're all moving toward this thing, the PEOC.

"And we get down in there," Bush continued. "This is through doors and guards, and you know, and it's just—whew! And we get—of course, she [Laura] can't see anything. And I see it all."

The president suspected it was a false alarm. Why would the terrorists suddenly be attacking again? All planes had been grounded and accounted for. The only aircraft in the sky were American military planes, which would shoot down any intruder, if necessary, long before it got near the White House. Bush began to look for a phone so he could get some answers. He dreaded the prospect of trying to sleep on the bunker's medieval couch-bed.

"And we get down in there and the guy goes—I bet you, forty-five seconds after we get there—he goes, 'Mr. President.' I said, 'What's going on?'

"And an airman pops up: 'Mr. President, it was a friendly!'" Bush recalled.

"It was one of our F-16s. People were on alert. They were conscious of the threat. Let me say: They were on super-alert. And so it was our own plane.

"And so then we turned right around and trudge right back up and go to sleep," the president said. "But it was kind of a humorous event—in retrospect."

Chapter Four

The Evildoer vs.
Head of International Infidels

AS A CAREER TERRORIST, Osama bin Laden had reached the pinnacle of his profession. In the space of a single hour, the lanky forty-four-year-old had struck a stunning blow against the mightiest infidel of them all—America. He accomplished this with minor expenditures (a paltry $300,000) and almost no infrastructure (he spent much of his time in caves), but an abundance of cunning and audacity. In one bold stroke, he had transformed himself from a shadowy, semi-obscure figure whom most Americans could not identify into a bona fide household name—not just in the United States, but in every corner of the world. He had achieved a level of infamy not seen since Hitler, Stalin, or at the very least, Saddam Hussein. In short, Osama bin Laden was now the first certifiable megavillain of the twenty-first century. Even his nemesis, President Bush, was referring to him as "The Evildoer," which seemed to impart some mythical status to this shy, exceedingly polite father of ten. No question about it—Osama bin Laden had arrived. And although he considered himself a modest man, he now felt entitled to indulge in a bit of old-fashioned gloating.

"Its greatest buildings were destroyed," he crowed. "America! Full of fear from its north to its south, from its west to its east. Thank God for that."

Bin Laden was clutching a microphone and kneeling with his back to a rocky outcrop in the hinterlands of Afghanistan. Seated next to him was his second-in-command, Egyptian surgeon Ayman Al-Zawahiri. Next to Zawahiri sat Muhammad Atef, al Qaeda's director of training, whose daughter had married one of bin Laden's sons in Kandahar earlier in the year. The two aides sat silently as their boss, the most wanted man on the planet, gazed into the lens of a video camera and reveled in the carnage of September 11.

"What America is tasting now is something insignificant compared to what we have tasted for decades," he said.

Actually, for the first decades of bin Laden's life, he had tasted only luxury. Born in the capital city of Riyadh as one of fifty-four children to the richest construction magnate in all of Saudi Arabia, bin Laden was lavished with the finest servants, tutors, and horses money could buy. About the only thing he couldn't purchase was a pedigree. A Saudi bloodline was extraordinarily important in the upper-crust world inhabited by bin Laden, but he was the product of a Yemeni father and a Syrian mother. Even Osama's half brothers had a social edge, since they were descended from their father's first three wives, all of whom were Saudis.

Perhaps that was why the tall, slender, sensitive Osama was drawn to the foreign Islamic fundamentalists who stayed at his family's Jeddah home during annual pilgrimages to nearby Mecca. Bin Laden's father had contracts to refurbish the sacred mosques in both Mecca and Medina—the two holiest places in all of Islam. He turned the family's sprawling house into a sort of way station for a yearly parade of true believers from the larger Muslim world. These foreigners, who spoke passionately of waging jihad against infidels, were untroubled by young Osama's lack of a Saudi pedigree.

In 1968, bin Laden's father was killed in a helicopter crash, leaving the boy $80 million at the tender age of eleven. He was even wealthier by seventeen, when he took his first wife. He also took an interest in the Muslim Brotherhood, a radical organization dedicated to creating a pan-Islamic nation. His interest intensified when he enrolled in King Abdul Aziz University in Jeddah and fell under the spell of Sheikh Abdullah Azzam, an influential member of the brotherhood's Palestinian chapter. The former confidant of Palestinian leader Yasser Arafat gave fiery speeches and recorded them on audiocassette tapes. Bin Laden spent hours listening to these screeds, which had the effect of accelerating his radicalization.

In 1979, bin Laden graduated with a degree in civil engineering. He was expected to assume his place in the family business, which by now was a multinational, multibillion-dollar construction conglomerate known as the Bin Laden Group. But the twenty-two-year-old couldn't seem to shake his fundamentalist fever. There was great upheaval in the Islamic world that year. Much to bin Laden's chagrin, the adjacent Muslim nation of Egypt signed a peace accord with the hated Jews of Israel. Naturally, the treaty was brokered by America. Even worse, the godless Soviet Union invaded the Muslim nation of Afghanistan. It was as if Islam were under assault from all sides. The year's only bright spot, as far as bin Laden was concerned, was the Iranian revolution. Inspired by the ousting of the shah, bin Laden figured the same could be done to the Soviets. So he gathered up his fortune, turned his back on the family business, and headed in the direction of Afghanistan.

He did not proceed directly to the front lines. But he did get as far as Peshawar, Pakistan, a strategic way station for mujahedeen freedom fighters on their way to Kabul, Afghanistan, via the Khyber Pass. Some of the ringleaders turned out to be the same Islamic fundamentalists who had stayed with the bin Laden family during their pilgrimages to Mecca. Bin Laden wrote down their names to keep track of the true believers. He made several trips back to Saudi Arabia to raise additional funds from family members, mosques, and the royal family. By 1984, he had set up a series of safe houses in and around Peshawar for fellow Arabs and other Muslim warriors on their way into Afghanistan. His list of names grew longer.

Eventually, bin Laden joined the fight inside Afghanistan. But instead of commanding infantry, he took charge of the army's corps of engineers. He used Bin Laden Group bulldozers—which were brought in on transport planes—to build crude roads for the freedom fighters. In 1986, he also began constructing the first of half a dozen training camps inside Afghanistan.

While bin Laden's largesse was significant, the rebels' real benefactor was America. The CIA supported the freedom fighters as a way of rolling back the spread of Soviet communism. Bin Laden was only too happy to make use of American tax dollars, although he detested the United States even more than the Soviet Union. After all, Washington was the world's biggest supporter of Israel.

By 1988, bin Laden's list of names had become the foundation of what he called al Qaeda, or "the base," a loose network of men willing to give up everything—even their own lives—to advance their puritanical strain of Islam. He brought the list back to Jeddah after the Soviets withdrew from Afghanistan in 1989.

Having spent millions on a successful holy war far from home, the prodigal son returned a conquering hero. He took his place in the family business and began expanding his personal wealth. He also expanded his family, which soon included four wives and ten children. But he came to resent the Saudi royal family—not because it was an increasingly corrupt and repressive regime but because it did not espouse bin Laden's particularly virulent strain of Islamic fundamentalism. Despite the protestations of his own worried family members and friends, bin Laden began openly to support antigovernment organizations. He sided with Saudi Arabia's most radical clerics, the ones who propagated fatwas, or religious rulings, undermining the authority of the royal family.

On August 2, 1990, Iraq invaded Kuwait and seemed capable of attacking Saudi Arabia next. Bin Laden had an inspiration: he would summon all his mujahedeen brethren from Afghanistan and Pakistan and the rest of the Muslim world to defend the Arabian peninsula. He offered such assistance in a letter to the Saudi royal family. He figured this would also smooth over any hard feelings the regime might still harbor toward him because of his public criticism.

But instead of taking bin Laden up on his offer, the royal family invited U.S. forces to use Saudi Arabia as a staging ground in their war against Iraq. The first Americans arrived on August 7, a mere five days after the invasion. Over the next five months, hundreds of thousands of troops from the United States and other Western nations poured into Saudi Arabia with the full blessing of the ruling monarchy. It was incomprehensible to bin Laden that this teeming mass of filthy, blasphemous infidels should be allowed even to set foot, much less establish long-term military bases, on the sacred soil of Mecca and Medina.

"The Arabian peninsula has never—since God made it flat, created its desert, and encircled it with seas—been stormed by any forces like the crusader armies now spreading in it like locusts, consuming its riches and destroying its plantations," bin Laden seethed in one of his own fatwas. "The United States has been occupying the lands of Islam in the holiest of places, the Arabian peninsula, plundering its riches, dictating to its rulers, humiliating its people, terrorizing its neighbors, and turning its bases in the peninsula into a spearhead through which to fight the neighboring Muslim peoples."

Bin Laden's rage only intensified when the Americans—after expelling Saddam Hussein from Kuwait in early 1991—showed no signs of leaving Saudi Arabia. It was worse than the Russians refusing to leave Afghanistan. He began to speak out more boldly against the acquiescent Saudi regime. Alarmed by bin Laden's penchant for troublemaking, the royal family barred him from traveling outside of Jeddah. He was under virtual house arrest, but he managed to pull some family strings that allowed him to slip out of the country in April 1991. He took with him $250 million.

Bin Laden returned to Afghanistan by way of Pakistan. But when he arrived in the nation he had helped liberate just two years earlier, he found it hopelessly mired in bitter disputes among rival Afghan factions. He tried to assert himself as mediator of these disputes, and got nowhere. To complicate matters, he became convinced that Saudi agents were trying to kidnap or assassinate him. By late 1991, bin Laden had decided to flee, although there were not a lot of nations rolling out the red carpet. He could no longer return to Saudi Arabia. And he considered both Afghanistan and Pakistan too dangerous. He was rapidly becoming an international pariah.

Bin Laden decided to try Sudan, where the National Islamic Front (NIF) had seized power in a military coup two years earlier. Since then, hundreds of Islamic militants had found refuge in Sudan, which waived visa requirements for all Muslims as a show of Islamic solidarity. Aware that bin Laden was worth $250 million, the NIF welcomed him to Khartoum. He soon used his money and engineering expertise to establish a road construction company that helped the government with public works projects. But he also set up a number of investment firms and foreign bank accounts that collectively amounted to a charitable foundation for terrorists. True believers from all over the world essentially applied for grants and then used the money to buy explosives, chemicals, and weapons. Bin Laden founded an agricultural firm to provide cover for some of the chemical transactions and a transportation firm that helped him to move terrorists throughout the world. The income from his various businesses was funneled into ongoing terrorist operations. It also allowed him to build three new al Qaeda training camps in Sudan, modeled after his facilities in Afghanistan. Now bin Laden had a total of nine camps in which an international network of terrorists could be trained to fight the infidels. It was time to start putting all this training to use.

On December 29, 1992, two graduates of bin Laden's Afghanistan training camps detonated a bomb inside a hotel where U.S. troops had been staying in Aden, Yemen. Bin Laden was chagrined to learn that by the time the bomb exploded, the Americans had left the hotel and were on their way to Somalia. The blast ended up killing a pair of Austrian tourists and injuring the Yemeni terrorists, both of whom were arrested. It was an inauspicious start to bin Laden's career in terrorism.

But another alumnus of bin Laden's Afghanistan training camps, Ramzi Yousef, was already plotting a far more lethal and spectacular terrorist attack—the obliteration of the World Trade Center. Bin Laden provided money and safe houses to Yousef, an Islamic militant who began executing his plan for this brazen assault immediately after the failed bombing in Yemen. The idea was to blow out the base of the World Trade Center's north tower, causing it to topple into the south tower so that both would crash to the ground. On the morning of February 26, 1993, a Ryder rental van packed with explosives was parked in the building's underground garage. At noon, terrorists used a timer to detonate the bomb, which killed six people, injured one thousand others, and trapped a group of traumatized schoolchildren in a smoky elevator for several hours. But the towers did not fall.

Bin Laden's frustration intensified. His first two terrorist attacks had killed a grand total of just eight people. The bombing in Yemen hadn't taken the life of a single American. He was particularly galled that the U.S. soldiers had been able to continue unmolested to Somalia, the latest Muslim nation to be infested with infidels. The Americans claimed to be conducting a humanitarian mission to feed starving Somalis, but bin Laden saw it as yet another desecration of Islamic soil. As far as he was concerned, the infidels had to be expelled.

He had already sent Muhammad Atef, al Qaeda's training director, to Mogadishu, Somalia, in late 1992 to plan attacks on American forces stationed there. After reporting back to bin Laden's headquarters in Khartoum, Atef was dispatched on a second trip to Somalia in early 1993. By spring, he was training and arming Somalis to kill American soldiers. In October, the Somalis got a chance to put their al Qaeda expertise to work. Firing machine guns and rocket-propelled grenade launchers, they swarmed over a small contingent of Americans who were trying to arrest two lieutenants of a local warlord in Mogadishu. The U.S. soldiers were vulnerable because their request for heavy armor had been turned down by the Clinton administration. The routine roundup mission degenerated into the longest sustained firefight involving U.S. forces since Vietnam. Two U.S. Black Hawk helicopters were shot down and eighteen GIs were killed. Mortified by news footage of ecstatic Somalis dragging an American corpse through the streets, Clinton quickly pulled out of Somalia. His defense secretary, Les Aspin, resigned after less than a year on the job. Bin Laden had scored his first major victory against the United States.

By this time the al Qaeda training camps were churning out graduates from half a dozen nations. Emboldened by his growing influence, bin Laden renewed his criticism of the Saudi regime for continuing to allow U.S. troops to defile the holy birthplace of Islam. But his outspokenness proved costly. In April 1994, the Saudi government stripped him of his citizenship. It also seized his lands and all financial assets he had left behind. Undaunted, bin Laden responded by establishing a network of training camps and safe houses near the Saudi border in northern Yemen in 1995. He issued a communiqué condemning the royal family's decision and warning that if the government refused to expel Americans, others would step up and do the job.

Inspired by this communiqué, four Saudi terrorists later that year detonated a 220-pound car bomb at a military base in Riyadh. Five Americans and two Indians were killed in the city of bin Laden's birth.

Almost immediately, the United States and Saudi Arabia began applying intense pressure on Sudan to expel bin Laden. The United Nations threatened to impose costly sanctions if Sudan's National Islamic Front continued to harbor the man who was quickly becoming the world's most notorious terrorist. As much as the Sudanese leaders enjoyed bin Laden's wealth, they finally asked him to leave. In May 1996, bin Laden fled to Afghanistan with his four wives and more than one hundred of his fiercest fighters. Spurned by yet another Muslim nation, the pariah settled in Jalalabad.

One month later, an enormous truck bomb exploded in Dhahran, Saudi Arabia, killing nineteen service members at an American military residence called Khobar Towers. Although bin Laden denied any involvement, he praised the Saudis who conducted the operation. Moreover, he formally declared war on America two months later. He issued a fatwa insisting that Saudis have the right to kill American troops as a way of driving the infidels from the Arabian peninsula. The signed statement also called for the overthrow of Saudi Arabia's royal family, the "liberation" of Muslim holy sites, and the support of Islamic radicals worldwide.

Bin Laden did not feel terribly safe in Afghanistan. Factional squabbles had ended in the formation of a weak government, which was now under siege by the Taliban, a fundamentalist student faction based in the southern Afghan province of Kandahar and headed by Mullah Muhammad Omar. Omar's supporters came primarily from Pakistani religious schools known as madrasses, which taught a particularly hateful form of Islam. There was only one thing stopping him from extending the Taliban's reach to Kabul and seizing control of the Afghan government—a dearth of funding.

Sensing an opportunity, bin Laden donated several million dollars to Omar. On September 11, 1996—exactly five years before the terrorist strikes in New York and Washington—the Taliban seized Jalalabad and pledged to protect the city's most generous resident, Osama bin Laden. Reinvigorated by their new benefactor's largesse, the Taliban went on to overrun the capital, Kabul, by the end of the month. Soon it controlled 90 percent of the country, with only the northernmost regions still run by the rebel Northern Alliance.

The Taliban imposed a reign of terror on Afghanistan, becoming one of the most repressive governments in the world. Men were forbidden to shave their beards. Women were forced to wear shapeless, head-to-toe garments called burkas. Girls were barred from attending school. Television, radio, and music were outlawed. Citizens were beaten or killed for minor infractions of draconian laws, all of which were enforced with the help of bin Laden's cash.

Al Qaeda displayed a flair for the dramatic in its next big terrorist attack, which took place in 1998. Bin Laden even scheduled it for August 7, the eighth anniversary of his life's defining moment—the arrival of U.S. troops in Saudi Arabia. To commemorate that dark day, bin Laden masterminded the simultaneous bombings of U.S. embassies in two African capitals more than 400 miles apart. This time the death toll was higher than all the others combined—224 corpses, including a dozen Americans. The blasts in Nairobi, Kenya, and Dar es Salaam, Tanzania, also injured more than five thousand people. Bin Laden had been planning the attacks since November 1994, when he sent Atef to Nairobi to confer with the local al Qaeda cell.

In America, news of the brazen attacks knocked Monica Lewinsky from atop the headlines for the first time in days. In the Rose Garden of the White House, President Clinton ignored reporters' shouted questions about Lewinsky—who had testified against him before a federal grand jury the previous day—and branded the bombings "cowardly." He added, "We are determined to get answers and justice."

Thirteen days later, Lewinsky returned to the grand jury and the top of the headlines. Clinton, without consulting Congress, ordered attacks on Afghanistan and Sudan. He insisted on two targets because bin Laden had bombed two embassies. But intelligence on one of the targets—a supposed chemical weapons plant in Sudan—was shaky at best. Nonetheless, thirteen Tomahawk cruise missiles leveled the facility—which turned out to be an aspirin factory—and killed a night watchman. Another seventy missiles slammed into three training camps in Afghanistan, killing twenty-four people. The missiles missed bin Laden and his top al Qaeda lieutenants, who were more than one hundred miles away.

Eager to dampen speculation that the president was contriving a military crisis to divert attention from a sex scandal—a practice known as "wagging the dog"—White House officials insisted the August 20 missile strikes would be followed by a sustained military campaign against terrorism. They said Clinton no longer regarded terrorism as a series of criminal acts, but as war. Yet during his remaining two and a half years in office, Clinton did not launch a single follow-up military strike. His Justice Department treated the embassy bombings the same way it had treated every other bin Laden attack since Clinton took office—as infractions of the U.S. criminal code. The FBI conducted investigations, and the Justice Department announced indictments against bin Laden and other terrorists around the world. In some cases, suspects were captured, extradited, and put on trial in American courts. A few were given long prison sentences and slapped with multimillion-dollar fines. But they were treated as criminals, not combatants. They ended up with more amenities in American prisons than they ever enjoyed in Afghan caves.

By late 2000, it was obvious to bin Laden that Clinton's threat of "war" had been empty. The terrorist decided it was time to up the ante. On October 12, a small boat laden with explosives pulled up alongside the USS *Cole*, which was refueling in Aden, Yemen. At 11:18 A.M., the skiff detonated, ripping an enormous hole in the side of the destroyer. Seventeen American sailors were killed and thirty-nine others were injured.

As heinous as all of these attacks were, none of them escalated jihad to the level bin Laden desired. In fact, after nearly nine years in the terrorism business, he could claim credit for the deaths of fewer than one hundred Americans. Each al Qaeda attack had killed under a dozen Americans, on average, and none more than a score. While bin Laden had become notorious among policy wonks who paid attention to global terrorism, a lot of people in the world still didn't even know his name.

All that changed, of course, on September 11—bin Laden's crowning achievement. He went from killing dozens of Americans to thousands. He terrorized millions more. He flattened both towers of the World Trade Center and staved in the side of the mighty Pentagon. In one fell swoop, the shy boy who lacked a Saudi pedigree etched his name into the annals of history. Yes, he had come a long way from that first, hapless terrorist strike in 1992, when the bomb didn't even explode until after the Americans had departed. So he had no compunction about treating himself to a victory lap.

"God has blessed a group of vanguard Muslims, the forefront of Islam, to destroy America," he enthused to the video camera on the rocky outcrop in Afghanistan. "May God bless them and allot them a supreme place in heaven."

Bin Laden held the microphone in his right hand, partially obscuring his salt-and-pepper beard that extended, in accordance with strict Taliban law, a full fist below his chin. The left-handed terrorist wagged a finger at the camera as he complained about the world's knee-jerk reaction to suicide bombers in places like Israel.

"When such people stood in defense of their weak children, their brothers and sisters, and retaliated for what they have suffered in Palestine and other Muslim nations, the whole world went into an uproar, the infidels followed by the hypocrites."

The infidels, of course, were America and the other Western nations. The hypocrites, as far as bin Laden was concerned, were "moderate"

Muslims who denounced such acts and who failed to protest U.S.-led sanctions against Iraq—which had been imposed on August 6, 1990, the day before American forces arrived in Saudi Arabia.

"A million innocent children are dying as we speak, killed in Iraq without any guilt. We hear no denunciation, we hear no edict from the hereditary rulers. And every day, Israeli tanks rampage across Palestine, in Ramallah, Rafah, and Beit Jala, and many other parts of the land of Islam, and we do not hear anyone raising his voice or objecting.

"But when the sword fell upon America," he added malevolently, "hypocrisy raised its head up high."

According to bin Laden, Muslims who grieved for the dead of the World Trade Towers and the Pentagon did not recognize the slain Americans for what they really were: "Killers who toyed with the blood, honor, and sanctities of Muslims."

In a way, bin Laden considered moderate Muslims more despicable than the infidels who had no Islamic beliefs whatsoever. After all, Americans and Israelis were *expected* to oppose him. But for fellow Muslims to denounce his fight for a pan-Islamic state was nothing short of treason.

"The least that can be said about those hypocrites is that they are apostates who followed the wrong path. They backed the butcher against the victim, the oppressor against the innocent child. So God has given them back what they deserve."

Bin Laden kept wagging his finger in front of the white tail of his turban, which flowed down from the back of his head, traversed his torso, and disappeared amid the folds of his baggy trousers. Instead of a traditional tunic, he wore a GI's garment over his willowy frame—camouflage fatigues, mottled in green, brown, and black. A black watch was strapped to his right wrist. At his side, leaning against the craggy rock face, was his trusty, Soviet-era, Kalashnikov rifle.

Despite his bravado, a trace of worry could be detected in bin Laden's rant. Prior to September 11, all his attacks had occurred during the era of Bill Clinton, who never responded forcefully. Indeed, Americans back then seemed averse to getting their fingernails dirty. The missiles of 1998 had been fired from warships docked safely out in the Red and Arabian seas. The Somalia firefight of 1993 had been largely an al Qaeda offensive that ended in a rout of the Americans. Instead of regrouping for a punishing counterattack, the infidels fled the Muslim nation with their tails between their legs. So much for the vaunted military prowess of the world's sole superpower.

And yet Clinton's successor was giving every indication that this time would be different. He immediately declared war on terrorism and did not wait for a federal indictment to conclude that bin Laden was the prime suspect. He also showed no interest in one-shot, retaliatory pinpricks. To the contrary, he was openly exhorting his fellow infidels to prepare for a crushing and sustained counterattack. He bluntly warned of U.S. casualties and a long conflict. For once, the Americans seemed willing to get their fingernails dirty.

But bin Laden couldn't give voice to such concerns here on this rocky outcrop, at least not while the camera was rolling. So he reiterated his contempt for "the senior officials in the United States of America, starting with the head of international infidels—Bush."

Having been branded "The Evildoer" by Bush, bin Laden had come up with a reciprocal moniker for the president of the United States—"Head of International Infidels." It was an extraordinary personalization of a war that both men portrayed as a titanic struggle between good and evil.

Bin Laden, who had once tried to obtain nuclear weapons, derided the United States for dropping atomic bombs on Hiroshima and Nagasaki fifty-six years earlier.

"In a nation at the far end of the world, Japan, hundreds of thousands, young and old, were killed. And this is not a war crime?" he said incredulously. "Or a million children in Iraq. To them, this is not a clear issue.

"But when a few more than ten were killed in Nairobi and Dar es Salaam, Afghanistan and Sudan were bombed," he added, referring to the fact that of the 224 people killed in the African embassy bombings, only twelve were Americans. "And hypocrisy stood behind the head of international infidels, the modern world's symbol of paganism—America—and its allies."

Clearly, bin Laden had issues about moderate Muslim nations sharing in America's outrage over terrorist attacks.

"These events have divided the world into two camps—the camp of the faithful and the camp of infidels," he said, warming to his climax. "Every Muslim must rise to defend his religion. The wind of faith is blowing, and the wind of change is blowing, to remove evil from the peninsula of Muhammad."

Unyielding to the end, bin Laden closed with a threat.

"As to America, I say to it and its people a few words: I swear to God that America will not live in peace before peace reigns in Palestine, and before all the army of infidels depart the land of Muhammad, peace be upon him.

"God is the greatest. And glory be to Islam."

Chapter Five

"The Middle Hour of Our Grief"

A FUNEREAL RAIN WAS FALLING when President Bush arrived at the National Cathedral in Washington and slipped inside the English oak doors. He was led into a small sacristy, where the heavy chains of iron chandeliers cast strange shadows across gothic arches. An easel was set up at one end of the room, and church officials began sketching out the logistics of the unprecedented service that was about to begin. Bush had declared today, September 14, a National Day of Prayer and Remembrance. He would be delivering his first formal speech since September 11 and hoped it would be a turning point for a grieving nation. But he also realized that if this hastily organized service did not strike exactly the right note, it would be a painful setback in the healing process.

When a dignitary walks to the pulpit in an Episcopal church, he is led by a verger, a church official who carries a sort of scepter, or verge, over the shoulder. The practice dates to the Middle Ages, when cathedrals teemed with so many undesirables that a church official actually had to swing a club from side to side in order to clear a path for the bishop. Stephen Lott, the head verger at the National Cathedral, explained that he would be leading Bush up to the pulpit when it came time for his speech.

"No," the president said. "I want to go by myself."

Lott and the other church officials were taken aback. None of them could remember any other dignitary refusing a verger. Bill Clinton had spoken here twice when he was president and both times he was led by a verger, although the first time the verger had to stick an elbow out to keep Clinton from walking next to him. Church officials are very strict on this point—the dignitary must walk behind the verger. But Bush seemed determined and impatient, so Lott moved on to the rest of his briefing.

The president had shed a lot of tears over the past seventy-two hours, not all of them in private. A day earlier, during a question-and-answer session with reporters in the Oval Office, Bush had briefly lost his composure while the cameras rolled. Having just announced the National Day of Prayer and Remembrance, the president was taken aback by a question from Francine Kiefer of the *Christian Science Monitor*, the reporter who had recently asked him whether he was "taking any naps in the afternoon." This time her question was much more substantive.

"About the prayer day tomorrow, Mr. President," she began. "Could you give us a sense as to what kind of prayers you are thinking? And where your heart is for yourself, as you—"

"Well, I don't think about myself right now," said Bush, notoriously wary of public introspection. "I think about the families, the children."

Suddenly the president's eyes grew misty. Standing with his fingertips resting on the top of his desk, he looked away to regain his composure. After several beats, he blinked hard and shook his head slightly, as if he had considered saying something but then thought better of it. A TV cameraman instinctively zoomed in for a tight shot of the president's flushed face.

"Um," Bush managed. "I am a—I'm a loving guy."

The corners of his mouth drooped involuntarily. His eyes were now brimming with tears. Having taken a tentative step onto terra touchy-feely, he was already losing control of his emotions. So he tried to change course.

"And I am also someone, however, who has got a job to do," said the president, leaning forward. "And I intend to do it."

Although he was trying to appear resolute, Bush was still struggling with his emotions. It was time to wrap this up.

"But this country will not relent"—he blinked—"until we have saved ourselves and others from the terrible tragedy that came upon America."

As he said the word "America," the right side of his upper lip twitched. Instead of waiting around for another question, Bush fled the room.

When Kiefer wrote her pool report for the rest of the White House press corps, it was conspicuously devoid of the smart-alecky tone that had characterized the pre-September 11 pool reports of journalists like Dana Milbank of the *Washington Post*. Instead of sarcastically referring to Bush as "the compassionate president," Kiefer wrote in respectful, almost reverential terms.

"It was a defining moment of his presidency," her report began. She wrote of "the deep anguish the president is feeling for his country at this historic moment." After describing the scene in poignant detail, Kiefer ended her report by remarking upon the significance of the president's answer.

"It seemed a moment in which the full weight of the office of the presidency was felt."

But there was an added significance that was not yet evident. For the first time, all three major television networks had broadcast live and uninterrupted coverage of an informal exchange between Bush and the press. For sixteen solid minutes, ABC, CBS, and NBC showed Bush without the usual filter of White House correspondents, producers, anchors, and analysts. Before September 11, the press routinely dissected, edited, and rearranged the president's daily utterances before serving them up on the evening news, usually in an unflattering context. One of the networks even refused to carry his August address to the nation on stem cell research. But now they were all showing raw, uncut footage of "Bush unplugged." As a result, the public had a chance to take the full measure of the man, with all his strengths and weaknesses. From that day forward, the public's approval of President Bush would rise dramatically. The press shrugged this off as a "rally round the flag" effect that would naturally follow any attack on America. But the White House was convinced it was because the public finally began to see the real George W. Bush. Sure, the cable news networks, which needed to fill twenty-four hours with fresh content, had been showing unedited coverage of Bush's routine speeches and chats with reporters since the beginning of his presidency. But Fox News Channel, CNN, and MSNBC each had audiences in the hundreds of thousands. ABC, CBS, and NBC had audiences in the millions. And now, with virtually everyone in America glued to TV sets, the broadcast networks had audiences in the tens of millions. If the normally cynical press was moved by the president's heartfelt display of emotion, so was much of the nation.

"It was just an honest reaction," Bush told me later. "I mean, standing behind the desk, I got very emotional when I started thinking about the families whose lives had been affected—thousands of people. I think a lot of Americans felt that way."

Indeed, one poll found that three out of four American adults, including men, admitted shedding tears over the tragedy.

"I guess that's what America appreciated—I was expressing their sentiments," Bush said. "America was hot. And we were sad. We cried."

The president's tears resurfaced the next morning, when he convened his first cabinet meeting since the attacks.

"I walk in, and the cabinet gives me a standing ovation, which caused me to tear up," Bush told me. "You know, I don't know why I got emotional. I guess because it was an emotional moment. I was tired and I was so appreciative."

Secretary of State Colin Powell became concerned that Bush might become an emotional basket case during his "Prayer and Remembrance" speech scheduled for later in the day.

"He leans over and says, you know, 'Are you okay?' I said, 'Yes, I'm fine,'" Bush recalled. "He said, 'Are you going to be okay for the National Cathedral speech?' I say, 'Yes.'

"He said, 'Well, take all words out of your speech that are emotional.' And I leaned over to him and said, 'Don't worry about it— I've already got my emotions out.' And he kind of laughed and I laughed. It was sweet of him to do that. He was concerned about the speech."

Truth be told, so was Bush.

"This is another incident, like the first speech right after the attack, that I had to set the right tone on the speech," the president told me.

"It's a very important speech. And I had worked on the speech and it was a good speech."

The trick for Bush was to talk about the nation's grief without wallowing in it. At the same time, he wanted to stir America to action without seeming insensitive to the mourners.

"I prayed a lot before the speech because I felt like it was a moment where I needed, well, frankly, for the good Lord to shine through," he told me.

All of this was on Bush's mind at the conclusion of the preservice briefing. He stepped into the cathedral's north transept and surveyed his breathtaking surroundings. One hundred and fifty thousand tons of hand-carved Indiana limestone, without a shred of steel reinforcement, were held together by sheer gravity and flying buttresses. It was the sixth-largest cathedral in the world and second-largest in America—only St. John's in New York was larger. It spanned a tenth of a mile and soared thirty stories to the highest point in all of Washington. In fact, when planes started hitting tall buildings in New York and then others headed for the District, church officials were terrified their magnificent structure would be destroyed barely a decade after construction had been completed—a feat that had taken eighty-three painstaking years. But the National Cathedral dodged a bullet. And now Bush stood beneath its 150-foot ceiling and wondered if this unprecedented service would work after all.

He took a deep breath, grabbed Laura's hand, and headed for the nave. Rounding the corner of a mammoth stone pier nineteen feet in diameter, Bush came face to face with former president Bill Clinton in the front pew. He and his daughter, Chelsea, jumped to their feet, although Senator Hillary Rodham Clinton remained seated. The president's parents, who were also in the front pew, stood as their son reached the center aisle. Bush paused to shake hands with former presidents Carter and Ford in the third pew, which also contained Al Gore. As a children's choir sang "Father in Thy Gracious Keeping," Bush greeted his own father. Then he and everyone else in that powerful front pew—including Hillary, who by now was on her feet—took their seats. The elder George Bush, nicknamed "41" for his place in the presidential pantheon, reached over and squeezed the hand of Laura, who was sitting between him and the younger Bush, otherwise known as "43."

"A-a-a-a-men," the children concluded.

In the silence that followed, Bush put on a pair of old-fashioned, circular, wire-rimmed spectacles and studied his program. The service had been thrown together in thirty-six hours by the two most important women in his life—Laura Bush and Karen Hughes—and looked like a case study in politically correct diversity. The first six speakers were a female bishop, a black minister, a Muslim imam, a rabbi, another black minister, and a Catholic bishop. The White House did not want to be accused of excluding anyone at this moment of national anguish.

"President Bush, all of us who have come here this day want you to know that we are grateful that you have called for this service and that you have brought such a multitude of God's children to this cathedral," began Jane Holmes Dixon, bishop of the Episcopal Diocese of Washington, pro tempore. "Those of us who are gathered here—Muslim, Jew, Christian, Sikh, Buddhist, Hindu—indeed, all people of faith—know that love is stronger than hate."

The Very Reverend Nathan D. Baxter, dean of the cathedral, prayed, "Guide our leaders, especially George our president. Let the deep faith that he and they share guide them in the momentous decisions they must make for our national security."

From a political standpoint, the most important preacher in the church was Imam Muzammil Siddiqi, of the Islamic Society of North America. Bush felt strongly that Americans should see a Muslim at the service because he wanted to send a message that the enemy was terrorism, not Islam. He did not want a repeat of World War II, when Japanese-Americans suffered widespread discrimination and some were even placed in internment camps. Bush had chosen one of those internees, Democrat Norman Mineta, to be his transportation secretary.

"With broken and humble hearts and with tears in our eyes, we turn to you, O Lord, to give us comfort," Siddiqi said. "Keep us together as people of diverse faiths, colors, and races."

The seventh and final preacher was the Reverend Billy Graham, who had changed Bush's life sixteen years earlier by inspiring him to turn to God and, eventually, away from the bottle. Graham, who had been a Bush family friend for years, was invited to spend a summer weekend at the family's retreat in Kennebunkport, Maine. One evening, the elder Bush asked Graham to answer questions from a large group of family members.

"He sat by the fire and talked. And what he said sparked a change in my heart," the younger Bush recalled in his memoirs. "I don't remember the exact words. It was more the power of his example. The Lord was so clearly reflected in his gentle and loving demeanor."

The next day, Bush and Graham strolled along Walker's Point, a rocky promontory on which the family home was built.

"I knew I was in the presence of a great man," Bush recalled. "He was like a magnet; I felt drawn to seek something different. He didn't lecture or admonish; he shared warmth and concern. Billy Graham didn't make you feel guilty; he made you feel loved."

Now Graham was eighty-two and his hair had turned snow white. He needed the verger to help him to the pulpit. In fact, because of Graham's infirmity, church officials had directed all speakers, including the president, to use the lower and less ornate of two stone pulpits. Thus, the ten-foot-tall Canterbury pulpit, where Martin Luther King Jr. delivered his last Sunday sermon before he was assassinated, went unused for the biggest event since the cathedral was built.

"I've become an old man now and I've preached all over the world and the older I get the more I cling to that hope that I started with many years ago," Graham said. "My prayer today is that we will feel the loving arms of God wrapped around us, and will know in our hearts that he will never forsake us as we trust in him.

"We also know that God is going to give wisdom and courage and strength to the president and those around him," Graham concluded. "And this is going to be a day that we will remember as a day of victory."

As Graham struggled down the steps of the pulpit, someone in the first pew stood up and began clapping loudly. Bush officials turned and were mortified to discover that the person leading what was now a standing ovation was none other than Bill Clinton. They considered this a contemptible breach of protocol. If anyone should start a standing ovation at this service, it should be President Bush. Bush aides were furious that the notoriously self-absorbed Clinton would draw attention to himself on this, the current president's day. Nonetheless, Bush stood up with the rest of the congregation to join Clinton's ovation.

When it finally came time for Bush to speak, he traversed the "crossing," an expanse of Italian marble formed by the intersection of the cathedral's nave, transepts, and choir. Since he had refused a verger, Bush strode alone across the large Jerusalem cross pattern in the floor. He looked puny beneath the 300-foot ceiling of the central tower, which was taller than any medieval cathedral in the world. He ascended the nine steps to the pulpit and gazed out over the most powerful collection of people he had ever seen assembled. Senators, congressmen, cabinet secretaries, generals, Supreme Court justices, diplomats, captains of industry—everyone who was anyone in official Washington was there.

"I usually am the kind of speaker that tries to connect with the audience to see how I am doing," Bush told me. "Frankly, if I see somebody that doesn't think I'm doing well, I'll switch to another person.

"And I saw—I can't remember her name—one of the press advance girls, who was just weeping," he recalled. "I felt that I wasn't going to be able to deliver—completely deliver the speech."

Searching for another focal point, Bush dared not gaze at the first pew.

"My biggest concern was looking at my parents," he explained. "If I looked down at my mother and dad, and they'd be weeping, then I'd weep.

"And so I didn't look at them," he added. "And I, you know, didn't look at much."

As a result, the president's voice was firm and seemed to fill the entire cathedral as he began the carefully crafted speech.

"We are here in the middle hour of our grief. So many have suffered so great a loss, and today we express our nation's sorrow. We come before God to pray for the missing and the dead, and for those who love them.

"On Tuesday, our country was attacked with deliberate and massive cruelty. We have seen the images of fire and ashes, and bent steel.

"Now come the names, the list of casualties we are only beginning to read. They are the names of men and women who began their day at a desk or in an airport, busy with life. They are the names of people who faced death, and in their last moments called home to say, 'Be brave, and I love you.'

"They are the names of passengers who defied their murderers, and prevented the murder of others on the ground. They are the names of men and women who wore the uniform of the United States, and died at their posts.

"They are the names of rescuers, the ones whom death found running up the stairs and into the fires to help others. We will read all these names. We will linger over them, and learn their stories, and many Americans will weep.

"To the children and parents and spouses and families and friends of the lost, we offer the deepest sympathy of the nation. And I assure you, you are not alone.

"Just three days removed from these events, Americans do not yet have the distance of history. But our responsibility to history is already clear: to answer these attacks and rid the world of evil.

"War has been waged against us by stealth and deceit and murder. This nation is peaceful, but fierce when stirred to anger. This conflict was begun on the timing and terms of others. It will end in a way, and at an hour, of our choosing.

"Our purpose as a nation is firm. Yet our wounds as a people are recent and unhealed, and lead us to pray. In many of our prayers this week, there is a searching, and an honesty.

"At St. Patrick's Cathedral in New York on Tuesday, a woman said, 'I prayed to God to give us a sign that He is still here.' Others have prayed for the same, searching hospital to hospital, carrying pictures of those still missing.

"God's signs are not always the ones we look for. We learn in tragedy that His purposes are not always our own. Yet the prayers of private suffering, whether in our homes or in this great cathedral, are known and heard, and understood.

"There are prayers that help us last through the day, or endure the night. There are prayers of friends and strangers that give us strength for the journey. And there are prayers that yield our will to a will greater than our own.

"This world He created is of moral design. Grief and tragedy and hatred are only for a time. Goodness, remembrance, and love have no end. And the Lord of life holds all who die, and all who mourn.

"It is said that adversity introduces us to ourselves. This is true of a nation as well. In this trial, we have been reminded, and the world has seen, that our fellow Americans are generous and kind, resourceful and brave.

"We see our national character in rescuers working past exhaustion; in long lines of blood donors; in thousands of citizens who have asked to work and serve in any way possible. And we have seen our national character in eloquent acts of sacrifice.

"Inside the World Trade Center, one man who could have saved himself stayed until the end at the side of his quadriplegic friend. A beloved priest died giving the last rites to a firefighter.

"Two office workers, finding a disabled stranger, carried her down sixty-eight floors to safety. A group of men drove through the night from Dallas to Washington to bring skin grafts for burn victims.

"In these acts, and in many others, Americans showed a deep commitment to one another, and an abiding love for our country. Today, we feel what Franklin Roosevelt called the warm courage of national unity. This is a unity of every faith, and every background.

"It has joined together political parties in both houses of Congress. It is evident in services of prayer and candlelight vigils, and American flags, which are displayed in pride, and wave in defiance.

"Our unity is a kinship of grief, and a steadfast resolve to prevail against our enemies. And this unity against terror is now extending across the world.

"America is a nation full of good fortune, with so much to be grateful for. But we are not spared from suffering. In every generation, the world has produced enemies of human freedom. They have attacked America, because we are freedom's home and defender. And the commitment of our fathers is now the calling of our time.

"On this national day of prayer and remembrance, we ask almighty God to watch over our nation, and grant us patience and resolve in all that is to come. We pray that He will comfort and console those who now walk in sorrow. We thank Him for each life we now must mourn, and the promise of a life to come.

"As we have been assured, neither death nor life, nor angels nor principalities nor powers, nor things present nor things to come, nor height nor depth, can separate us from God's love. May He bless the souls of the departed. May He comfort our own. And may He always guide our country.

"God bless America."

No one clapped when the president finished. He closed his leather folder, descended from the pulpit, and walked in total silence. Clinton, gnawing on his lower lip, had his eyes pinned on Bush, as did

Chelsea. Hillary looked straight ahead. When the president sat down, his parents were beaming. Forty-one reached across Laura and patted 43 on the arm. The younger Bush took his father's hand and shook it, although neither man said a word. The son dared not look at the father for fear of welling up. Laura, smiling serenely and looking straight ahead, discreetly patted her husband's leg eight or nine times with the back of her hand. It was her way of telling him he had hit a home run.

"It was a touching moment," Bush told me.

From behind the "rood screen," a carved wooden partition separating the crossing from the choir, filed sixteen men and women in crisp white uniforms. These members of the U.S. Navy Sea Chanters assembled in pairs on the steps and opened songbooks that looked like big black menus. The solemn snap of a snare drum broke the silence, followed by a fanfare of trumpets and the stentorian chords of the cathedral's 10,600-pipe Great Organ. And then the choir began to sing.

> *Mine eyes have seen the glory of the coming of the Lord*
> *He is trampling out the vintage where the grapes of*
> *wrath are stored*
> *He hath loosed the fateful lightning of His terrible*
> *swift sword*
> *His truth is marching on*
> *Glory! Glory! Hallelujah! Glory! Glory! Hallelujah!*
> *Glory! Glory! Hallelujah! His truth is marching on....*

"The Battle Hymn of the Republic" is one of those patriotic songs that is so well known that most Americans are inured to the power of its lyrics. And yet when the people in that church got to the part about loosing "the fateful lightning of His terrible swift sword," they got goose bumps. House Majority Whip Tom DeLay, who is considered such a tough guy that he is nicknamed "The Hammer," had tears streaming down his cheeks as he sang. The White House was later criticized in some corners for choosing such a "warlike" song in a house of worship, but Bush was unapologetic. He could think of no better hymn with which to conclude this service, which combined the healing power of prayer with the cold resolve of retribution.

I have read a fiery Gospel writ in burnished rows of steel
"As ye deal with My contemners, so with you My grace shall deal"
Let the Hero, born of woman, crush the serpent with His heel
Since God is marching on....

Defense Secretary Donald Rumsfeld, who was already planning the war that Bush had assigned him, seemed to relish this righteous anthem about smiting one's "contemners" and crushing "the serpent." He was singing for all he was worth. But he wasn't alone. Jimmy Carter and Trent Lott and George Herbert Walker Bush and almost everyone else in attendance were belting out this bellicose hymn with gusto. From one end of the National Cathedral to the other, voices rang out and tears streamed down.

... Glory! Glory! Hallelujah! Glory! Glory! Hallelujah!
Our God is marching on.
On! On!! On!!! ON!!!!

There was a clashing of cymbals and horns and drums, all of which rose into a great crescendo that culminated in one final explosion of sound. When it ended, the note echoed through the limestone edifice and reverberated off the stained-glass windows.

The service concluded with the steady tolling of a bell, solemn and mournful, from deep in the gloam of the Gloria in Excelsis Tower. It reminded the Washington power brokers who lingered in the pews, as well as the millions of rapt Americans watching the ninety-minute service on TV, that they were still, as Bush had phrased it, "in the middle hour of our grief." And yet somehow that hour now seemed shorter. There is something about a long, moving church service, especially one in which tough issues are tackled, that makes attendees feel cleansed and refocused when it is over. America still faced a very long road to recovery. But it felt good to take that first step.

When Bush walked outside, the funereal rain had been replaced by glorious sunshine and a bright blue sky. His day was just getting started.

Chapter Six

"I Scammed My Way In"

"BRIDGE CLOSED."

Well, wasn't that just perfect. How was Bob Beckwith supposed to get to Ground Zero if he couldn't even cross from Brooklyn over to Manhattan? How could he join the rescue effort if the Williamsburg Bridge was blocked off with orange cones and this big sign proclaiming, "BRIDGE CLOSED"?

Maybe he should have listened to his wife and kids after all. Maybe they were right—he *was* too old. Sure, he had diabetes and hypertension, but for a retiree pushing seventy, Beckwith considered himself in pretty good shape. Certainly strong enough to grab a shovel and help dig his brethren out of that hulking slag heap once known as the World Trade Center. Hundreds of his fellow firemen were missing and Beckwith hoped some of them were still alive. It had been, after all, less than seventy-two hours since the attacks.

The attacks still astonished Bob Beckwith. After thirty years in the New York City Fire Department, he thought he had seen it all. But when he added up all the flames and smoke and death and destruction he had witnessed over those three decades, it didn't come close

169

to this megadisaster. The mightiest skyscrapers in the history of the city—*the friggin' Twin Towers!*—had been flattened. And Beckwith had been reduced to helplessly watching the whole sickening spectacle unfold on live television.

Talk about a day that went from bad to worse.

"On September 11th, I was awakened early, around 7 o'clock, by my daughter, that my grandson was hit by a car around the corner from where I live," said Beckwith, a resident of Baldwin, Long Island. "He was ridin' his bike to school and he was clipped by a car. So I ran around the corner and there was a big crowd, of course—police cars and ambulance. I ran up and I got through, and he was sittin' up and I said, Joe, are you okay? And he said yeah. But they took him to the hospital and I said, Okay, I'm goin' to the hospital also, but I just wanna go home and get somethin' to eat."

As a diabetic, Beckwith needed to get some food in his stomach before heading to the emergency room, where he might be waiting for hours on end.

"So I came home and put the radio on and I hear the weatherman—not the weatherman, the traffic man in the area. He's in a helicopter sayin' it looks like a small plane just went into the Twin Towers. And so I came in the den and I turned on the TV and they had cameras on it already. And I saw smoke, and then the wind took the smoke away, and I said, boy, that's a pretty big small plane that went into that thing. It looked like that was some-sized hole. And I says wow."

Beckwith remembered the last time a plane crashed into a New York City skyscraper—back in 1945, when he was thirteen years old. He had run outside and looked up at the skyline, but the fog was so thick he couldn't see the top portion of the building. Neither, evidently, could the pilot. But September 11 was sunny, without a cloud in the sky. How could any pilot overlook the World Trade Center on such a beautiful day?

"And I'm sittin' there watchin' the thing and I see an explosion in the second building. And I said, Oh my God. I didn't see the plane go in and I figures, Uh-oh, what's this all about? And then they pointed out that somebody had seen a plane go in on the second tower. I says, Oh my God. And they pointed it out and you did see the plane actually go into the building, and then the explosion. And I was just beside myself. I says, Oh boy."

Beckwith's heart was racing just like in the old days, when the alarm would sound at Ladder 117, the firehouse in Queens where he had served for twenty-three years, or Ladder 164, also in Queens, where he spent the final seven years of his career. He knew that firemen from all over the city were speeding to the World Trade Center at this very moment. Some were older men who had served with him. Others were the sons of his fellow retirees. None had ever faced anything like this.

It was difficult for Beckwith to tear himself away from the Sony television in the den of his modest brick home—a cross between a saltbox and a colonial—in the tidy working-class town of Baldwin. But he had to see his grandson. So he got into his 1995 Saab and made the twenty-minute drive up to Winthrop Hospital in Mineola. In the emergency room, doctors were concluding that Joe Clancy had suffered no broken bones or other serious injuries. Beckwith sat at his grandson's bedside and watched the television in the room, which continued to show smoke pouring from the Twin Towers.

"What a mess," Beckwith thought. "It's like watchin' a movie, ya know? I thought, I don't believe this is goin' on.

"And then a little later on, I'm still sittin' there and I watch the first tower go down," he said. "I says, Oh man. I knew I had a lot of guys in there, ya know?"

In that moment, as most Americans blinked in disbelief at their TV screens, Bob Beckwith knew his brothers were dying. He didn't know how many. But he knew that some members of the New York City Fire Department—perhaps a great many—were being crushed to death as he sat there in the emergency room of Winthrop Hospital in Mineola, Long Island. Firemen are paid to run into burning buildings while others run out. Beckwith sensed in his sixty-nine-year-old bones that no matter how many civilians were able to get out of that tower before it collapsed, there were firemen still inside. He also figured there were additional firemen outside who were too close to the structure to escape when it crashed. As far as Beckwith was concerned, there were only two questions. How many were dying? And how many were trapped?

Half an hour later, the old-timer sat rapt with revulsion as the north tower collapsed. Another batch of brothers was being crushed to death.

"Oh my God," he whispered to himself. "We took some beatin' on this one."

Over the next three days, Beckwith began to learn the identities of the missing firemen.

"Most of the guys who were killed in the Twin Towers were not the guys I worked with for thirty years, but their sons. I said, Oh my God. One of the first ones I heard was Jimmy Boyle—Jimmy Boyle's kid was missing. Now, Jimmy Boyle was president of our union. And I was a delegate in the union. I was a battalion delegate, so I knew Jimmy very well. I said oh, man, *his* kid is missin'?"

For three long days—Tuesday, Wednesday, and Thursday—Beckwith watched the tube and worked the phone. Although it had been seven years since he hung up his fire helmet, a thought began to grow in his mind.

"I gotta get these guys outta that hole. They're in the hole and I gotta get these guys out. That's the only thing that was on my mind. I have to get down there. I have to see what I can do to help to get these guys outta there.

"For a coupla days, I couldn't believe what I saw. I was sittin' there, listenin' to the reports, and I said to my children—my children are all big now—and I said to them, I gotta get down there. I'm goin' down there. And they'd tell me, Don't go down, you're too old. That's a young man's job. An old-timer like you should stay home.

"So on the 14th, the mornin' of the 14th, I got up and I said to my wife, I'm outta here. She said, You're nuts. She says, You're too old to be down there. I was sixty-nine years old. I said I don't care. I'm outta here."

The only item of firefighting gear Beckwith still possessed was his battered black helmet, which bore the number of his old ladder company, 164. He pulled on a scroungy blue sweatshirt that also had the 164 logo over the heart. Donning blue jeans—Beckwith called them dungarees—and a sturdy pair of work boots, the retired fireman climbed into his 1995 Saab, and left for the city at 6:30 A.M. But when he got off the Brooklyn Queens Expressway to take the Williamsburg Bridge into Manhattan, he was stopped cold by the "BRIDGE CLOSED" sign and all those orange cones. It was as if the entire world were conspiring to keep him away from Ground Zero.

Just then a police car, followed by a black Chevy Suburban, drove up and cut between the cones to get on the bridge. Instinctively,

Beckwith maneuvered his own car between two cones and fell in behind this little caravan. He was flying along at 65 mph, faster than he ever remembered driving on this normally congested thoroughfare.

"I'm sayin', if they think I'm a terrorist, let them stop me, lock me up, do what they gotta do. But nobody stopped me. The cops were down at the end of the bridge, but nobody stopped me. I kept goin'."

Having driven the streets of New York for half a century, Beckwith had mastered the art of what he called "offensive driving."

"You gotta have a little gall," he explained. "You gotta be a little pushy. I get away with it. I've been gettin' away with it for years."

Besides, Beckwith figured no self-respecting New York City cop would go to the trouble of actually arresting a sixty-nine-year-old retired New York City fireman once he explained he was only trying to help out at Ground Zero. So he plowed ahead, utterly unmolested, and found himself on Delancey Street, in lower Manhattan. This was where he used to come as a kid to buy clothes from the Jewish merchants. They sold pants, shirts, belts, socks, and underwear cheaper than anyone else. Back in those days, people used to call this area "Jew town," although Beckwith suspected that was no longer considered politically correct.

He headed west and onto the Bowery, where his father had grown up. The old man had told young Bob over and over that if he didn't study in school, he would end up here, with the bums and derelicts and winos. Not that an education would necessarily keep him out of the Bowery. Beckwith had known of learned men—even college professors—who ended up here, down on their luck, drinking themselves to death on the vilest wine imaginable.

After passing from the Lower East Side into Little Italy—which Beckwith pronounced "*It*-lee"—he parked next to the Engine 55 firehouse and stuck a firefighter placard on the dashboard to ward off ticketers and tow trucks. He walked inside the ancient station, which was twenty-five feet wide—barely big enough to hold its only truck. Or rather, its only former truck. Engine 55's pumper had been buried beneath the hellish rain of debris from the World Trade Center.

"How'd you guys make out?" Beckwith asked.

"We lost four guys and a pumper," one of the firemen replied.

"I'm sorry," the old-timer said.

Although Beckwith had not personally known the fallen firemen, he paid his respects at a makeshift memorial that had been erected on the sidewalk just outside at the station. Then, donning his old helmet, he asked the surviving firemen for advice on how to get to Ground Zero. They knew he was retired, but also could see that he was aching to go to work. So they told him to go down to West Street and make his way south along Battery Park. All in all, it would be about a mile walk.

But within two blocks of his journey, Beckwith discovered that police had set up a security perimeter that extended well beyond Ground Zero. So he began to cut in and out of streets in an effort to get closer to the action. The old man had an intimate knowledge of New York's streets. Although he was born in the Astoria section of Queens, he attended St. Gabriel Catholic Elementary School in the Bronx and later graduated from Rice High School in the heart of Harlem, the all-boys school run by the Irish Christian Brothers. Unlike most firemen, who join the force in their early twenties, Beckwith spent years driving a delivery truck for United Parcel Service, which gave him an even greater knowledge of the city's streets. By the time a couple of his firefighting buddies finally convinced him to take the fire department examination, Bob Beckwith was a thirty-two-year-old father of five, with a sixth child on the way. He thought long and hard before leaving the security of his UPS job, which paid well and made him a member of the Teamsters union. But once Beckwith took the plunge, he found that he liked firefighting. His firehouse was pretty busy, so he ended up spending a lot of time on these streets he knew so well.

Still, no matter which way he turned, Beckwith could not penetrate the perimeter. On Canal Street, police stopped him at a checkpoint and told him he was not allowed inside.

"But I gotta get in there," Beckwith pleaded, showing them his old fire department ID card.

The cops eyeballed the battered card, which had been issued a quarter century earlier. It featured a laminated photo of a much younger man with a mustache and considerably more hair than Beckwith now possessed. They looked the old-timer up and down. He wasn't even wearing a uniform. But he did have an ancient helmet above that careworn face. He obviously wanted to help. What harm could one retired fireman cause? Besides, there was a strong bond between cops and firemen, who often found themselves jointly responding to calls.

"Okay," one of the cops finally said. "Go ahead."

But Beckwith didn't get very far.

"I went another block and who's set up a perimeter but the National Guard. And you wanna see a tough nut. They wouldn't let me through for beans. I didn't tell 'em I was retired. I told 'em I was active duty. But they didn't want to let me in. I showed 'em my card—my identification card with my picture on it—and they passed it around. I said, Okay, if I don't get in there, I'm gonna be in a lotta trouble. So they softened up a little bit. And a coupla guys said, Okay, go ahead in.

"So I got in. I scammed my way in."

Beckwith progressed through Chinatown, which in recent years had been taking over much of Little Italy. In a lifetime on these streets, he had never seen them so deserted. It was like a ghost town. And the farther he walked, the more everything was covered with wet ash.

At length, Beckwith finally came face to face with the scene that had kept him glued to his television for three days. But now, instead of viewing a miniaturized image of Ground Zero on the twenty-seven-inch Sony in his den on Long Island, he was suddenly dwarfed by a hulking mountain of smoldering debris that loomed before him like a grotesque colossus. Smoke still clung to the filthy heap, nearly overpowering him with its acrid stench. It shrouded huge hunks of the building's exoskeleton that jutted skyward at drunken angles. As his liquid blue eyes began to focus, Beckwith noticed things he had not seen on TV, the specific flotsam and jetsam that made up this misshapen mountain. There were rusted I-beams, still welded together; a street vendor's cart, upended like a child's toy; and looking closer, Beckwith could make out family photo albums and even individual business cards. He also noticed that the day's rain had transformed the thick coating of ash into a viscous mud that fouled the slag heap even further and cloyed the streets. But even as the old fireman marveled at the massive scope of the carnage, he couldn't help wondering how a pair of 110-story buildings had been compressed into something just five stories high. The sheer density of the rubble was remarkable. How could anyone survive such a crushing, pulverizing, stupendous force? And yet Beckwith clung to a glimmer of hope.

"I figured there's still guys under there that are alive. There's air pockets. You got up to a week where you can find guys alive. And that was in the back of my head. So I'm sayin', Let's go, let's go! I'm a natural-born boss."

Clambering over the wreckage were the bucket brigades, lines of men passing five-gallon plastic pails to one another. Since Beckwith was under no one's command, he headed straight to the front of one of the lines, pulled on his work gloves, and began scooping handfuls of muck into a bucket. Once filled, the buckets were passed back, hand over hand, and eventually dumped out to be sifted for body parts, badges, and other items of identification. After a while, Beckwith noticed a shovel that someone had left unattended, so he grabbed it and began using it to fill the buckets. He found two identification cards of civilians who had worked in the Twin Towers. He also found portions of bones from arms and legs. He wondered if they belonged to the many jumpers who had chosen to end their lives instead of waiting to be burned or crushed to death. At one point he found most of a right hand, containing the last three fingers. At another point he found a human heel. Beckwith segregated these remains from the muck he was scooping into the buckets and carefully placed them in body bags for later identification by investigators employing DNA analysis.

Every so often he and the other diggers would bang pieces of steel against the twisted girders that protruded from the smoking rubble. Then they paused and cocked their ears, hoping survivors would return the signal by banging on the other end of the girders. But no one ever did. Oh, a couple of times, Beckwith and the others thought they heard something and even called in dogs to sniff the area in question. But it always turned out to be background noise or the sounds of underground pockets burning and collapsing or the groaning and shifting of nearby buildings that were weakened by severe collateral damage. Beckwith and the others fell into a sort of rhythm. Dig, bang, listen. Dig, bang, listen. The routine was periodically interrupted when the men were ordered to take cover because of recurring fears that yet another building was about to collapse. Each time the alarm passed, the men waded back into the rubble and resumed their routine. Dig, bang, listen.

At lunchtime, Beckwith and several firemen with whom he had once worked wandered into a vacant, damaged building where volunteers were serving free food and drinks.

"So we went and had lunch and yakked away for a while. And then I said, Okay, I'm outta here, I'm back to work. And I went back to work. And I found another shovel in another area and I started diggin' and bangin'. And we had the dogs there, you know, they were smellin' around."

As they dug, Beckwith and the other workers uncovered a fire truck that had been crushed beneath the rubble. It had been a pumper, carrying water to the scene of the disaster. Now it was barely recognizable.

"The crane operator picked up the pumpah and brought it out to the street and put it on West Street. And we went right back to work."

As the afternoon wore on, a rumor spread among the rescue workers that President Bush would be visiting Ground Zero. This did not faze Beckwith, who had voted for Al Gore in the election ten months earlier. The old-timer had joined the Democratic Party at the age of eighteen and never once voted for a Republican presidential candidate. More than two decades ago, a political boss promised Beckwith's son a job as a garbageman if the fireman would join New

York's Conservative Party. Beckwith agreed, but never actually went through with the party switch. Nonetheless, the boss "bought it" and gave Beckwith's son the job. Years later, after retiring from the fire department, Beckwith felt guilty enough to finally switch parties. But he kept right on voting for Democrats.

Still, a president was a president, even if Beckwith had voted against him. The retired fireman figured Bush would appear at a tent in the distance that served as the command post. He kept digging until one of the fire chiefs announced that the president was nearby and would appear before the hardhats momentarily.

"And so I went out to the street, I looked around and didn't see him. And the pumpah was out there and I said, Oh, that's a good spot. I'll be able to see him from there. So I jumped up on the pumpah and I'm standin' there. I didn't have much room to stand because there was so much garbage on it. And I said, Oh boy, I've got a pretty good spot here."

He noticed that the rest of the firemen and rescue workers gathered in clusters around their commanding officers. But since Beckwith was a freelancer, he stood by himself. After a while, a middle-aged man in a blue windbreaker walked over and removed a couple of bricks from the chassis of the pumper where Beckwith was standing. The man, who had sandy-blond hair and wire-rimmed glasses, dusted off a place next to the old fireman's feet.

"Is this safe?" the man asked.

"Yeah," Beckwith replied.

"Show me," the man demanded. "Jump up and down on it."

Beckwith was a little puzzled, but he complied, demonstrating that the chassis of the pumper was indeed sturdy.

"Okay," the man said. "Somebody's coming over here. And when that somebody comes over here, you help them up. And when they come up, you come down."

Beckwith shook his head knowingly. He had heard that a Long Island congresswoman, Representative Carolyn McCarthy, was on the scene. Beckwith figured McCarthy would want this vantage point so she could get a clear view of Bush over at the command post.

Soon he heard a commotion.

"I see people movin', but you can't see who they are, 'cause there's a million people down there. And all of a sudden, I dunno, I'm just standin' there and I'm lookin' around and I hear the ironworkers. They're standin' down there and they're screamin', USA! USA! USA! So I figured the president was there—I just didn't see him.

"I didn't see him until he came around the corner. He came right in front of the pumpah. I said, Oh my God, that's the president.

"And he puts his hand up and I pull him up and I turn him around. And I said, Are you okay, Mr. President?—I picked that up on the *West Wing*, you know—and he says, Yeah.

"And so I start to get down and he says, Where you goin'? I said, I was told to get down. He puts his arm around my shoulder and says, No, you stay right here with me.

"I was bedazzled. I didn't know what to say. I just stood there. I really was set back. I said, Oh my God.

"And he had his arm around me and he started in with the bullhorn—somebody had passed him a bullhorn. I didn't even see the guy who handed it to him. All of a sudden he had a bullhorn in his hand.

"And he still had his arm around my shoulder," Beckwith marveled. "And then he started to speak."

Chapter Seven

"I Can Hear *You!*"

PRESIDENT BUSH WAS TEN MILES out when the stench hit him. He had never smelled anything quite like the sharp, sulfurous stink that filled his nostrils as Marine One thumped over the Atlantic Ocean. It grew even stronger as the helicopter touched down at the base of a pier in Manhattan.

The Secret Service pulled a Chevy Suburban right up to the stairs of the chopper so that Bush wouldn't have to fight his way through the throng. But as the motorcade started to pull away, the president looked out his left window and noticed a dozen ash-caked firemen lined up in their gear and oxygen tanks. He ordered the driver to stop.

Bush hopped out, walked over, and began to greet the firefighters. When he got to the fourth one—a big burly guy—the president stopped in his tracks. Two enormous tears were rolling down the brute's cheeks. Bush reached up and cupped the fireman's face in his hand. The scene prompted a number of grown men to break down. One of them was Deputy White House Chief of Staff Joe Hagin, himself a former fireman. The president managed to keep his own emotions in check as he

183

finished greeting the firemen and walked back to the motorcade for the trip to Ground Zero.

"I remember us all cramming into a smaller Suburban," Bush told me. "Pataki and me and Giuliani and the police and commissioner of the firemen, we're crammed in there. I remember sloshing around."

Bush had wanted to come to Ground Zero sooner, but didn't want to disrupt the rescue operations. He feared that a presidential visit would divert precious resources from the search for survivors. So he stayed away as long as possible. But his advisors were worried that if he didn't visit Ground Zero soon, his absence might become a political issue. They were still smarting over accusations that Bush had been afraid to return to Washington on September 11. Perhaps Democrats would begin suggesting Bush was afraid to go to Ground Zero as well. Clinton had never bothered visiting the World Trade Center after al Qaeda exploded a bomb in the parking garage in 1993, killing six, for which he was criticized. Republicans didn't want Democrats to be able to say the same thing about Bush. But they needn't have worried. On September 13, without warning his staff, Bush told Giuliani and Pataki during a televised conference call that he would visit the next day.

The president arrived at the disaster site as a fighter jet roared overhead. He got out of the suburban and waded into the sea of police, firefighters, paramedics, and rescue workers who had descended on the site from all over the nation. It was a motley crew of unshaven men with haggard expressions and filthy clothing. Bush was glad he had changed clothes during the flight from Washington, swapping his suit and tie, which he had worn early that day during his speech at the National Cathedral, for a plain gray windbreaker, adorned only with a small brass collar pin in the shape of an American flag.

"It was so surreal," he told me. "Smoke coming out—it was like a movie set, except it was real."

He added, "It was unbelievable. It was gray. It was ash. And there was slosh all over the ground, and soot, and emotion. It was just a very, very strange experience there, just watching—looking at this."

As the president moved from man to man, he clapped them on the shoulder or draped an arm around them. At one point he briefly donned a fireman's hat. Again and again, he heard the men say things like "God bless you," and "We're proud of you." One man called out, "Don't let 'em get away with it, George!" The informality was astounding. These hardhats were addressing the most powerful person on the planet by his first name.

Bush had not prepared any formal remarks for this occasion, and yet the rescue workers seemed eager to hear from their president. Although Bush was doing his best to greet them one at a time, the crowd was just too large. For every hardhat the president thanked in person, hundreds more were clamoring for a mere glimpse of him. They pressed in from all sides.

Secret Service protocols went right out the window. It would have been almost impossible to extract the president from this crowd if something had gone wrong. For starters, most of the presidential motorcade, which was normally positioned just a few steps away from Bush in case he needed to make a speedy getaway, had been left behind. There was simply no room to maneuver a dozen vehicles in this cramped and confusing war zone. Secondly, the setting itself was profoundly dangerous. There were fires burning beneath the rubble. Smoke was everywhere. The whole place was shrouded in a toxic haze. Underground cavities were still collapsing. Badly damaged buildings were in danger of toppling over at any moment.

To bring a sitting president into such a volatile environment was unprecedented.

To complicate matters, Bush was trailed by New York's congressional delegation, including Senator Hillary Rodham Clinton. Several senior White House officials noted with dismay that Representative Jerrold Nadler seemed to be maneuvering into camera shots of the president. They felt the hulking Democrat was getting in the way of the Secret Service, which was already on edge because so many people surrounding Bush in this chaotic scene had not been subjected to security sweeps—a highly unusual occurrence. One Bush aide told Nadler three times to give the president some space.

"I'm a U.S. congressman," Nadler protested.

"I don't give a shit *who* you are!" the aide shot back.

The president seemed oblivious to the dustup. He felt somehow protected as he moved among these rough-hewn, jostling men who kept calling him by his first name. His presence seemed to stir their weary souls into a state of excitement that verged on rowdiness, especially among the ironworkers. As Bush slowly made his way toward the epicenter of destruction, some of the ironworkers took up a chant: "USA! USA! USA!"

Nina Bishop, a member of the White House advance team, could sense the crowd's excitement. She approached Karl Rove, the president's top political advisor, and Andy Card, the White House chief of staff, and suggested that Bush speak to the hardhats as a group. Both men agreed, but there was a problem: No public address system had been set up. So Bishop began darting into various tents that had been erected by rescue agencies and utilities until she found one with a bullhorn. She managed to borrow the device, but when she tested it by blowing into the mouthpiece, she discovered it did not work very well. The bullhorn must have been running low on power, because Bishop found it difficult to amplify her voice. Still, it was the only bullhorn she could find, and the president was nearing the spot where Rove and Card had decided he should speak. So she hustled over and passed the defective bullhorn up to the president.

Bush took it in one hand and reached up with his other to an old fireman with a stunned look on his craggy face. It took a moment for the old-timer to regain his composure, but then he grabbed the president's hand and pulled him atop what appeared to be a twisted pile of steel and bricks, steadying him as Bush found his footing.

"Are you okay, Mr. President?" the fireman said.

"Yeah," Bush replied. When he saw the fireman begin to climb down, he added, "Where you goin'?"

"I was told to get down," the old-timer explained.

"No," said Bush, draping his arm around the fireman's shoulder. "You stay right here with me."

Bush looked out over the crowd, which was again chanting, "USA! USA! USA!"

"Thank you all," he said through the bullhorn.

"Go get 'em, George!" shouted a beefy man in a powder blue hardhat and kelly green windbreaker. Such informality! Back in Washington, no one dared call the president of the United States by his first name, at least not in public. And yet here on this smoldering slag heap, a total stranger in a ludicrous blue hardhat was calling him George. Only it came out as *"Jawj!"*

"I, uh, I want you all to know—" Bush began.

"Louder!" shouted another hardhat off to the president's right.

Bush turned to his heckler and shrugged. "It can't go any louder."

The hardhats chuckled. The president plowed on.

"I want you all to know that America today—America today—is on bended knee in prayer for the people whose lives were lost here, for the workers who work here, for the families who mourn," Bush said. Although he held the bullhorn just inches from his mouth and slowly swept it from side to side, it didn't seem to project his voice very well. Forty years earlier, Bush had learned to use a megaphone as head cheerleader of Phillips Academy, then an elite, all-male prep school in Andover, Massachusetts. But this bullhorn was no megaphone. And these hardhats were no preppies.

"Go get 'em, Jawj!"

"This nation stands with the good people of New York City and New Jersey and Connecticut as we mourn the loss—"

"Can't hear you!" called a voice in the distance.

"—of thousands of our citizens," Bush continued.

"Can't hear you!" came another voice.

This was degenerating in a hurry. Although Bush rather enjoyed the exuberance of these brutes, he could not very well tolerate their constant interruptions. He had to get control of the crowd or else the situation would turn into a free-for-all.

"George!" hollered another hardhat off to his left. "We can't hear you!"

Bush swung around to face his tormentor, pulling the bullhorn close to his lips and pumping as much volume into his voice as possible.

"I can hear *you!*" he yelled.

At long last, the bullhorn seemed to be working. The crowd erupted in laughter at the president's flip reply, which silenced the hecklers. Even the old fireman at his side chuckled. The laughter gave way to appreciative cheers, whistles, claps, and waves. Relieved, Bush managed a smile. As the cheer crested and began to subside, he decided to fill the conversational void before the hecklers could start in again.

"I can hear you," the president repeated, holding one finger aloft. "The rest of the world hears you," he continued, now extending two fingers. "And the people—"

Bush was now pointing behind him at the hulking wreckage of the World Trade Center. The men were cheering and whistling and clapping again, with several screaming: "Yeah!" Bush let the applause rise and fall before continuing.

"—and the people who knocked these buildings down will hear *all* of us soon!" he vowed, jabbing his index finger in the air.

"YEAAAHHH!!!" the men roared in a thunderous primal scream. They punched their fists skyward and let loose with bloodcurdling war whoops. When one of them began barking like a dog, others quickly took up the savage cry.

"*WOOF! WOOF! WOOF! WOOF! WOOF! WOOF! WOOF!*"

The catharsis was extraordinary. After three days of grimly digging bits of their brethren from this filthy, smoldering slag heap, the workers were suddenly overflowing with righteous indignation. Grown men were baying at the top of their lungs like a pack of junkyard dogs! It was as if their commander in chief had finally given them permission to vent all the rage and frustration and sorrow and whatever else was coursing through their exhausted bodies and shell-shocked brains. Bush lifted the bullhorn to his lips and was about to say something more when a lone voice rang out: "USA! USA!"

Someone else picked up the chant: "USA! USA!"

In a heartbeat, the whole lot of them were throwing back their heads and roaring lustily: "*USA! USA! USA! USA!*"

Bush dropped the bullhorn to his side and surveyed the spectacle before him. He had never witnessed such an overt, spontaneous display of raw patriotism. These were not the same tired, disaffected men who had heckled him just moments earlier. These were *patriots*—the wild-eyed, go-for-broke sort that America hadn't seen in sixty years. Bush couldn't believe it. He and his speechwriters had spent so much time carefully crafting his address for the VIPs back at the National Cathedral. His aides had been so worried about striking just the right note. And now he was here at Ground Zero, firing off a few impromptu remarks through a defective bullhorn to a bunch of hard-core New York union workers—virtually all of them Democrats who had probably voted for Al Gore. And yet in this imperfect, electrifying moment, America seemed to come *alive* again. Bush later told me, "It was one of those defining moments in American history."

"USA! USA! USA! USA! USA!"

Then, as suddenly as it had risen, the chant subsided. The president lifted the bullhorn to his mouth one final time.

"The nation," he began, pulling Beckwith close. "The nation sends its love and compassion—"

"God bless America!" screamed a hardhat. It was a guttural cry of defiance, tinged with anguish.

"—to everybody who is here," Bush said. "Thank you for your hard work. Thank you for making the nation proud. And God bless America."

The cheers rose again, along with the now familiar shouts of "George!" The president smiled and raised his arm to acknowledge the applause. Then he turned to the ancient fireman at his side and cocked his right hand in the gesture that says: Get ready for a big ol' handshake. It took a moment for the man to comprehend that the president of the United States wanted to shake his hand, right then and there, at the climax of this extraordinary moment. Bush's hand swooped down like an eagle spearing a salmon. He gave the old-timer's paw a firm shake and then turned to clamber down from this mound of twisted metal and bricks. A forest of hands shot up to help the president down, although he stopped when he saw that one of the hands was offering him a small American flag on a stick. Bush took it, straightened back up, and waved it aloft. It was only a foot wide, but in that moment it might as well have been a mile. The crowd went ballistic.

"USA! USA! USA! USA! USA! USA! USA! USA! USA! USA!"

The only journalists to witness this scene were a small pool of reporters assembled by the White House. Jonathan Alter of *Newsweek* shook his head and said to White House Press Secretary Ari Fleischer, "This is one of those scenes that's a turning point in history."

"What are you talking about?" said Fleischer, who had been so consumed with the nightmarish logistics of the president's movements that he had missed the significance of the moment.

Alter insisted, "This is a turning point in history."

Another journalist told Fleischer it was like Reagan's exhortation, "Mr. Gorbachev, tear down this wall!" But there was a major difference—Reagan's line had been written in advance.

Since there was no live feed for this scene, David Gregory of NBC News held up his cell phone so that TV viewers could at least hear the president's electrifying words. Bush had nicknamed the reporter Little Stretch because he stood 6-feet-5-inches, or one inch shorter than Dick "Stretch" Keil of Bloomberg. But "Little Stretch" kept his cell phone some nine feet in the air until Bush finally clambered down from the wreckage.

"It was just one of those spontaneous things where it just popped right out," Bush told me later. "It wasn't planned, it wasn't thought about, it wasn't scripted. It just happened.

"And maybe that's the way it should be," he added. "The American people don't like to be kind of fooled. They don't want script, particularly in these moments. I believe they want feeling and emotion and emotion and honesty—honesty isn't the right word, but honest feeling. And so this moment was an opportunity. It was just one of those God-given moments where it worked out fine because it sent the right kind of message to the country."

Bush handed off the bullhorn and headed back to the truncated motorcade, which drove him three miles north to the Jacob K. Javits Convention Center. He got out and greeted firefighters from urban search-and-rescue teams who had traveled here from states like Ohio and California. The press pool tagged along.

"Mr. President," David Gregory ventured, "I wonder what some of your impressions are, sir."

"Well, I'm shocked at the size of the devastation," Bush said. "And it's hard to describe what it's like to see the snarled steel and broken glass and twists of the building, silhouetted against smoke.

"I said that this was the first act of war on America in the twenty-first century and I was right—particularly having seen the scene. However, out of the rubble and ash and ugliness, there's a lot of good—starting with the guys from L.A. that are here. They've come all the way over from California to help brothers and sisters in need. And that's a symbol of the greatness of the country. This is a country that's coming together.

"I was also struck by how angry many of the workers were, in spite of the fact that they had worked to exhaustion. Yeah, they're angry. They're angry at the people who did the crime. They're angry at the people who destroyed life. They're angry at the people who caused the devastation. And, as I said, I heard their anger. And America will feel the same way. And our response will be one that is justified."

"Sir, what's your level of satisfaction on how the investigation is progressing and how the intelligence gathering is going?" Gregory asked.

"I am satisfied that America has rallied during this terrible tragedy. I'm satisfied that the compassion of the nation has risen to the surface. I'm satisfied that in any community, if we ask for help, we would find it.

"I'm also satisfied that the four thousand FBI agents are working tirelessly to gather all the evidence that can be gathered, to find those who may still be in our country, if they are here. I'm satisfied that our planning for possible future actions is going on course.

"But most of all, I'm satisfied and I'm pleased to be an American. This is a proud moment for our country. Out of this terrible devastation and ruin, the greatness of America shines forth.

"I'm here just to—as best as I possibly can—to thank the American people who are helping here. And to give comfort to those who hurt.

"A lot of the firefighters that we saw had tears in their eyes because they lost loved ones and their brothers are missing. And, you know, it's a sad moment to be with them. And the least I can do is give 'em a hug and maybe encourage them some."

As Bush began to walk away, he heard another question.

"Are you close to determining who did this?" a reporter asked.

"We're gathering all possible evidence," Bush said as he continued walking. "And at the appropriate time, we will let America know what the evidence says."

"Do you feel like you know who did it?"

"We know," Bush began, but then corrected himself as a cryptic smile crossed his countenance. "We got a suspect."

With that, the president ended his exchange with the press and went back to greeting the firefighters, including a group from Sacramento, California.

"How's your family?" one of the firemen asked as he shook Bush's hand.

"Freaked out, the girls are," the president replied matter-of-factly. "My wife's okay. She understands we're at war and she's got a war mentality. So do I. Thanks for asking."

Bush told the fireman about the "great strength of the country" and how the tragedy had resulted in a "lot of people pulling together."

"That's the thing about these bad events," the fireman said. "People pull together and, in that sense, really shine through."

Bush agreed and kept moving. He eventually worked his way over to a "pipe-and-drape" enclosure that contained several hundred people who had lost loved ones in the attacks.

"I don't want any press in here," Bush instructed a White House staffer. "I don't want a lot of elected officials in here. We're not gonna make a spectacle out of this."

The idea was for the president to spend thirty minutes bucking up the spirits of these anguished family members, all of whom had gut-wrenching stories. Instead, he spent two hours crying right along with them.

"It was hard," Bush told me. "Now, the interesting thing about this, Bill, was that everybody felt like their loved one was alive at this point. And I had just come from a scene of incredible devastation."

In other words, the president realized these anguished souls were in denial. More than seventy-two hours had passed since the attacks. Although the hardhats were technically still conducting a "rescue" operation, it was beginning to seem more like an effort to recover the bodies. Yet many of these family members refused to give up hope. They were the same sort of shell-shocked people who for days had been wandering the streets of Manhattan like zombies, clutching family photos and asking passersby for any sign of the missing. Now these photos were being thrust at the president.

"I came up with a formula as to how to deal with that," Bush told me. "And that was to say, 'Let me sign this for you, and when you get Bill back, or Joe back, or John back, you tell him he's not going to believe that you saw the president, and this will be proof.'"

"That was kind of my way of saying, you know, I'm with you, I hope you're right, and at the same time, kind of add a little humor," he explained. "There's something about the presidency—not necessarily the president, but the presidency—which brings out kind of a predictable response. People want their picture, people want their autograph—in times of happiness and in mourning. And so, we had a lot of pictures taken, and a lot of signing of autographs."

Ravaged by sorrow and sleep deprivation, some of the people in the enclosure were literally holding one another up as the president worked the crowd.

"My son is a marine," one lost soul said. "If anybody can get out, he can."

A black woman asked the president to sign a picture of her husband. He complied and she tucked the photo into her purse.

"I'm sure we're gonna get him out of there," Bush assured her. "We're gonna get him out."

A beefy guy carried a small child, four or five years old, who pointed to a picture of the man's brother and announced, "That's my daddy."

The raw emotion in the room was overwhelming. Again and again, the president asked the lost souls to tell him about their loved ones. Again and again, he listened and cried and hugged them. Virtually everyone in the enclosure was bawling. The Secret Service, which normally hovers behind the president, pulled back in order to allow a modicum of privacy.

"I mean, I wept with family members, I hugged dads," Bush told me. "I was supposed to be there for, like, thirty minutes. We stayed for a couple of hours. And it was the right thing to do. I saw every single person there."

This included a nine-year-old girl and her eleven-year-old brother who were so nervous about meeting the president that they clung to their mother, who tried to nudge them toward Bush. At length, the boy summoned his courage and approached the most powerful person on the planet. He was clutching a small brown teddy bear in one hand and a photo of his father in the other. Bush looked at the departmental photo of a fireman in uniform and inquired about the father's name. Then he signed it and handed it back.

The boy looked at the picture and burst into uncontrollable sobs. Bush reached out, grabbed him around the head and waist, and pulled him close. The president held him for a long time. He hugged the girl as well. But the boy never stopped crying. The mother and a variety of onlookers also went to pieces. Even the Secret Service agents—those supposedly emotionless Terminators with coiled wires coming out of their ears—were blubbering like babies.

As Bush worked the room, families stood in clusters and respectfully kept their distance while others were being comforted. After nearly two hours, the president had covered just about everyone in the room except for one family.

An elegantly dressed woman sat off to one side. She was surrounded by several grown sons and a variety of grandchildren, all of whom were wearing suits and ties. They could have been posing for a family portrait. And they never approached the president.

So Bush, who knew it was time to leave, approached them. The woman introduced herself as Arlene Dillon, the mother of New York police officer George Howard. She pulled out something and pressed it into the president's hand, closing her palm over his.

"This is my son's shield," she said quietly as the president leaned close. "It was on him and I want you to have it, just to remember. My son would want you to have it, too."

Bush took the shield, which had been unearthed by the bucket brigades, and put it in his pocket. There wasn't a whole lot he could say to this woman, who was beaming at him instead of crying.

It was dark by the time the president finally departed the convention center. His motorcade headed north on Twelfth Avenue and then turned east on Forty-Second Street. The sidewalks were filled with people, five and six deep, clutching candles and signs that said "God bless America," "God bless the USA," and "God bless you, President Bush." The president was accustomed to seeing knots of well-wishers whenever his motorcade departed some city for the local airport. But such crowds normally thinned after a few blocks. Tonight, however, the crowd grew denser as the motorcade progressed through the city. There were thousands and thousands of candles. At Times Square, people were lined up forty deep; some were openly weeping. As the president approached, a great roar filled the air. It rose high above the motorcade to a giant neon news ticker that was scrolling the latest headline: "BUSH CALLS UP 50,000 RESERVISTS." The winds of war were blowing through Times Square.

The president eventually made his way back to the helicopter, which lifted him above the ocean and on to McGuire Air Force Base in New Jersey. As he walked across the tarmac from Marine One to Air Force One, he was intercepted by Ari Fleischer, who told him that Congress had just voted to authorize the use of force. The resolution passed the Senate 98-0 and the House 420-1. The lone dissenter was California Democrat Barbara Lee, a leftist radical from the ideological fever swamps of Berkeley. Fleischer had already drafted a presidential reaction for the press and needed Bush to sign off on it.

"I am gratified that the Congress has united so powerfully by taking this action," the draft said. "It sends a clear message—our people are together, and we will prevail."

Bush approved the statement and the two men talked for a while about the meeting with family members at the convention center. The president said he felt "whipped" by that emotionally draining experience, not to mention everything else that had happened throughout the long day. It had begun with a tearful cabinet meeting and speech about "the middle hour of our grief." It was ending with Congress uniting behind his desire to unleash the "terrible swift sword" of the United States military.

Yes, Bush felt "whipped," but he also felt good, he confided to Fleischer. Friday, September 14, seemed more like a month than a single day. The president, as well as the nation, had experienced every emotion imaginable. The tears of grief, the laughter of embarrassment, the pride of patriotism, the rush of defiance, the anger of righteousness.

Bush knew that September 11 was the day everyone would remember for eternity. But as far as he was concerned, September 14 was nearly as important. For it was the day America began to shake off its despair and set about the task at hand—fighting back.

Chapter Eight

"The Hour Is Coming"

THE STANDING OVATION LASTED a full five minutes, with Democrats applauding just as rhapsodically as Republicans. President Bush stood in the well of the House chamber and drank it all in. Could this be the same place where, just eight months earlier, sixteen Democrats stormed out of a joint session of Congress to protest the certification of Florida's electoral votes and Bush's presidential victory? Could this possibly be the same chamber where, less than seven months ago, scattered boos and hisses greeted Bush during his first address to a joint session of Congress? The transformation was nothing short of remarkable. This time around, instead of booing and hissing, there was applause that seemed to grow ever louder. Democrats desperately groped for the president's hand as he strode down the center aisle of this magnificent chamber—a chamber that had been so hastily evacuated a scant nine days earlier.

Behind Bush stood House Speaker J. Dennis Hastert, the beefy Illinois Republican who had invited the president to make this rare wartime address to a joint session of Congress. Hastert had extended the invitation the day after the attacks and Bush had accepted immediately, although he cautioned that he wouldn't give the speech until he had something to say. The president eventually decided he would have something to say at 9 P.M. on September 20.

Under normal circumstances, Vice President Cheney, who also served as president of the Senate, would have the seat next to Hastert. But tonight the Senate's president pro tem, West Virginia Democrat Robert Byrd, had that spot. The last time a president addressed a joint session of Congress without his vice president sitting on the dais behind him was in 1974, after Gerald Ford replaced Richard Nixon as president because of the Watergate scandal. Twenty-seven years later, Vice President Cheney was at an "undisclosed location" because of security concerns. If a terrorist somehow took out Bush and those around him, Cheney would be able to assume the presidency and the nation would be spared a broader decapitation of its government. But first the terrorist would have to get past the soldiers in full combat gear, Secret Service agents brandishing machine guns, SWAT teams in bulletproof vests, bomb-sniffing police dogs, fighter jets, attack helicopters, police cruisers, fire trucks, ambulances, and black Chevy Suburbans that encircled the Capitol in an unprecedented show of force.

"Mr. Speaker, Mr. President Pro Tempore, members of Congress, and fellow Americans," Bush began. "In the normal course of events, presidents come to this chamber to report on the state of the Union. Tonight, no such report is needed. It has already been delivered by the American people.

"We have seen it in the courage of passengers, who rushed terrorists to save others on the ground—passengers like an exceptional man named Todd Beamer. And would you please help me to welcome his wife, Lisa Beamer, here tonight."

Congress leaped to its feet for another ovation as Bush nodded to a pregnant blond woman in a black dress whose husband had died aboard one of the hijacked planes. Todd Beamer's story was as inspirational as it was chilling. When the thirty-two-year-old software manager realized that United Airlines Flight 93 was being hijacked, he swiped his credit card through an in-flight telephone mounted in the back of one of the plane's seats. Failing to get authorization for the call, the father of two was routed to an operator, who listened to his story and then transferred him to a supervisor for GTE Verizon, Lisa Jefferson. During the thirteen-minute conversation that ensued, Jefferson told Beamer about the three other hijacked planes that had already been crashed into the World Trade Center and the Pentagon. Beamer informed Jefferson that a passenger on board Flight 93 was already dead. At least two knife-wielding hijackers were in the cockpit. Beamer explained that another hijacker was in the rear of the plane claiming to have a bomb—a red box strapped to his torso with a belt. He said he and some other passengers were going to jump the man, adding, "I know I'm not going to get out of this." At Beamer's request, Jefferson joined him in reciting the Lord's Prayer.

Our Father, who art in heaven,
Hallowed be Thy name.
Thy kingdom come, Thy will be done
On earth as it is in heaven.
Give us this day our daily bread,
And forgive us our trespasses,
As we forgive those who trespass against us.
And lead us not into temptation
But deliver us from evil....

Deliver us from evil! No wonder Bush referred to the terrorists as "evildoers." Beamer was about to confront pure, unadulterated evil. But first he made Jefferson promise to call his wife and sons, ages three and one, back in their New Jersey home. Then he put the phone down, leaving the line open. The last words Jefferson heard Beamer say were, "Are you ready, guys? Let's roll." Investigators believe Beamer and his fellow passengers, including a man named Jeremy Glick, overpowered the hijacker at the back of the plane and then stormed the cockpit. "Get out of here!" screamed one of the hijackers in a scuffle that was picked up by the cockpit voice recorder. "Get out of here! *Get out of here!*" The 757 then crashed in a rural field near Shanksville, Pennsylvania. All forty-four people on board perished. It was the only hijacked plane that didn't claim the life of a single person on the ground.

Bush was deeply moved by the story of Todd Beamer, especially his last words, "Let's roll." The succinct phrase seemed to encapsulate the nation's defiant, can-do attitude in the wake of the terrorist attacks. It was a plucky slogan the president would repeat many times in the coming months as he exhorted America to prosecute the war against terrorism with maximum gusto.

"We have seen the state of our Union in the endurance of rescuers, working past exhaustion. We have seen the unfurling of flags, the lighting of candles, the giving of blood, the saying of prayers—in English, Hebrew, and Arabic. We have seen the decency of a loving and giving people who have made the grief of strangers their own.

"My fellow citizens, for the last nine days, the entire world has seen for itself the state of our Union—and it is strong."

Up until now, Bush had refrained from appearing too bellicose in his public statements, preferring instead to let the nation grieve for a while. But six days after commemorating "the middle hour of our grief," the president served notice that the grieving process, as far as he was concerned, was officially over.

"Tonight we are a country awakened to danger and called to defend freedom. Our grief has turned to anger, and anger to resolution. Whether we bring our enemies to justice, or bring justice to our enemies, justice will be done."

Bush had already demanded that the Taliban, the fundamentalist Islamic regime that ruled most of Afghanistan, turn over Osama bin Laden and the rest of the terrorists in the al Qaeda network. Now he was warning that if the Taliban refused to give these terrorists up, America would simply come and get them.

"I thank the Congress for its leadership at such an important time. All of America was touched on the evening of the tragedy to see Republicans and Democrats joined together on the steps of this Capitol, singing 'God Bless America.' And you did more than sing; you acted, by delivering $40 billion to rebuild our communities and meet the needs of our military.

"Speaker Hastert, Minority Leader Gephardt, Majority Leader Daschle, and Senator Lott, I thank you for your friendship, for your leadership, and for your service to our country."

Bush had come into office vowing to "change the tone" of Washington, where Democrats had resorted to character assassination of Republicans during the impeachment of President Clinton. While Bush made some progress in his first months in office, the terrorist attacks had the effect of instantly eradicating all remaining vestiges of partisan politics, at least for the foreseeable future. Moreover, the president's job approval, which had fallen to its low point of 51 percent just before the attacks, skyrocketed to 86 percent immediately afterward, according to Gallup. That was almost as high as his father's 89 percent rating at the end of the Persian Gulf War in March 1991—the highest of any president since Gallup began measuring job approval in 1938. But the elder Bush went on to lose his bid for reelection to a relative unknown named Bill Clinton just twenty months later. The fleeting nature of soaring poll numbers had been a bitter lesson for the younger Bush, who promised himself that if he ever amassed such a wealth of political capital, he would not hoard it like his father. So the president decided to spend his newfound political riches on enlisting not just the nation, but the larger world, in his war against terrorism.

"And on behalf of the American people, I thank the world for its outpouring of support. America will never forget the sounds of our National Anthem playing at Buckingham Palace, on the streets of Paris, and at Berlin's Brandenburg Gate.

"We will not forget South Korean children gathering to pray outside our embassy in Seoul, or the prayers of sympathy offered at a mosque in Cairo. We will not forget moments of silence and days of mourning in Australia and Africa and Latin America.

"Nor will we forget the citizens of eighty other nations who died with our own: dozens of Pakistanis; more than 130 Israelis; more than 250 citizens of India; men and women from El Salvador, Iran, Mexico, and Japan; and hundreds of British citizens."

The president had spent the last week trying to assemble a coalition for the inevitable counterattack, although he quickly realized it would not be a wartime alliance in the conventional sense. Rather, it would be a series of smaller, "floating" coalitions of nations providing dramatically different levels of assistance, some overt and some covert, some short-term and some open-ended. There was one nation, however, that gave its support completely and virtually unconditionally.

"America has no truer friend than Great Britain. Once again, we are joined together in a great cause."

The president gestured to Tony Blair, who was sitting in the visitors' gallery next to Laura Bush.

"I'm so honored the British prime minister has crossed an ocean to show his unity of purpose with America," Bush said as Congress rose for another ovation. "Thank you for coming, friend.

"On September the 11th, enemies of freedom committed an act of war against our country. Americans have known wars, but for the past 136 years, they have been wars on foreign soil—except for one Sunday in 1941."

Although the White House was trying to discourage comparisons between tonight's address and the "Infamy" speech by President Roosevelt, Bush knew the press would draw parallels anyway. After all, this was the first time in nearly sixty years that an attack had taken place on American soil. Still, as far as Bush was concerned, there were more differences than similarities between December 7, 1941, and September 11, 2001.

For starters, Pearl Harbor was attacked more than seventeen years before Hawaii had become a state. That meant the last time the United States proper was attacked by a foreign enemy was the War of 1812, which saw the White House burned by the British. The last war waged on the American mainland, aside from battles with Indians during the push West, was the Civil War, which ended in 1865.

"Americans have known the casualties of war—but not at the center of a great city on a peaceful morning. Americans have known surprise attacks—but never before on thousands of civilians. All of this was brought upon us in a single day—and night fell on a different world, a world where freedom itself is under attack."

Poetic phrases like "night fell on a different world" came from the pen of Michael Gerson, the president's top speechwriter, who helped craft this night's address with White House Counselor Karen Hughes.

Encouraged by the unexpected success of the president's August stem cell speech, which was largely explanatory, Bush and his speechwriters decided to make a significant portion of this address a primer on terrorism.

"Americans have many questions tonight. Americans are asking: Who attacked our country? The evidence we have gathered all points to a collection of loosely affiliated terrorist organizations known as al Qaeda. They are the same murderers indicted for bombing American embassies in Tanzania and Kenya, and responsible for bombing the USS *Cole*.

"Al Qaeda is to terror what the mafia is to crime. But its goal is not making money; its goal is remaking the world—and imposing its radical beliefs on people everywhere.

"The terrorists practice a fringe form of Islamic extremism that has been rejected by Muslim scholars and the vast majority of Muslim clerics—a fringe movement that perverts the peaceful teachings of Islam. The terrorists' directive commands them to kill Christians and Jews, to kill all Americans, and make no distinction among military and civilians, including women and children.

"This group and its leader—a person named Osama bin Laden—are linked to many other organizations in different countries, including the Egyptian Islamic Jihad and the Islamic Movement of Uzbekistan. There are thousands of these terrorists in more than sixty countries. They are recruited from their own nations and neighborhoods and brought to camps in places like Afghanistan, where they are trained in the tactics of terror. They are sent back to their homes or sent to hide in countries around the world to plot evil and destruction.

"The leadership of al Qaeda has great influence in Afghanistan and supports the Taliban regime in controlling most of that country. In Afghanistan, we see al Qaeda's vision for the world.

"Afghanistan's people have been brutalized—many are starving and many have fled. Women are not allowed to attend school. You can be jailed for owning a television. Religion can be practiced only as their leaders dictate. A man can be jailed in Afghanistan if his beard is not long enough.

"The United States respects the people of Afghanistan—after all, we are currently its largest source of humanitarian aid—but we condemn the Taliban regime. It is not only repressing its own people, it is threatening people everywhere by sponsoring and sheltering and supplying terrorists. By aiding and abetting murder, the Taliban regime is committing murder."

Now that the distinction between ordinary Afghans and their despotic rulers was out of the way, Bush went straight for the jugular.

"And tonight, the United States of America makes the following demands on the Taliban:

"Deliver to United States authorities all the leaders of al Qaeda who hide in your land.

"Release all foreign nationals, including American citizens, you have unjustly imprisoned.

"Protect foreign journalists, diplomats, and aid workers in your country.

"Close immediately and permanently every terrorist training camp in Afghanistan, and hand over every terrorist, and every person in their support structure, to appropriate authorities.

"Give the United States full access to terrorist training camps, so we can make sure they are no longer operating.

"These demands are not open to negotiation or discussion," Bush said, drawing thunderous applause. "The Taliban must act, and act immediately. They will hand over the terrorists, or they will share in their fate."

Mindful of warnings that his war plans would roil the "Arab street" throughout the Middle East, Bush hastened to add that he had no quarrel with Muslims in the larger Arab world.

"I also want to speak tonight directly to Muslims throughout the world. We respect your faith. It's practiced freely by many millions of Americans, and by millions more in countries that America counts as friends. Its teachings are good and peaceful, and those who commit evil in the name of Allah blaspheme the name of Allah.

"The terrorists are traitors to their own faith, trying, in effect, to hijack Islam itself. The enemy of America is not our many Muslim friends; it is not our many Arab friends. Our enemy is a radical network of terrorists, and every government that supports them.

"Our war on terror begins with al Qaeda, but it does not end there. It will not end until every terrorist group of global reach has been found, stopped, and defeated."

In other words, Bush was not about to preemptively limit his global war against terrorism to the borders of Afghanistan—overtures to the Arab street notwithstanding. So he tried to make the argument that bin Laden's attack on the United States was merely the opening salvo in a wider reign of terror against other nations.

"Americans are asking: Why do they hate us? They hate what we see right here in this chamber—a democratically elected government. Their leaders are self-appointed. They hate our freedoms—our freedom of religion, our freedom of speech, our freedom to vote and assemble and disagree with each other.

"They want to overthrow existing governments in many Muslim countries, such as Egypt, Saudi Arabia, and Jordan. They want to drive Israel out of the Middle East. They want to drive Christians and Jews out of vast regions of Asia and Africa.

"These terrorists kill not merely to end lives, but to disrupt and end a way of life. With every atrocity, they hope that America grows fearful, retreating from the world and forsaking our friends. They stand against us, because we stand in their way.

"We are not deceived by their pretenses to piety. We have seen their kind before. They are the heirs of all the murderous ideologies of the twentieth century. By sacrificing human life to serve their radical visions—by abandoning every value except the will to power—they follow in the path of fascism, and Nazism, and totalitarianism. And they will follow that path all the way, to where it ends: in history's unmarked grave of discarded lies."

This was supposed to be one of the more memorable lines from the speech, although "history's unmarked grave of discarded lies" didn't exactly roll off the tongue like "a date which will live in infamy." Still, Congress applauded ecstatically.

"Americans are asking: How will we fight and win this war? We will direct every resource at our command—every means of diplomacy, every tool of intelligence, every instrument of law enforcement, every financial influence, and every necessary weapon of war—to the disruption and to the defeat of the global terror network.

"This war will not be like the war against Iraq a decade ago, with a decisive liberation of territory and a swift conclusion. It will not look like the air war above Kosovo two years ago, where no ground troops were used and not a single American was lost in combat."

Bush later told me it was important to overcome the public's aversion to even minimal American casualties. He realized that air strikes alone would not be enough to eradicate the Taliban.

"We needed to unleash the mighty military in a way that would bring them to justice—which meant a change of policy," he told me.

"And the policy changes were boots on the ground. We had gone through this kind of antiseptic vision of war. I was asked, Do you think you'll suffer lives? And the answer was: I hope not, but yes, I do think we'll suffer life. If you knew what I knew—which was the commitment of ground troops, people willing to go into those caves, like the 10th Mountain Division—somebody is going to lose their life."

The president told the joint session of Congress, "Our response involves far more than instant retaliation and isolated strikes."

This was a pointed reference to former president Bill Clinton's failed military strike against bin Laden three years earlier. It happened on August 20, 1998, the day after Monica Lewinsky testified before a federal grand jury in the sex-and-lies case that led to Clinton's impeachment. The president was widely accused of "wagging the dog," contriving a military crisis to divert attention from his sexual misdeeds. White House aides vehemently disputed this theory, insisting the cruise missiles that rained down on bin Laden's terrorist training camps in Afghanistan and a "chemical weapons" plant in the Sudan were merely the opening salvo in what would become a sustained and comprehensive campaign against worldwide terrorism. But as the months passed, there were no follow-up strikes. And it became clear that the training camps in Afghanistan had been mostly empty when the cruise missiles hit. The "chemical weapons" plant in the Sudan turned out to be an aspirin factory; its owner, a Saudi businessman, successfully sued the Clinton administration to release $24 million in assets the White House had frozen at the time of the attacks. No, Bush was determined to refrain from quick and dirty retaliations that would amount to another embarrassing display of American impotence. He insisted on giving Rumsfeld enough time to put together a war plan that could actually do some serious damage to the enemy.

At the same time, the president was abandoning his long opposition to open-ended military adventures. Less than a year earlier, during a debate with Vice President Gore, Bush had derided the Clinton administration's penchant for overdeploying U.S. forces on nebulous "nation-building" missions. "Our military is meant to fight and win war," candidate Bush said. "I'm going to be judicious as to how to use the military—it needs to be in our vital interest, the mission needs to be clear and the exit strategy obvious."

And yet there was nothing obvious about the exit strategy for the war against terrorism. In fact, the president explicitly told Congress that this new kind of war would have no exit strategy whatsoever.

"Americans should not expect one battle, but a lengthy campaign, unlike any other we have ever seen. It may include dramatic strikes, visible on TV, and covert operations, secret even in success. We will starve terrorists of funding, turn them one against another, drive them from place to place, until there is no refuge or no rest. And we will pursue nations that provide aid or safe haven to terrorism.

"Every nation, in every region, now has a decision to make. Either you are with us, or you are with the terrorists. From this day forward, any nation that continues to harbor or support terrorism will be regarded by the United States as a hostile regime."

This "with us or against us" rhetoric would become known as the Bush Doctrine. While it was hailed for its moral clarity, the president would eventually grant temporary exemptions to his own doctrine, starting with Palestinian leader Yasser Arafat and continuing with strategic U.S. allies like Saudi Arabia. But none of these messy complications were on anyone's radar screen just yet.

"Our nation has been put on notice: We are not immune from attack. We will take defensive measures against terrorism to protect

Americans. Today, dozens of federal departments and agencies, as well as state and local governments, have responsibilities affecting homeland security. These efforts must be coordinated at the highest level. So tonight I announce the creation of a cabinet-level position reporting directly to me—the Office of Homeland Security.

"And tonight I also announce a distinguished American to lead this effort, to strengthen American security: a military veteran, an effective governor, a true patriot, a trusted friend—Pennsylvania's Tom Ridge. He will lead, oversee, and coordinate a comprehensive national strategy to safeguard our country against terrorism, and respond to any attacks that may come."

Bush had called Ridge the night before and asked him to take the job. Having lost the vice presidential slot to Cheney because of his support for abortion, Ridge had long ago ruled out working for the administration in any other capacity. But now Bush made him an offer he couldn't refuse, calling a second time that very morning to seal the deal. The Republican agreed to resign as governor in order to shore up the nation's domestic defenses.

"These measures are essential. But the only way to defeat terrorism as a threat to our way of life is to stop it, eliminate it, and destroy it where it grows.

"Many will be involved in this effort, from FBI agents to intelligence operatives to the reservists we have called to active duty. All deserve our thanks, and all have our prayers.

"And tonight, a few miles from the damaged Pentagon, I have a message for our military: Be ready. I've called the armed forces to alert, and there is a reason. The hour is coming when America will act, and you will make us proud."

A day earlier, the Pentagon had ordered more than one hundred warplanes to the region surrounding Afghanistan—the most obvious first step of the war plans that Bush and his lieutenants had been quietly drawing up for nearly nine days. As the president later explained to me during an interview in his office aboard Air Force One, the need for war plans was obvious from the outset.

"There's no question about fighting," he told me. "On this airplane, at this desk, airborne out of Florida—I knew. That night in the bunker below the White House, we discussed, and I asked for, plans. And on the 16th, I saw the beginnings of the plans. So there's no question about that."

The only question was how.

"How do you fight a guerrilla war with conventional forces? I knew we were going to fight, and the question is, How are we going to win? And that was probably the most, kind of, questionable thing for me. And Tommy Franks and Rumsfeld had worked it hard, worked it really hard.

"The other interesting thing that became apparent was that the CIA would play an operational role in this war. In other words, not just the military," Bush recalled. "When I said 'hunt them down,' I also was speaking to an intelligence community that had had some experience in the area. What's interesting is that when we look back on the design of the strategy to win the war in this theater, the CIA had a major planning role."

The president said linking "the intelligence team with the military enabled us to develop a plan which became one that worked."

Although some were calling for immediate strikes against Afghanistan, Bush insisted on getting his ducks in a row first. After all, only nine days had elapsed since the terrorist strikes.

"I knew we could not rush the military," he told me. "On the other hand, I didn't want the military planners to spend an inordinate amount of time.

"Secondly, it turned out by not rushing, but by being careful in how we planned it, it gave the world the view that we were rallying a coalition—which we were. We did a lot of diplomatic work.

"Thirdly, in any type of attack, there's a lot of logistical concerns: Uzbekistan, overfly rights, Pakistan," he added, referring to efforts to turn Afghanistan's neighbors against the Taliban. "There's a lot of things that we had to get in place that the planning time allowed us to get in place. In other words, there was a lot of things happening concurrently."

Not all of them, however, were proceeding as smoothly as Bush wanted. Securing Uzbekistan as a staging ground for American forces, for example, was a typically vexing component in the quest to assemble a fighting force on the other side of the globe.

"How to get them on the ground—that became the difficulty. I remember in Uzbekistan it took us a while," he told me. "The weather at first, and then the permission, and then the something, and then the who, and how."

In an effort to make this task easier, Bush used his address to the joint session of Congress to remind other nations that they had a stake in the success of the coming counterattack.

"This is not, however, just America's fight," he told Congress. "And what is at stake is not just America's freedom. This is the world's fight. This is civilization's fight. This is the fight of all who believe in progress and pluralism, tolerance and freedom.

"We ask every nation to join us. We will ask, and we will need, the help of police forces, intelligence services, and banking systems around the world. The United States is grateful that many nations and many international organizations have already responded—with sympathy and with support. Nations from Latin America, to Asia, to Africa, to

Europe, to the Islamic world. Perhaps the NATO Charter reflects best the attitude of the world: An attack on one is an attack on all."

On September 12, for the first time in NATO's history, the alliance invoked Article V of its charter, which equates an armed attack against any member of NATO to "an attack against them all." Thus, at the very least, Bush could count on the other eighteen members of NATO in the war against terrorism. But he had also enlisted the support of leaders like Russian President Vladimir Putin, one of the first to call on September 11.

"The civilized world is rallying to America's side. They understand that if this terror goes unpunished, their own cities, their own citizens may be next. Terror, unanswered, can not only bring down buildings, it can threaten the stability of legitimate governments. And you know what? We're not going to allow it.

"Americans are asking: What is expected of us? I ask you to live your lives, and hug your children. I know many citizens have fears tonight, and I ask you to be calm and resolute, even in the face of a continuing threat.

"I ask you to uphold the values of America, and remember why so many have come here. We are in a fight for our principles, and our first responsibility is to live by them. No one should be singled out for unfair treatment or unkind words because of their ethnic background or religious faith."

This was the latest in a long line of presidential exhortations to leave peace-loving Muslims alone.

"I ask you to continue to support the victims of this tragedy with your contributions. Those who want to give can go to a central source of information, libertyunites.org, to find the names of groups providing direct help in New York, Pennsylvania, and Virginia.

"The thousands of FBI agents who are now at work in this investigation may need your cooperation, and I ask you to give it. I ask for your patience, with the delays and inconveniences that may accompany tighter security; and for your patience in what will be a long struggle.

"I ask your continued participation and confidence in the American economy. Terrorists attacked a symbol of American prosperity. They did not touch its source. America is successful because of the hard work, and creativity, and enterprise of our people. These were the true strengths of our economy before September 11th, and they are our strengths today."

Actually, the economy was in a free fall. The terrorist attacks had shut down the New York Stock Exchange for an unprecedented four days. When it finally reopened on Monday, the Dow Jones Industrial Average plummeted 684 points, the worst one-day drop in history. It had been falling ever since, losing another 383 points in the hours before the president's speech. All in all, the Dow had lost more than an eighth of its value in just four business days and was well on its way toward its worst week since the Great Depression. Trillions of dollars of wealth had been wiped out. More than 100,000 workers had been laid off by the airlines and other industries over the preceding week, with more job cuts looming in the immediate future. The anemic economy that Bush had inherited from Clinton was almost certainly headed for recession after a decade of dot-com expansion and what Federal Reserve Chairman Alan Greenspan called "irrational exuberance." So now, like a Depression-era banker urging panicked customers not to start a run on the bank, Bush was imploring the nation to keep its economic wits.

"And finally, please continue praying for the victims of terror and their families, for those in uniform, and for our great country. Prayer has comforted us in sorrow, and will help strengthen us for the journey ahead.

"Tonight I thank my fellow Americans for what you have already done and for what you will do. And ladies and gentlemen of the Congress, I thank you, their representatives, for what you have already done and for what we will do together.

"Tonight, we face new and sudden national challenges. We will come together to improve air safety, to dramatically expand the number of air marshals on domestic flights, and take new measures to prevent hijacking. We will come together to promote stability and keep our airlines flying, with direct assistance during this emergency.

"We will come together to give law enforcement the additional tools it needs to track down terror here at home. We will come together to strengthen our intelligence capabilities to know the plans of terrorists before they act, and find them before they strike.

"We will come together to take active steps that strengthen America's economy, and put our people back to work."

All of this coming together was expensive. The day after the terrorist attacks, Bush decided to seek $20 billion in emergency military spending and disaster relief. Less than twenty-four hours later, New York's two Democratic senators, Hillary Rodham Clinton and Charles Schumer, met Bush in the White House and asked him for another $20 billion for their state. The president unhesitatingly said yes. Thus had Bush, one week after the terrorist strikes, signed a $40 billion emergency spending bill. But that was only the beginning. Congress was poised to pass a multibillion-dollar airline-bailout package the day after Bush's speech. And there was talk of spending tens of billions in additional federal funds to resuscitate the economy. In order to pay for all this, Democrats and Republicans set aside their squabble over "raiding" the Social Security surplus, which had been such a divisive issue before September 11.

"Tonight we welcome two leaders who embody the extraordinary spirit of all New Yorkers: Governor George Pataki and Mayor Rudolph Giuliani."

The crowd rose for its most raucous ovation of the night. The two Republicans, who were sitting next to Laura Bush, looked awkwardly at each other and smiled.

"As a symbol of America's resolve, my administration will work with Congress, and these two leaders, to show the world that we will rebuild New York City.

"After all that has just passed—all the lives taken, and all the possibilities and hopes that died with them—it is natural to wonder if America's future is one of fear. Some speak of an age of terror. I know there are struggles ahead, and dangers to face. But this country will define our times, not be defined by them. As long as the United States of America is determined and strong, this will not be an age of terror; this will be an age of liberty, here and across the world.

"Great harm has been done to us. We have suffered great loss. And in our grief and anger we have found our mission and our moment. Freedom and fear are at war. The advance of human freedom—the great achievement of our time, and the great hope of every time—now depends on us. Our nation—this generation—will lift a dark threat of violence from our people and our future. We will rally the world to this cause by our efforts, by our courage. We will not tire, we will not falter, and we will not fail.

"It is my hope that in the months and years ahead, life will return almost to normal. We'll go back to our lives and routines, and that is good. Even grief recedes with time and grace. But our resolve must not pass. Each of us will remember what happened that day, and to whom it happened. We'll remember the moment the news came—where we were and what we were doing. Some will remember an image of a fire, or a story of rescue. Some will carry memories of a face and a voice gone forever."

Pulling something from his pocket, Bush added, "And I will carry this: It is the police shield of a man named George Howard, who died at the World Trade Center trying to save others. It was given to me by his mom, Arlene, as a proud memorial to her son. This is my reminder of lives that ended, and a task that does not end.

"I will not forget this wound to our country or those who inflicted it. I will not yield; I will not rest; I will not relent in waging this struggle for freedom and security for the American people.

"The course of this conflict is not known, yet its outcome is certain. Freedom and fear, justice and cruelty, have always been at war, and we know that God is not neutral between them.

"Fellow citizens, we'll meet violence with patient justice—assured of the rightness of our cause, and confident of the victories to come. In all that lies before us, may God grant us wisdom, and may He watch over the United States of America.

"Thank you."

For the thirty-second time that evening, Bush stood in the well of the House and let the adulation wash over him. He had just delivered the speech of his life, an address that was widely considered more important than his National Cathedral remarks or even his "I can hear *you*" exhortation at Ground Zero. Some would call tonight's rare, wartime address to a joint session of Congress the best speech they had ever heard. They were struck by its content as well as its delivery. It contained 2,990 words, and George W. Bush, notorious mangler of the English language, had mispronounced nary a one. Not even the press could continue to suggest the president was not up to the challenge. All of Congress was on its feet as cheers of "Bravo!" filled the air.

My, how things had changed.

Chapter Nine

"We Will Not Tire"

OF ALL DAYS TO BE LATE, this was undoubtedly the worst. White House Press Secretary Ari Fleischer knew how much his boss loathed tardiness, even on ordinary days. But today was Sunday, October 7, the day America would begin bombing Afghanistan. Since Fleischer had been privy to this closely guarded secret in advance, there was absolutely no excuse for him to show up late at the West Wing this morning. He tried to console himself with the knowledge that he was not technically late—Bush was simply early. But it was a meaningless distinction. Fleischer's job was to be at the White House *before* the notoriously punctual president, who had spent the night at Camp David and the morning laying a wreath at a firefighters' memorial in Emmitsburg, Maryland. Fleischer should have anticipated that Bush—who was undoubtedly preoccupied with the imminent counterattack—might cut short his scheduled chitchat with fire officials after the memorial service and make a beeline for Marine One. The chopper was already in the air and headed for the White House, more than an hour ahead of schedule. Fleischer was still at home when he found out, so he hurried to his car and did something he had never done before.

As he sped through the streets of Washington toward the White House, the mild-mannered presidential spokesman switched on his car's emergency blinkers and began running red lights. The bald, bespectacled press secretary was breaking the law in order to play his part in history. He was supposed to alert the media that America was about to unleash a massive barrage of missiles and bombs on Afghanistan. If he got pulled over, Fleischer wouldn't be able to explain a word of this to a District cop, of course. Bush took tremendous pride in running a nearly leakproof White House. It would be unthinkable for Fleischer to prematurely disclose the most momentous decision of the young presidency just to get out of a traffic ticket. So he just kept blowing through the red lights and hoping he wouldn't get caught.

The forty-year-old spokesman arrived at 10:45 A.M., just as the president was stepping off Marine One on the South Lawn. Fleischer intercepted him in the Diplomatic Reception Room and walked with him into the Oval Office, where Bush informed him the attack would begin shortly.

"I gave them fair warning," he reminded Fleischer. "They chose not to heed it."

He had also given Secretary of State Colin Powell and the rest of his administration enough time to put together a team of allies, a task that had been completed just days earlier.

"We had the coalition built at this point in time," Bush told me later. "I had made the case to our country and to the world that we would take the actions we took, eventually took. And the only constraint at that point was the plan."

But even the military plan was finished by October 2, a mere three weeks after the terrorist strikes. It was on that day, during a meeting in the White House Situation Room, that Bush tentatively decided to go ahead and execute the plan. Before pulling the trigger, he dispatched Rumsfeld to the region for one last round of consultations with the front-line allies, just to make sure they were all on board and ready to rumble.

On October 5, as Rumsfeld was wrapping up this mission, Bush met again in the Situation Room with his military planners. This time he was less tentative about his decision to launch a counterattack.

"He turned to General Myers, the chairman of the Joint Chiefs, looked him right in the eye, and said, 'Dick, is Tommy Franks ready to go?'" recalled National Security Advisor Condoleezza Rice. "And General Myers said, 'Yes, sir, he's ready to go.'"

Rice said this was the "moment he knew that it was now time to start this next phase of this war on terrorism." She added, "He gave the go-ahead. And at that point then, of course, military operations actually began."

Well, sort of. Bush waited until Rumsfeld returned from the region and could participate—via teleconference—in a National Security Council meeting that the president chaired from Laurel Lodge at Camp David on October 6. He quizzed Rumsfeld on what kind of cooperation he could count on from the allies in the region. He solicited final assessments from Powell, Director of Central Intelligence George Tenet, and Myers. He wanted every member of his war council to be able to assure him that the United States was indeed positioned to destroy the Taliban.

Bush told me the conversation went like this: "I said, 'Are you confident with the plan you developed?' They said yes. I said, 'That's the plan.'"

The president was especially interested in Rumsfeld's assessment of the military's readiness.

"The timing of the counterattack was: 'When ready.' And that's important to know," he told me. "Don Rumsfeld said, 'We are ready.' And I said, 'Fine, we're going.'

"It wasn't: 'We're ready, and then, Mr. President, go out there and try to figure out a convenient time for you.' In other words, my only point was, was that this didn't require any focus group work. And the reason I bring that up is because I remember Vietnam and I remember politicians making military decisions.

"Mine was: 'You're ready? You tell me. When you're ready, I'm ready.' It wasn't: 'You tell me you're ready and then I'll try to figure out whether it's okay or not.'"

He added, "So moving from September the 11th to October 7th turned out to be a relatively quick turnaround, from the moment of 'let's go' to actually going."

Bush ended that fateful NSC meeting by ordering the bombers to leave their bases. At 12:27 P.M. the next day, Tomahawk cruise missiles began slamming into Taliban targets in Afghanistan. Rumsfeld called the White House to confirm that the attack was underway. Bush instructed Fleischer to make arrangements for a televised presidential address to the nation.

Fleischer knew that as soon as he called the TV networks to request broadcast time for the president's speech, the entire media would instantly realize the counterattack was at hand—even though Fleischer couldn't reveal the topic of the address. So he and White House Counselor Karen Hughes had choreographed the news right down to the minute. One of Fleischer's underlings would go to the microphone in the "lower press" office and announce over the intercom to reporters in the building that Fleischer would be making a statement in the press briefing room in two minutes. Then Fleischer would speed-dial the network newsrooms, letting them know the president would soon be addressing the nation. Lastly, he would race to the podium in the James S. Brady briefing room, stand before that famous blue curtain and presidential seal, and make a cryptic announcement that would impart very little specific information, yet leave no doubt in anyone's mind that the day of reckoning had finally arrived. Fleischer decided to model his statement on the famous utterance of the elder President Bush's press secretary, Marlin Fitzwater, who had gone to the same podium a decade earlier to announce the start of the Gulf War thus: "The liberation of Kuwait has begun."

The White House press briefing room is a cramped and cluttered dump. It is radically different from the regal, pristine chamber routinely portrayed in movies and TV shows about the White House. The first thing one notices is how small the place is. There are only eight rows of six seats. Behind these seats, at the back of the room, an elevated platform is crammed with tripods, cameras, and TV monitors. The side aisles are choked with spools of heavy cable and battered aluminum ladders used by photographers during presidential events in the adjacent Rose Garden. Between the podium and the front row is a trapdoor that leads to a subterranean swimming pool. The pool was built so Franklin D. Roosevelt could exercise his crippled legs, but covered over by Richard Nixon, who disliked swimming so much he once wore a business suit to the beach. Instead of water, the pool was now filled with miles of electrical cables of every color and gauge imaginable.

Most of the time, the briefing room has very few occupants. The journalists who work in the White House spend the majority of their hours in unbelievably tiny booths and cramped compartments just east of the famous chamber. On weekday mornings, some of these reporters wander out of their pathetic workspaces and take their assigned seats in the briefing room in order to spend fifteen minutes asking Fleischer questions. This is known as the "gaggle," which is on the record but off camera. It is an informal session, with Fleischer in shirtsleeves, giving reporters a heads-up on the president's schedule and providing the administration's initial reaction to the headlines of the morning. Until September 11, the gaggle was always held in the press secretary's "upper press" office in the West Wing. Reporters would crowd around Fleischer, who was seated at his desk near tall arched windows overlooking the North Lawn, and pelt him with questions and the occasional wisecrack. But after the terrorist strikes, so many reporters began crowding into Fleischer's office each morning that it practically turned into a mosh pit. So the gaggle was moved to the briefing room and another Washington tradition fell victim to the age of terrorism. Of course, the briefing room's main purpose is the formal afternoon question-and-answer session, with Fleischer wearing a suit and facing reporters for about thirty minutes in a performance that is usually televised live by the cable news channels. But the cameras do not capture the seediness of the room, which has all the ambience of a bus station. After each gaggle and briefing, cameramen lounge in the chairs, perusing the sports pages of dog-eared newspapers that are strewn everywhere. Some doze on the floor around the base of the podium. Technicians pass the time playing DVD movies in the bewildering nests of electronic equipment jammed into the back of the room.

On weekends, there are far fewer journalists in the West Wing. This is especially true on Sundays, when the press area is practically deserted. So when a voice came over the intercom at 12:39 P.M. on October 7, alerting the press that Fleischer would be at the podium in two minutes, there were precious few journalists on hand to witness this sliver of history. A handful had been given a wink and a nod in advance to signal that today just might be the day. They instantly realized the announcement could mean only one thing—war! TV news crews literally sprinted into the briefing room and began working desperately to connect the tangled spaghetti of cables necessary to broadcast this historic moment to the waiting world. Technicians who had been lounging on an otherwise lazy Sunday afternoon were suddenly thrown into unmitigated panic, shouting to one another as they struggled to hook up live microphones for correspondents who took their positions at the front of the briefing room. One poor guy lunged across the front-row seat normally occupied by veteran reporter Helen Thomas and dived headlong under the second row to grab a fistful of multicolored cables. As the seconds ticked by, ABC News correspondent Terry Moran looked down at the elevated derriere of this dedicated technician and couldn't help but chuckle. The man's pants were drooping perilously low. History was about to be made in the James S. Brady briefing room, and yet the focal point of the moment was the "plumber's crack" of a frantic technician. It was the only light moment in an otherwise tense two minutes.

When Fleischer arrived, the vast majority of seats in the briefing room were empty. The usually unflappable spokesman seemed a bit nervous as he stepped behind the podium at 12:41 P.M.

"Ladies and gentlemen, we are beginning another front in our war against terrorism, so freedom can prevail over fear," he blurted. "The president will address the nation at 12:50 P.M. Thank you."

It wasn't as memorable as Fitzwater's "the liberation of Kuwait has begun," but it got the point across. Fleischer abruptly turned and stepped away without taking questions, although the reporters were so awed that none attempted even a halfhearted query until the spokesman was practically out the door. Besides, everyone in the room instantly grasped the significance of the moment. Twenty-six days after the worst terrorist attack in history, America was striking back.

Bush left the West Wing for the Executive Residence and took the elevator up two floors. His aides wanted a forum other than the Oval Office, where he had addressed the nation on that terrible night of September 11. They chose the Treaty Room, so named because it was where various presidents had signed historic treaties, including the 1972 Anti-Ballistic Missile Treaty that Bush now wanted to scrap. The president, who routinely did much of his work in this room, sat in a carved wooden chair that was mounted on a slightly elevated platform. There were small strips of wood fastened around the four legs to prevent the chair from moving while Bush spoke. To his right, just off camera, stood a tiny table with a glass of water and a printed copy of his speech. Flanked by Old Glory and the presidential flag, Bush settled in front of a large window that looked over the South Lawn and was framed by the Doric columns and wrought-iron balustrade of the South Portico. The Jefferson Memorial could be seen in the background. Growing impatient, he ordered one of his personal assistants, Logan Walters, to empty the room of various aides and technicians.

"Clear 'em out, Logan," the president barked.

Then he faced the camera and waited for the red light on top to turn on. When it did, the president's image was beamed to tens of millions of TV sets across America and beyond. Even the New York Yankees, who were about to play the Tampa Bay Devil Rays in Florida, looked up at the Jumbotron over Tropicana Field to watch a thirty-foot image of Bush on Fox News Channel. The ballplayers, like the rest of America, suddenly realized the long wait was over.

"Good afternoon. On my orders, the United States military has begun strikes against al Qaeda terrorist training camps and military installations of the Taliban regime in Afghanistan."

Bush had decided not to blast bridges, electrical plants, or other components of Afghanistan's civilian infrastructure, which was already in tatters from decades of constant warfare. Besides, the president wanted to punish the Taliban, not innocent Afghan civilians.

"These carefully targeted actions are designed to disrupt the use of Afghanistan as a terrorist base of operations, and to attack the military capability of the Taliban regime."

Unlike Saddam Hussein's regime, a decade earlier during the Gulf War, the Taliban did not have a lot of conventional military assets that could be targeted. But there were some tanks, armored personnel carriers, and aging warplanes. There were also some communications and antiaircraft facilities, both of which were primitive by American standards. Finally, there were the al Qaeda training camps, safe houses, and meeting places.

"We are joined in this operation by our staunch friend, Great Britain. Other close friends—including Canada, Australia, Germany, and France—have pledged forces as the operation unfolds. More than forty countries in the Middle East, Africa, Europe, and across Asia have granted air transit or landing rights. Many more have shared intelligence. We are supported by the collective will of the world."

Although Bush had assembled the largest coalition in history, critics complained that it was a mile wide and an inch deep. Britain was the only ally helping with the initial bombing. And Bush had to twist a lot of arms and overlook a lot of sins in order to bring some of the

Arab nations on board. For the first time, he openly called for the creation of a Palestinian state, which angered Israeli Prime Minister Ariel Sharon. The administration also made overtures to Iran, Syria, and even Sudan, each of which harbored its own terrorists.

"More than two weeks ago, I gave Taliban leaders a series of clear and specific demands: Close terrorist training camps; hand over leaders of the al Qaeda network; and return all foreign nationals, including American citizens, unjustly detained in your country.

"None of these demands were met. And now the Taliban will pay a price."

It was the kind of line that would have drawn thunderous applause from Congress or any group of Americans in a live setting. But with the president sitting alone in the Treaty Room, his words had a sobering effect on the rapt nation.

"By destroying camps and disrupting communications, we will make it more difficult for the terror network to train new recruits and coordinate their evil plans."

Bush knew the press sneered at his use of the term "evil," just as it had sneered at President Reagan's characterization of the Soviet Union as the "evil empire." For weeks, White House correspondents in their cramped booths and compartments would guffaw whenever the word "evil" or "evildoer" crept into the president's remarks, which were piped into speakers in the West Wing's press area. But Bush was defiantly unembarrassed about his moral clarity. He also seemed to sense that if the word "evil" made the press squirm, it was probably okay with the majority of the American people.

"Initially, the terrorists may burrow deeper into caves and other entrenched hiding places. Our military action is also designed to clear the way for sustained, comprehensive, and relentless operations to drive them out and bring them to justice."

Rumsfeld had come up with a plan to pulverize everything remotely connected to al Qaeda, hoping the terrorists would eventually be flushed out into the open.

"At the same time, the oppressed people of Afghanistan will know the generosity of America and our allies. As we strike military targets, we'll also drop food, medicine, and supplies to the starving and suffering men and women and children of Afghanistan."

Bush had been telling his top advisors for days that he would not allow the bombing mission to begin until arrangements had been made for humanitarian assistance. The self-described "compassionate conservative" was not about to let his political critics begin portraying him as a heartless warmonger.

"The United States of America is a friend to the Afghan people, and we are the friends of almost a billion worldwide who practice the Islamic faith. The United States of America is an enemy of those who aid terrorists and of the barbaric criminals who profane a great religion by committing murder in its name."

The president was at pains to differentiate between good Muslims and bad Muslims. He had already been taken to the woodshed by the press for using the word "crusade" in offhand remarks about his war against terrorism. And the Pentagon had been forced to scrap the military operation's code name, "Infinite Justice," because it was considered vaguely offensive to Muslims who believed only Allah could achieve infinite justice. Even in the midst of the greatest American crisis in more than half a century, political correctness knew no bounds.

"This military action is a part of our campaign against terrorism, another front in a war that has already been joined through diplomacy, intelligence, the freezing of financial assets, and the arrests of known terrorists by law enforcement agents in thirty-eight countries."

Since September 11, hundreds of millions in terrorist funds had been seized and hundreds of suspected terrorists around the globe had been detained. Bush was keen on describing these as fronts in his war against terrorism, although most Americans still did not think of criminal arrests, financial seizures, intelligence gathering, and diplomatic pressure as war. As far as the nation was concerned, the real "war" had begun just minutes ago.

"Given the nature and reach of our enemies, we will win this conflict by the patient accumulation of successes, by meeting a series of challenges with determination and will and purpose. Today we focus on Afghanistan, but the battle is broader."

This was code for Iraq. The president had spent much of the past twenty-six days listening to his top advisors make war recommendations. Most favored concentrating on Afghanistan, at least initially, because the September 11 terrorist attacks had been perpetrated by bin Laden's al Qaeda network. But some conservatives in the administration, notably Deputy Defense Secretary Paul Wolfowitz, were eager to go after Saddam Hussein as well. They argued that unlike bin Laden, Saddam had already gained weapons of mass destruction, as evidenced by his use of poison gas against his own people. Wolfowitz was still irked that Saddam had not been taken out of power at the conclusion of the Gulf War. He had argued for the dictator's ouster back then, when he was a top deputy to Defense Secretary Dick Cheney. But Colin Powell, then chairman of the Joint Chiefs of Staff, had opposed Wolfowitz and supported the elder President Bush's decision to end the war after expelling Iraqi forces from Kuwait. Now Wolfowitz and Powell were locking horns all over again on the same old debate—whether to go after Saddam. Wolfowitz wanted to use the war against terrorism to simultaneously eliminate bin Laden and

Saddam. But Powell supported the younger President Bush's instincts to initially focus on Afghanistan. There was no convincing evidence that Saddam had anything to do with bin Laden's attack on America. Besides, it was hard enough attacking one country at a time. Powell was already having difficulty keeping the Arab nations in the coalition. If the United States simultaneously attacked Afghanistan *and* Iraq, worldwide support for the war might collapse. Most of the other top presidential advisors agreed with Powell rather than Wolfowitz.

So the decision was made to focus on Afghanistan for now. The White House explicitly reassured Arab states it had no plans to attack Iraq, although the message to the American public was intentionally more ambiguous. The administration chose not to disabuse the press of its constant speculation that an attack on Iraq could happen at any time. This ambiguity kept hawks on Wolfowitz's side from becoming critics—and one of these hawks, interestingly, was Connecticut Senator Joseph I. Lieberman of the late Gore-Lieberman ticket that Bush had defeated. Besides, by refusing to be pinned down about his intentions for Iraq, Bush kept Saddam Hussein off balance and sowed the seeds for wider public support of a future attack on Iraq, if that should be necessary. While polls showed that a whopping 94 percent of Americans favored the campaign against Afghanistan, the White House worried such support would erode if the war were prematurely broadened.

"There was very little debate about extending the first battlefield of the war of the twenty-first century," Bush told me later. "All of us understood. And I don't ever think that I allowed much debate. I believe that first things first."

"We needed to stay focused," he recalled. "There was no dissension that we ought to defend America and seek justice—no dissension.

And there's no dissension that we needed to use all the resources available to us."

He added, "There was no dissension as to where we ought to—what we ought to do."

At least not for the initial counterattack, anyway.

"Every nation has a choice to make," Bush told the nation. "In this conflict, there is no neutral ground. If any government sponsors the outlaws and killers of innocents, they have become outlaws and murderers themselves. And they will take that lonely path at their own peril."

Bush did not consign Saudi Arabia to that lonely path, even though the Saudi government continued to give millions to the families of Palestinian suicide bombers. It was another overlooked sin in the urgent quest to destroy al Qaeda.

"I'm speaking to you today from the Treaty Room of the White House, a place where American presidents have worked for peace. We're a peaceful nation. Yet, as we have learned, so suddenly and so tragically, there can be no peace in a world of sudden terror. In the face of today's new threat, the only way to pursue peace is to pursue those who threaten it.

"We did not ask for this mission, but we will fulfill it. The name of today's military operation is Enduring Freedom."

After much anguished consultation with the PC police in the press and academia, "Enduring Freedom" had been deemed a sufficiently bland moniker to replace the discredited "Infinite Justice."

"We defend not only our precious freedoms, but also the freedom of people everywhere to live and raise their children free from fear. I know many Americans feel fear today."

It was an extraordinary presidential admission to a nation that had once been reassured by Franklin Roosevelt, "The only thing we have to fear is fear itself—nameless, unreasoning, unjustified terror, which paralyzes needed efforts to convert retreat into advance." Bush, who used FDR's old desk in the Oval Office, was breaking an important American taboo against admitting fear—even in the face of catastrophic attack.

"And our government is taking strong precautions. All law enforcement and intelligence agencies are working aggressively around America, around the world, and around the clock. At my request, many governors have activated the National Guard to strengthen airport security. We have called up Reserves to reinforce our military capability and strengthen the protection of our homeland."

The National Guardsmen, four thousand of whom had been called up at the end of September, were only a temporary solution until civilian security could be hardened. Democrats seized on this as an opportunity to unionize tens of thousands of airport security workers, a move that Bush would initially oppose but eventually allow.

"In the months ahead, our patience will be one of our strengths—patience with the long waits that will result from tighter security; patience and understanding that it will take time to achieve our goals; patience in all the sacrifices that may come.

"Today, those sacrifices are being made by members of our Armed Forces who now defend us so far from home, and by their proud and worried families. A commander in chief sends America's sons and daughters into a battle in a foreign land only after the greatest care and a lot of prayer.

"We ask a lot of those who wear our uniform. We ask them to leave their loved ones, to travel great distances, to risk injury, even to be prepared to make the ultimate sacrifice of their lives. They are dedicated, they are honorable; they represent the best of our country. And we are grateful.

"To all the men and women in our military—every sailor, every soldier, every airman, every coast guardsman, every marine—I say this: Your mission is defined; your objectives are clear; your goal is just. You have my full confidence, and you will have every tool you need to carry out your duty.

"I recently received a touching letter that says a lot about the state of America in these difficult times—a letter from a fourth-grade girl, with a father in the military: 'As much as I don't want my dad to fight,' she wrote, 'I'm willing to give him to you.'"

Bush had been so moved by the letter that he instructed Hughes to make sure it was included in today's speech.

"This is a precious gift, the greatest she could give. This young girl knows what America is all about. Since September 11th, an entire generation of young Americans has gained new understanding of the value of freedom, and its cost in duty and in sacrifice.

"The battle is now joined on many fronts. We will not waver; we will not tire; we will not falter; and we will not fail. Peace and freedom will prevail.

"Thank you. May God continue to bless America."

The red light on the camera went off, but Bush continued to sit motionless in the chair so that news photographers could snap a few pictures for the next morning's editions. Afterward, he went back down to the West Wing to await a televised press conference by Rumsfeld and General Myers. The session would not begin for another ninety minutes and Bush was getting hungry.

"Let's have lunch," he announced to his senior staff.

So sandwiches were brought in and there were a couple of updates on the progress of the bombing campaign. But after weeks of round-the-clock planning and intensive, behind-the-scenes strategizing, the president's top advisors suddenly found themselves with nothing to do. They had worked tirelessly to help Bush prepare the nation for war—especially over the past forty-eight hours—but now that the war was underway, the ball was no longer in their court. Bush was adamant about letting the military wage the war on its own terms, without a lot of second-guessing by politicians and other civilians. And so, as bombs and cruise missiles rained down from Kabul to Kandahar, from Jalalabad to Mazar-i-Sharif, the president and his advisors were reduced to munching on sandwiches that were sent in from the White House kitchen.

Karen Hughes looked impatiently at the big-screen TV. The Pentagon press conference had still not begun. Nervously, she glanced around the room.

"What do we need to do now?" she said to no one in particular.

The answer came from National Security Advisor Condoleezza Rice.

"Now," she mused, "we wait."

Chapter Ten

The Press Tires

BEFORE THE MONTH OF OCTOBER was out, the press had tired of the war against terrorism. Reporters quickly discarded what the president had counseled during that first hour of bombing: "In the months ahead, our patience will be one of our strengths." Indeed, the patience of the press did not even survive the opening weeks of the campaign. In an age of instant information and gratification, the media wanted the war wrapped up in time for the six o'clock news.

Bush could see the coverage heading south. He rose before dawn each day, took Barney and Spot into the Rose Garden, brought coffee to Laura, and then perused the morning papers. None was more influential in setting the tone for the rest of the media than the *New York Times*, which on October 31 posed the following question on its front page: "Another Vietnam?"

"Like an unwelcome specter from an unhappy past, the ominous word 'quagmire' has begun to haunt conversations among government officials and students of foreign policy, both here and abroad," began R. W. "Johnny" Apple Jr., the paper's chief Washington correspondent. "Could Afghanistan become another Vietnam? Is the

United States facing another stalemate on the other side of the world?"

Although America's involvement in Vietnam had lasted years, the fighting in Afghanistan was less than a month old. Yet Apple, who once worked as the *Times* Saigon bureau chief, had already concluded that the role of Special Operations forces in Afghanistan "sounds suspiciously like that of the advisors sent to Vietnam in the early 1960s."

"Despite the insistence of President Bush and members of his cabinet that all is well, the war in Afghanistan has gone less smoothly than many had hoped," he continued. "Signs of progress are sparse."

So this is what it had come to. One month after America was blindsided by the worst attack in sixty years, its most prestigious newspaper was already likening the president's counterattack—all of twenty-five days old—to the "quagmire" of Vietnam.

" 'Quagmire,' 'Vietnam,' " Bush muttered to me later. "I mean, we were at this thing for three weeks, and all of sudden there was kind of a breathless condemnation of the strategy."

Perhaps he should have known this would happen. He should have realized that the media's uncharacteristic patience and patriotism in the first days after September 11 would prove fleeting. The conduct of journalists had seemed so promising, even inspirational, in the immediate aftermath of the terrorist attacks. Brave correspondents risked life and limb to cover the destruction of the World Trade Center. Grave anchormen exhibited a sobriety that was appropriate to the magnitude of the tragedy. American journalists who had never been comfortable with patriotism suddenly seemed united with the rest of the nation.

"God Bless America," blared the headline on the cover of the September 15 *Newsweek*, which bore the famous photo of three firemen raising Old Glory amid the rubble of the World Trade Center. "One

Nation, Indivisible," proclaimed the September 17 *Time* cover, which featured a photo of a flag-waving Bush with Bob Beckwith at Ground Zero. The first three letters of "TIME" were done up in red, white, and blue.

Even CBS News anchor Dan Rather got swept up in the patriotic fervor. On September 17, during an appearance on the David Letterman show, Rather repeatedly broke down in tears while reciting lyrics from "America the Beautiful" and lauding the heroism of firefighters. He also effusively praised the president's moral clarity in the war against terrorism.

"He looked the camera straight in the eye, unblinking, and said, 'Osama: Dead or alive,'" Rather recalled. "George Bush is the president. He makes the decisions. And, you know, it's just one American, wherever he wants me to line up, just tell me where. And he'll make the call."

For an anchorman of a major news network to place himself at the beck and call of a Republican president was nothing short of extraordinary. Rather was particularly emphatic in endorsing Bush's call for patience.

"This is for the long haul," the newsman said. "We have the firepower, we've mustered the willpower, and unlike the Gulf War, we will have the staying power."

Lance Morrow of *Time* was even more blunt.

"Let's have rage," he wrote. "What's needed is a unified, unifying, Pearl Harbor sort of purple American fury—a ruthless indignation that doesn't leak away in a week or two, wandering off into Prozac-induced forgetfulness or into the next media sensation."

But alas, the forgetfulness would soon set in. One of the first news agencies to forget the impact of September 11 was Reuters, which ordered its reporters to stop calling the hijackers "terrorists" and the attacks acts of "terrorism."

"We all know that one man's terrorist is another man's freedom fighter and that Reuters upholds the principle that we do not use the word terrorist," wrote Stephen Jukes, Reuters's director of global news, in an internal memo to its 2,500 employees. "To be frank, it adds little to call the attack on the World Trade Center a terrorist attack."

In an interview with media writer Howard Kurtz of the *Washington Post*, Jukes actually suggested moral equivalence between America and al Qaeda.

"We're trying to treat everyone on a level playing field, however tragic it's been and however awful and cataclysmic for the American people and people around the world," he said.

And yet the wire service had no compunction about its reporters describing the Taliban's war against America as "holy." For example, one Reuters dispatch told of pro-Taliban fighters massing in Afghanistan "to wage holy war against the United States."

Perhaps sensing the repugnance of his moral-equivalence argument, Jukes introduced another defense of his policy—self-censorship. He suggested that Reuters banned the word "terrorists" to protect its journalists from reprisals by, well, terrorists.

"We don't want to jeopardize the safety of our staff," he said. "Our people are on the front lines, in Gaza, the West Bank, and Afghanistan. The minute we seem to be siding with one side or another, they're in danger."

If a news organization censored every word that might endanger its correspondents, dispatches from the front lines would quickly degenerate into little more than propaganda. By Jukes's logic, crime reporters should be forbidden from using words like "mafia." After all, everyone knows that one man's "mafia" is another man's legitimate business enterprise.

Whatever the reason, the ban on "terrorism" as a word to describe what happened on September 11 led to some awkward formulations in Reuters stories. One reporter was reduced to writing that "two hijacked planes attacked the twin towers," as if the aircraft themselves were living, breathing murderers.

Incidentally, Reuters had no trouble applying the term "terrorism" to the 1993 Oklahoma City bombing, which was perpetrated by Americans. In fact, the press in general had fewer qualms about applying the term "terrorist" to American Christians than to foreign Muslims. In the wake of the attacks on September 11, the Society of Professional Journalists issued guidelines urging reporters, "When writing about terrorism, remember to include white supremacists, radical anti-abortionists and other groups with a history of such activity." Yet these same guidelines also warned: "Avoid using word combinations such as 'Islamic terrorist' or 'Muslim extremist' that are misleading because they link whole religions to criminal activity." In other words, it was repugnant to use phrases that imply all terrorists are Islamic, or that all Muslims are extremists, but perfectly acceptable to use terms that imply that all whites are supremacists, or that all anti-abortionists are radical.

Reuters was not the only news agency that anguished over the word "terrorist." A second London-based organization, the BBC, adopted a similar ban on the word because it was too "judgmental." And according to a September 27 story in the *Wall Street Journal*, CNN "hasn't barred specific words but is aiming to 'define people by their actions,' a spokeswoman said. Those flying the planes that hit the World Trade Center and Pentagon, for example, would be 'alleged hijackers,' not 'terrorists,' because, the spokeswoman said, 'CNN cannot convict anybody; nothing has been judged by a court of law.'"

The day after the story appeared, the network issued the following clarification: "CNN has not 'banned' the use of the word 'terrorist.' In fact, CNN has referred to the persons responsible for the attacks on the World Trade Center and the Pentagon as 'terrorists' and the act as 'terrorism' since September 11."

That same day, Howard Kurtz of the *Washington Post* vowed to defy any Orwellian ban of the word "terrorist" on his weekly CNN show, *Reliable Sources*, which dissected media coverage.

"Excuse me, if you commandeer an airliner and you drive it into the building with an express intent of killing thousands of innocent civilians, what are you supposed to call these people—'High-octane tourists?'" Kurtz railed on the *Imus in the Morning* radio show. "One commentator came up with the phrase 'casualty facilitators.'

"I mean, I just think this kind of value-neutral reporting is hogwash. I mean, you don't want to convict people. But at the same time, what are we talking about here? There's no better explanation, word, description for these acts than the most, the rawest kind of terrorism."

"So what happens if you go on your show on CNN, *Reliable Sources*, and describe them as terrorists and they fire you?" asked host Don Imus.

"That's fine because I'm not going to use any other word," Kurtz declared. "The T-word is the word here."

"Well, good for you," Imus said.

Although ABC News allowed its journalists to use the T-word, it banned them from wearing tiny lapel pins in the shape of an American flag.

"Especially in a time of national crisis, the most patriotic thing journalists can do is to remain as objective as possible," ABC spokesman Jeffrey Schneider told the *Washington Post*. "That does not mean journalists are not patriots. All of us are at a time like this. But we cannot signal how we feel about a cause, even a justified and just cause, through some sort of outward symbol."

Ted Koppel, anchor of ABC's *Nightline*, agreed.

"I don't believe that I'm being a particularly patriotic American by slapping a little flag in my lapel and then saying anything that is said by any member of the U.S. government is going to get on without comment," he sniffed at the Brookings Institution, a liberal Washington think tank. "And anything that is said by someone from 'the enemy' is immediately going to be put through a meat grinder of analysis. Our job is to put it all through the meat grinder of analysis."

When he said "the enemy," Koppel raised his fingers in "air quotes," as if to signify the Osama bin Laden had just as much claim to the moral high ground as President Bush.

Asked about the flag flap by David Letterman, ABC's Cokie Roberts tried to have it both ways. On the one hand, she defended her network's ban on flag pins, saying, "The patriotic thing to do is to ask questions." On the other hand, she admitted she skirted the ban by wearing a lapel pin in the shape of another American symbol—the bald eagle. "ABC has decided that we shouldn't be wearing flags, so I wear an eagle," explained Roberts, who was later eased out of her cohosting duties at ABC's *This Week*.

The lapel pins were also banned by NBC News, whose president, Neal Shapiro, told *USA Today* that on-air correspondents sporting the flags risked "calling attention to what they're wearing and not their story."

NBC News anchor Tom Brokaw, who made a fortune collecting the patriotic stories of World War II veterans into his *Greatest Generation* books, decided there was nothing great about wearing a small American flag on TV.

"I wear the flag in my heart," he told Northwestern University's student newspaper. "I don't think a journalist ought to be wearing a flag, because it does seem to be—to me at least—a sign of solidarity toward whatever the government is doing, and that is not our role."

CBS News anchor Dan Rather took a similar stand.

"I have the flag burned in my heart, and I have ever since infancy," Rather told CNN. "And I just don't feel the need to do it. It just doesn't feel right to me. And I try to be—particularly in times such as these—and I have tried to be in touch with my inner self, my true inner self, and I tried to listen. And my inner self says, You don't need to do that. But I have absolutely no argument with anyone else who feels differently."

About the only TV news operation that was unembarrassed by the lapel flags was Fox News Channel. Brit Hume, anchor of *Special Report*, began wearing a pin immediately after the September 11 attacks. He told *USA Today* that Old Glory represents all of America, not just the White House, and suggested it was ludicrous for U.S. reporters to claim neutrality in the titanic struggle between the United States and al Qaeda.

"Our flag is not the symbol of the Bush administration," Hume said. "And Fox News is not located in Switzerland."

He added that if any Fox journalist opted to wear a flag pin, "their duties as a journalist remain the same—to be fair-minded, thoughtful and skeptical as ever."

ABC News sparked an even bigger controversy when its president, David Westin, waffled on whether the Pentagon had been a legitimate military target. During a speech to the Columbia University Graduate School of Journalism, Westin observed that the World Trade Center was not a legitimate military target, since thousands of innocent civilians had been killed.

"Do you believe the Pentagon was a legitimate military target?" asked a member of the audience.

"The Pentagon as a legitimate target?" Westin stalled. "I actually don't have an opinion on that. And it's important I not have an opinion on that as I sit here in my capacity right now."

Westin proceeded to equivocate on whether flying a hijacked plane into the Pentagon, which killed hundreds of innocent Americans, "was right or wrong." He added, "As a journalist, I feel strongly that's something that I should not be taking a position on. I'm supposed to figure out what is and what is not—not what ought to be."

Yet he had just finished taking the position that the terrorists ought not to have attacked the World Trade Center. He didn't stop at the mere observation that the Twin Towers had been destroyed; he denounced their destruction. He could not bring himself to say the same thing about the Pentagon, however, even though its victims were every bit as innocent as those in New York.

The journalism students were utterly unfazed by Westin's callous reply and went on to grill him about other topics, such as why the *New York Times*-led media consortium had indefinitely postponed publication of its "mother of all recounts" in the aftermath of September 11. When the speech was shown on C-SPAN, no news organization showed the slightest interest in the astonishing observation about the Pentagon by the head of a major news network. It took the Media Research Center, which monitors the press for bias, to publicize the item, which was then picked up by the *Drudge Report* and, eventually, the reluctant "mainstream" press. Within a week, Westin shifted into serious damage-control mode.

"I was wrong," he acknowledged in a written statement. "Under any interpretation, the attack on the Pentagon was criminal and entirely without justification. I apologize for any harm that my misstatement may have caused."

Westin's forced apology chilled others in the press, who fretted that the outpouring of American patriotism was cramping their journalistic style.

"Any misstep and you can get yourself into trouble with these guys and have the Patriotism Police hunt you down," griped MSNBC President Erik Sorenson to the *New York Times*. "These are hard jobs. Just getting the facts straight is monumentally difficult. We don't want to have to wonder if we are saluting properly. Was I supposed to use the three-fingered salute today?"

Dan Rather, perhaps coming to his senses after that overt display of patriotism on the David Letterman show, later echoed Sorenson's comments.

"There was a time in South Africa that people would put flaming tires around people's necks if they dissented," Rather told the BBC, recalling a practice known as "necklacing." "And in some ways the fear is that you will be necklaced here, you will have a flaming tire of lack of patriotism put around your neck."

Bill Maher, host of ABC's *Politically Incorrect*, felt he was necklaced by the Patriotism Police after describing American service members as "cowards." The remark came less than a week after September 11, on a day when Maher left one of his four guest chairs empty in honor of Barbara Olson, who had booked her doomed flight from Washington to Los Angeles in order to appear on his show. Maher dismissed suggestions that the terrorists who murdered Olson and thousands of other Americans were cowards.

"We're the cowards," he declared. "We have been the cowards. Lobbing cruise missiles from 2,000 miles away, that's cowardly. Staying in the airplane when it hits the building—say what you want about it—is not cowardly."

Nine days later, under intense criticism, Maher backpedaled by issuing a "clarification." "I am not unpatriotic," he insisted. "Patriotism does not involve shutting up, it involves speaking out."

But the damage had been done. Big advertisers like Sears and Federal Express pulled their commercials. Local ABC affiliates, including the one in Washington, dropped the show. Eventually, the misnamed *Politically Incorrect* would be canceled altogether.

Former president Bill Clinton didn't exactly help matters when he suggested white Americans were somehow culpable in the September 11 attacks because they had a long history of domestic terrorism. Joseph Curl of the *Washington Times* broke the story.

"Those of us who come from various European lineages are not blameless," Clinton said in a speech at his alma mater, Georgetown University. "Here in the United States, we were founded as a nation that practiced slavery. And slaves were, quite frequently, killed—even though they were innocent. This country once looked the other way when significant numbers of Native Americans were dispossessed and killed to get their land or their mineral rights. Or because they were thought of as less than fully human. And we are still paying the price today. Even in the twentieth century in America, people were terrorized or killed because of their race. And even today, though we have continued to walk, sometimes to stumble, in the right direction, we still have the occasional hate crime rooted in race, religion, or sexual orientation. So terror has a long history."

Less than two weeks after the September 11 attacks, the *New York Times* reported that Clinton "is described by friends as a frustrated spectator, unable to guide the nation through a crisis that is far bigger than anything he confronted in his eight-year tenure." Clinton had long craved a crisis that, unlike Monica Lewinsky, was of historic significance—something he could heroically solve on behalf of a grateful nation. He wanted, in short, an honorable legacy. Presidential aide George Stephanopoulos once wrote that Clinton "envied Lincoln his enemies, knowing that it takes a moral challenge to create a memorable presidency." Indeed, late in his administration, Clinton was said to have ruminated to friends that the only presidents who are ever judged "great" by historians are those who won wars or led the nation out of severe economic hardship. But Clinton took office twenty-two months into a decade-long economic expansion and presided over eight years of dot-com prosperity. And since Ronald Reagan had already won the Cold War, Clinton's biggest military adventures were the Balkans, which posed no threat to the United States, and a few errant missiles lobbed at Osama bin Laden. So he left office with an unenviable legacy—the only elected president to have been impeached.

And now, incredibly, George W. Bush, whom Clinton believed had lost the election to Al Gore, was given the monumental challenge of defending America against its most menacing threat since World War II, or at least since President Reagan defanged international communism. At the same time, Bush was expected to lead the nation out of a severe economic downturn, caused in no small part by the terrorist attacks themselves. For eight years, Clinton had presided over peace and prosperity. Yet after just eight months, Bush confronted war and recession—the two very tests of presidential greatness. Although it would be years before historians could judge whether Bush belonged in the pantheon of great presidents, unwanted circumstances had certainly thrust him into contention. Clinton, by contrast, never even got the chance. And now he was beside himself, according to Paul McCartney's fiancée, Heather Mills, who was hobnobbing with the former president in New York shortly after the terrorist attacks.

"I said to Clinton: 'Do you wish you were president now?' And he said: 'I feel I would be better trained for it, more prepared,'" Mills told Ananova news service. "It must be frustrating for him."

Meanwhile, the frustration of reporters was beginning to manifest itself at the White House, where Press Secretary Ari Fleischer's daily press briefings were eagerly watched by the nation. TV viewers were jarred by the effrontery of some of the reporters' questions. In late September, for example, a reporter pointed out that while bin Laden "was a known and indicted terrorist" when Bush took office, the new president did not immediately launch a war against terrorism.

"Why wasn't this done seven months ago?" the journalist demanded. "Why did it take this tragedy?"

Another reporter wanted to know whether Bush, who had already pushed through a multibillion-dollar bailout program for the airlines industry, would announce even more federal largesse during an upcoming visit with airline workers in Chicago.

"Is he simply going to feel their pain?" the reporter said. "Or is he going to try to help them in some other way?"

A couple of days later, as Fleischer was reiterating the administration's adamant opposition to negotiating with the Taliban, he was met with open skepticism by Helen Thomas, the doyenne of the White House press corps.

"We know that," she muttered. "We heard that in Iran-Contra, too, about ten thousand times before."

Some reporters were incredulous that the Bush administration would not publicly sketch out its vision for a post-Taliban government in Afghanistan, even before the counterattack began. They complained that the United States was not giving the citizens of Afghanistan assurances that had been given to other nations in previous conflicts.

"During World War II, many promises were made," a journalist said. "They would find freedom at the end of the road and so forth."

"We are offering nothing," the journalist opined. "All we're offering is destruction."

There were even aspersions cast on the U.S. military for the crash of the hijacked jetliner in Pennsylvania. Although the administration had made it clear for weeks that the jet crashed during a struggle between the hijackers and a group of brave passengers, including Todd Beamer, some in the press clung to conspiracy theories.

"Can you deny reports that it might have been shot down by us?" a reporter demanded.

Day after day, the questions kept coming. There were times when it seemed that the only unpatriotic people in America were the couple of dozen reporters sitting there in the James S. Brady press briefing room. Some of them aggressively challenged the administration's refusal to disclose all evidence against Osama bin Laden.

"You're asking everyone to trust you, but without supplying information to show why," protested one reporter.

That was too much for a TV viewer in Gulfport, Mississippi, who fired off an angry postcard addressed to the White House press corps.

"Your stupidity exceeds all I have ever seen," the card began. "How Ari Fleischer puts up with your stupid questions beats me."

The writer specifically complained about Helen Thomas's demanding proof that bin Laden was the primary suspect.

"That was nuts," the observer wrote. "President Bush should not expose his sources. These terrorists have just killed thousands of Americans. We have enjoyed more freedom than anyone on Earth. If this is to continue, we must stand behind our president. If we do not act now, the thugs will."

"Freedom comes with a price, but it's a price we must pay," the writer concluded. "Get real."

The card was posted on the bulletin board behind the press briefing room. A practical joker scribbled "Love, Gordon" at the bottom to make it look as though the missive had been penned by White House press wrangler Gordon Johndroe. Reporters read the card and chuckled in private, knowing that it was no longer acceptable to laugh at the administration in public.

This new reality was frustrating to journalists who until September 11 were accustomed to gleefully lampooning the president. Journalists were especially miffed that they could no longer make fun of Bush's penchant for mangling the English language.

"There's no doubt in my mind, not one doubt in my mind, that we will fail," Bush told employees at the Labor Department on October 4.

A TV correspondent shook his head and privately groused, "If he had said that prior to September 11th, we'd be all over it."

Instead, the White House press corps had to content itself with making fun of Bush off camera or outside of the copy they filed. They chortled at his repeated use of the non-word "misunderestimate" to describe bin Laden's assessment of American resolve. They rolled their eyes when he told airline workers that America will "win this war against freedom." They howled when he predicted that "ticket counters and airplanes will fly out of Ronald Reagan Airport."

But for the most part, public coverage of Bush remained positive. And why not? Two days after his address to a joint session of Congress, the president's approval ratings shot to 90 percent, the highest level since Gallup began taking such polls in 1938. That made him the most popular president in modern history, at least for the moment, and the press was not about to deny the obvious conclusion that the rest of the country had reached—namely, that Bush seemed to be handling the crisis extraordinarily well. Thus, as late September gave way to early October, journalists were spending more time anguishing over the meanings of patriotism and terrorism than over the effectiveness of President Bush.

When the counterattack began, the press jettisoned its tortured self-analysis and focused on covering the action on the ground. It didn't take long for ABC News to find something wrong with the operation. The day after the bombing commenced, anchor Peter Jennings archly observed that the dropping of food and medicine into Afghanistan by U.S. warplanes was "not popular with everyone. The international relief organization Doctors Without Borders, which won the Nobel Peace Prize for relief work, described it today as military propaganda designed to justify the bombing."

The next day, Jennings led his nightly newscast by intoning, "Are the U.S. food drops on Afghanistan making matters worse? Some relief agencies say yes." ABC correspondent Dan Harris added, "Some say the U.S. is actually doing more harm than good. The bombing raids have some truck drivers too scared to carry food into the country."

When it turned out that the Taliban was confiscating food trucks, ABC switched to reporting that errant U.S. bombs were killing innocent Afghan civilians. On October 10, ABC correspondent David Wright reported on Afghans fleeing to Pakistan.

"Many who are leaving say it would be one thing if the Americans were only bombing the terrorist camps in Afghanistan," Wright said. "But, they say, the killing of innocents is not okay."

The next day, ABC correspondent Bob Woodruff reported, "The Taliban believes more than a hundred civilians have died in the bombings, but there's no way to verify any of it."

This lack of verification did not stop ABC from continuing to report inflated casualty figures.

"The Taliban claims some 200 civilians in a village near Jalalabad were killed by a stray U.S. missile," Wright reported on October 14. "If that's true, it would be the deadliest strike so far in the war. The Islamic militia escorted the press to a residential area littered with shrapnel. Inside one house, a bloodstained pillowcase. Outside another, dozens of dead sheep and goats as well as what appeared to be body parts. Villagers were still digging through the rubble looking for bodies. The air has a rancid stench."

Meanwhile, the *Chicago Tribune* published a column that resurrected the Vietnam-era debate over whether journalists should put their profession above their status as Americans. The column was based on an interview with Loren Jenkins, senior foreign editor of National Public Radio, who oversaw thirteen journalists in and around Afghanistan and the Middle East. Jenkins told *Tribune* columnist Steve Johnson that his employees were expected to expose American forces in Afghanistan.

"The game of reporting is to smoke 'em out," Jenkins said. He was borrowing a phrase from President Bush, but applying it to U.S. troops instead of terrorists. "Since Vietnam, the Pentagon has made this harder and harder for reporters to do, mostly because they blame the press for losing the war in Vietnam," he added.

Jenkins was asked whether NPR would report the presence of an American commando unit it found in, for example, a village in northern Pakistan.

"You report it," the NPR boss replied matter-of-factly. "I don't represent the government. I represent history, information, what happened."

Jenkins later said his quotes were taken out of context, although he didn't claim to have been misquoted. NPR ombudsman Jeffrey Dvorkin, instead of expressing outrage at the influential journalist's appalling lack of judgment, shrugged: "Jenkins was sucker-punched and led with his chin."

The controversy recalled a similar uproar in 1989, when Mike Wallace of CBS's *60 Minutes* made clear he was a reporter first, American second. The admission came when Wallace and ABC's Peter Jennings appeared on a PBS show called *Ethics in America*. Moderator Charles Ogletree Jr., a Harvard professor, described a theoretical war between the "North Kosanese" and the U.S.-backed "South Kosanese." He asked the newsmen what they would do if they learned the enemy troops with whom they were traveling were about to launch a surprise attack on an American unit.

"If I was with a North Kosanese unit that came upon Americans, I think I personally would do what I could to warn the Americans," Jennings said.

But Wallace said any self-respecting TV news crew "would regard it simply as another story that they are there to cover." Turning to Jennings, he added, "I'm at a little bit of a loss to understand why, because you are an American, you would not have covered that story."

Ignoring the fact that Jennings was actually a Canadian, Ogletree said to Wallace, "Don't you have a higher duty as an American citizen to do all you can to save the lives of soldiers, rather than this journalistic ethic of reporting fact?"

"No, you don't have a higher duty," Wallace said without hesitation. "You're a reporter."

Jennings conceded: "I think he's right, too. I chickened out."

Fortunately, Jennings and Wallace were not allowed to accompany U.S. Special Forces into Afghanistan. But lack of access to the military did not stop such journalists from pooh-poohing the effectiveness of the bombing campaign.

Daniel Schorr, senior news analyst for National Public Radio, warned that the counterattack was riling the vaunted "Arab street."

"Whatever success the Anglo-American alliance is having pounding the Taliban into dust, it's having little success winning the hearts and minds of Islamic peoples," Schorr said on the October 15 edition of NPR's *All Things Considered*. "Most alarming of all, anti-American feeling is rising in Pakistan, where the Taliban came from, threatening the stability of the Musharraf regime."

But *New York Times* photographer Vincent Laforet said the press was wildly exaggerating anti-American protests in Pakistan.

"Don't trust anything you see on TV and be wary of some of the things you read," he wrote on a photojournalist web site. "I witnessed how sensationalistic the media can be during the Florida recount. It's even worse here. We covered a pro-Taliban demonstration last week attended by maybe 5,000 protesters. CNN stated there were 50,000. The BBC estimated 40,000. We're continually hearing of 'violent clashes with police' when the TV stations report on non-violent demonstrations we covered ourselves."

Although the war was still in its infancy, the press seemed determined to brand it a failure.

"So far, this is a war without any clear-cut victories or defeats," ABC's David Wright reported on the eighth day of bombing. "That's true of the bombings and of the battle for public sympathy."

On October 14, a mere week after the counterattack began, Johnny Apple of the *New York Times* became the first major journalist to compare it to Vietnam. "The experience of Vietnam is instructive," he wrote in a piece complaining that Bush, like President Johnson, had not sufficiently called on the nation for sacrifice.

Frustrated by this negative coverage, the Pentagon tried to emphasize hopeful signs in the bombing campaign.

"The series of strikes we've conducted over the past nine days have had a fairly dramatic effect on the Taliban," Marine Corps Lieutenant General Gregory S. Newbold told reporters on October 16. "The combat power of the Taliban has been eviscerated."

The word "eviscerated" would be thrown back in the Pentagon's face countless times over the next three weeks by journalists who insisted the Taliban was besting the Americans.

"Opposition Afghan leaders trying to fashion an anti-Taliban uprising say U.S.-led bombing has seriously undermined their efforts," began a *Wall Street Journal* dispatch from Peshawar on October 18. "Instead of a thankful Afghan population, popular support for the Taliban appears to be solidifying and anger with the U.S. is growing. And rather than a relatively quick Taliban collapse, the U.S. may have to settle for continued governance by the movement, perhaps shorn of its top two or three leaders."

Even Senator Joseph Biden, chairman of the Senate Foreign Relations Committee, was showing signs of impatience.

"How much longer does the bombing continue?" the Delaware Democrat asked on October 22. "Because we're going to pay every single hour. Every single day it continues, we're going to pay an escalating price in the Muslim world."

Addressing the Council on Foreign Relations, Biden said the bombing fuels criticism that "we're this high-tech bully that thinks from the air we can do whatever we want." He also questioned how long "the honeymoon, how long the unquestioning period of unabashed support for the president's policy, will continue."

Meanwhile, the military brass was caught in a no-win situation. Having lost all trust in the press after Vietnam, commanders were reluctant to take reporters into the Afghanistan theater to witness the progress of bombing raids. To fill the information void, many reporters simply got their "facts" from the Taliban and illustrated them with questionable video from Al-Jazeera, the Qatar-based Arab news network.

"Video phone footage from Al-Jazeera television today shows body bags lined up in a hospital hallway in Kandahar," ABC's Dan Harris reported on October 23. "There have been reports of civilian casualties before, but never these kinds of pictures. According to Al-Jazeera, U.S. attacks on a village near Kandahar killed ninety-three civilians on Tuesday, including eighteen members of one family. There has been no independent confirmation.

"Across the border in the Pakistani town of Quetta, five people arrived today at a hospital with injuries they say they suffered in another U.S. attack, this one about seventy-five miles north of Kandahar. They say twenty-nine people died when their village was hit Monday night. This boy is one of the injured. His uncle says he had heard American radio broadcasts promising civilians wouldn't be targeted. But he says his village was nowhere near any Taliban positions.

Abdul Jabar is the doctor in charge. How do you feel when you see these kids?"

"I feel very sad," Jabar said.

"Angry?" Harris prompted.

"Yes," Jabar said. "My sympathies are with the Afghanis."

"Angry at the United States?" Harris suggested helpfully.

"Yes," Jabar replied.

"Everyone we spoke with at this tiny hospital said the ongoing raids have made the population here and across the border angry at the U.S. and supportive of the Taliban," Harris concluded.

That same day, over at the Pentagon, reporters peppered Assistant Defense Secretary Victoria Clarke with questions about the bombing of civilians. She expressed outrage over all the play the allegations were getting.

"Most of the information that has come out from the Taliban—I daresay just about everything we've heard for the last few weeks—has been wrong and outright lies," she said. "They regularly throw out numbers about casualties, most of which are completely outrageous."

The Taliban, encouraged by the willingness of American journalists to air Al-Jazeera footage of bloody civilians, upped the ante by inviting selected TV networks on guided tours of dubious atrocities. ABC and CNN were among more than a dozen news agencies to take the tour, although Fox News Channel was discouraged from attending by demands for large sums of cash.

The Taliban-orchestrated coverage became so prevalent that by the end of October, CNN Chairman Walter Isaacson felt compelled to implore his staff for some semblance of balance.

"As we get good reports from Taliban-controlled Afghanistan, we must redouble our efforts to make sure we do not seem to be simply reporting from their vantage or perspective," Isaacson wrote in a memo to his international correspondents. "We must talk about how the Taliban are using civilian shields and how the Taliban have harbored the terrorists responsible for killing close to 5,000 innocent people."

When covering Afghan casualties, CNN should not "forget it is that country's leaders who are responsible for the situation Afghanistan is now in," Isaacson added.

Rick Davis, CNN's head of standards and practices, was not convinced the front-line reporters would take Isaacson's message to heart. So he wrote his own memo, gingerly pointing out that it "may be hard for the correspondents in these dangerous areas to make the points clearly."

To disabuse the public of growing perceptions that the press was siding with the enemy, Davis drafted disclaimers to be read by CNN's anchors: " 'We must keep in mind, after seeing reports like this from Taliban-controlled areas, that these U.S. military actions are in response to a terrorist attack that killed close to 5,000 innocent people in the U.S.,' or, 'We must keep in mind, after seeing reports like this, that the Taliban regime in Afghanistan continues to harbor terrorists who have praised the September 11 attacks that killed close to 5,000 innocent people in the U.S.,' or, 'The Pentagon has repeatedly stressed that it is trying to minimize civilian casualties in Afghanistan, even as the Taliban regime continues to harbor terrorists who are connected to the September 11 attacks that claimed thousands of innocent lives in the U.S.' "

Davis added, "Even though it may start sounding rote, it is important that we make this point each time."

The new policy was derided as "ill-advised" by former CNN correspondent Peter Arnett at a Brookings Institution forum in October. Arnett was best known for a 1991 CNN report parroting Saddam

Hussein's claim that America had bombed a Baghdad "baby milk factory," which turned out to be a biological weapons plant. He was fired by CNN in 1999 for falsely reporting on the air, and in *Time* magazine, that U.S. forces had used nerve gas to kill civilians in a Vietnam operation known as Tailwind.

On Sunday, October 28, exactly twenty-one days after the bombing campaign began, Cokie Roberts used the words "Vietnam" and "quagmire" in an interview with Defense Secretary Donald Rumsfeld.

"There have been stories over the weekend that give the perception that this war, after three weeks, is not going very well," she said on ABC's *This Week*. "That the Taliban is getting stronger, that Osama bin Laden is still at large, that one of the chief opposition leaders has been assassinated, and that the Red Cross warehouse has been hit by U.S. bombs. Is the war just not going as well as you had hoped it would at this point?"

"Oh, no, quite the contrary," Rumsfeld countered. "It's going very much the way we expected when it began. Three weeks is not a very long time, if one thinks about it. And the progress has been measurable. We feel that the air campaign has been effective."

Rumsfeld was hit with the same question, the same day, on CNN's *Late Edition*.

"Did the U.S. military underestimate the Taliban, Osama bin Laden, and his al Qaeda supporters?" demanded Wolf Blitzer.

"Not at all," Rumsfeld said. "We said it would be long; we said it would be difficult; we said it would be different. And indeed it is."

Blitzer then replayed the clip of Lieutenant General Newbold saying two weeks earlier that the Taliban had been "eviscerated."

"How long is this going to go on, in your opinion?" Blitzer pressed.

"It's going to take time and patience," Rumsfeld counseled. "And I must say, I hear some impatience from the people who are, of course, have to produce news every fifteen minutes, but not from the American people. I think the American people understand the fact that it's going to be long and hard."

That very day, on CBS's *Face the Nation*, Bob Schieffer wailed, "There must be someone out there saying, wait a minute, are we getting into another Vietnam?" Meanwhile, on ABC, White House correspondent Terry Moran flat-out asserted, "I think the bad guys are winning."

Maureen Dowd of the *New York Times* came to much the same conclusion that morning in a column portraying the president as a hopelessly aristocratic Ivy Leaguer who suddenly found himself in a down-and-dirty street fight.

"George W. Bush was brought up to believe in Marquess of Queensberry rules," she sniped. "Now he is competing against combatants with Genghis of Khan rules, who hide among women and children in mosques and school dormitories, and who don't need an executive order to betray and murder.

"Polo at Yale is a bit different than the Afghan version, bushkazi, a violent free-for-all with no rules in which galloping horsemen try to throw a headless goat's carcass over a goal."

Dowd was repeating the media mistake of a decade earlier, when reporters ominously intoned about Saddam Hussein's vaunted Republican Guard. She implied Bush had underestimated Afghan fighters.

"Now, like the British and Russians before him, he is facing the most brutish, corrupt, wily and patient warriors in the world, nicknamed dukhi, or ghosts, by flayed Russian soldiers who saw them melt away," she wrote from the comfort of her Washington office.

The next morning, the *Boston Globe* reported, "Some members of the U.S.-led antiterrorism coalition suggested that the battle in Afghanistan could become a quagmire and that the Bush administration had underestimated the resilience of the country's hard-line regime."

The *Los Angeles Times* was equally pessimistic.

"Stung by a week of setbacks in its Afghan campaign, the United States is adjusting both its military and political tactics, with shifts ranging from possible bombing pauses during the Muslim holy month of Ramadan to a more prominent diplomatic role for the United Nations.

"Even Bush administration officials acknowledge that last week's reverses were not encouraging. Air strikes went awry, hitting Red Cross warehouses, mine-sniffing dogs and Toyotas. A rebel offensive collapsed near the northern city of Mazar-i-Sharif. A charismatic Afghan military hero, apparently the first to plot a daring overthrow of the Taliban, was captured and executed shortly after sneaking into Afghanistan. And a drive to unite the anti-Taliban opposition bogged down in jealous wrangling."

That evening, Peter Jennings began ABC's *World News Tonight* by suggesting the Pentagon was picking on the press for daring to criticize the war effort.

"The secretary of defense said today that those people who are questioning the effectiveness of the U.S. bombing campaign in Afghanistan are too impatient," Jennings complained. "The bombing campaign against the Taliban is now entering its fourth week and the Taliban are still standing."

ABC's John McWethy added, "Two weeks after the Pentagon said Taliban forces had been 'eviscerated' by U.S. bombing, the Taliban still appear to be firmly in control."

On NBC's *Nightly News*, Pentagon reporter Jim Miklaszewski suggested the military had come around to the media's way of thinking. "Pentagon officials are now beginning to express some frustrations and doubts over the slow pace of the war. U.S. military officials tell NBC News for now the war in Afghanistan has ground to a stalemate.

"The officials say that in putting together the war plan, the Pentagon made two serious miscalculations. First, it was believed once the U.S. started the bombing, opposition forces like the Northern Alliance would aggressively attack the Taliban military," Miklaszewski said. "The second mistake—misreading the enemy. It was hoped intensive bombing would force large numbers of Taliban military to defect. Instead, the Taliban forces are digging in."

The skepticism became so pronounced that even Geraldo Rivera—an unabashed Clinton apologist during the Monica Lewinsky scandal—railed against what he called "a disturbing trend that I've seen in the press."

"The media is, I'm afraid to say, losing its nerve. And that malignant insecurity is already questioning a war effort that is scarcely three weeks old," Rivera said October 29 on CNBC. "You've all seen the melancholy reports over the last few days: Our bombing's not working. We're slaughtering innocent civilians. Our allies, the so-called Northern Alliance, are all bluster, no belly. The Taliban's winning. Ramadan is coming. Winter is coming. Woe is us!

"I think it's time for the naysayers to heed the famous philosopher who said, Get over it!" Rivera added. "As Defense Secretary Rumsfeld said today, 'This is a marathon, not a sprint.' And the only war we're losing so far is the battle not to lose our nerve."

Rivera, who had quietly inked a deal to soon join Fox News Channel, lambasted reporters for not suspecting the Taliban of storing weapons in a Red Cross warehouse that was bombed by American warplanes. He pointed out that the Taliban was already hiding weapons in mosques and schools. He was incredulous that the press refused to give the Pentagon "the benefit of the doubt," especially after the terrorists had killed "thousands of Americans."

"This isn't Vietnam," he said. "Vietnamese never took out the Golden Gate Bridge. They never hit a shopping mall. They never hit an office tower."

But it was no use. The press was impervious to criticism, even from its own ranks. Over at the Pentagon, a second batch of seemingly unpatriotic Americans pelted Rumsfeld with breathtakingly ignorant questions every couple of days.

"You said that the air strikes are deliberately designed not to hit residential centers," a reporter began on October 30. "But you also say that the Taliban is hiding weapons, stockpiling weapons in residential areas.

"Have you ruled out the possibility of dropping leaflets, days in advance of an air strike, to get residents out and saying, 'This could become a military target'? Is that something, without discussing future operations, could you see that possibly coming to fruition?"

Rumsfeld was rendered momentarily speechless by the sheer preposterousness of the question, which hung there in the air of the briefing room for what seemed like a very long time. He finally managed, "We drop leaflets?"

By this point in the war, Rumsfeld had publicly skewered numerous journalists for asking inane questions. But the query he now faced was so patently ridiculous that the blunt defense secretary decided it could not even be lampooned. So Rumsfeld instead adopted the manner of a patient adult addressing a particularly plodding child.

"Dropping those kinds of leaflets, of course, *would* tell the innocent people that they should stay out of mosques," he conceded.

"But it would also tell the *other* people *they* should stay out of mosques," he added, as gently as possible. "It is not quite clear to me how we would advantage ourselves."

It was as though some rare fever had addled the brains of the press corps, while leaving the rest of America with its common sense intact. There could no longer be the slightest doubt about the name of the insidious ailment that now gripped the Fourth Estate—Vietnam Syndrome. Truth be told, the press had never really been cured of the disease, although the symptoms went into remission between wars. The last time the press had suffered an outbreak this severe was at the dawn of the Gulf War, in 1991. Back then, the *New York Times*'s Johnny Apple wrote, "For all of President Bush's passionate insistence to the contrary, the war in the Persian Gulf has more than a few similarities to the war in Vietnam."

Ten years later, Apple evidently dug up this yellowed clipping and rearranged a few words for his updated version of "Another Vietnam?"

"Despite the insistence of President Bush and members of his cabinet that all is well, the war in Afghanistan has gone less smoothly than many had hoped," he wrote on October 31.

The next day, conservative columnist Robert Novak opined in the *Washington Post* that there was a "mood of foreboding in the fourth week of the aerial war." He summarized that "Afghanistan is surely not Vietnam, but the bad memories of a generation ago return in a war that is a long way from being won."

On November 4, *Los Angeles Times* editorial writer Jacob Heilbrunn concluded that the Bush administration had "bungled" the campaign in Afghanistan.

"The war effort is in deep trouble," he warned. "The United States is not headed into a quagmire; it's already in one. The U.S. is not losing the first round against the Taliban; it has already lost it."

Heilbrunn said "constant pinprick bombings" and the use of U.S. Special Forces were doomed strategies. He complained about the Pentagon's "irresolution." And he insisted that even if the bombing succeeded, "there does not appear to be a political force capable of replacing the Taliban."

"The U.S. is as poorly prepared for this conflict as for Vietnam," Heilbrunn concluded. "The U.S. is learning, once again, that an indigenous foe in a remote, inhospitable terrain is proving far more tenacious than it ever anticipated. The longer the Bush administration pursues its current strategy, the more confident the Taliban will grow."

On November 6, the top story on the front page of the *New York Times* asserted in its opening sentence that the Bush administration was "worried that public opinion abroad has turned against the American military campaign in Afghanistan." The next day, its lead story explored "signs overseas of waning popular support for the bombing of one of the world's poorest countries."

As the Bush administration struggled to cope with the avalanche of negative war coverage, it was also scrambling to make sense of a mysterious outbreak of anthrax. The attacks began a week after September 11 and eventually killed five people. Though fewer than twenty people fell ill, anthrax-tainted mail terrorized Congress, the U.S. Postal Service, and some of the biggest organizations in the news media, among others. Ordinary Americans were frightened to open their mail and looked to a bewildered federal government for reassurance. Missteps by various agencies spurred a new round of finger pointing by a stressed-out press.

To make matters worse, there were grumblings over warnings the administration kept issuing about elevated threats of additional terrorist attacks. Reporters complained that the warnings had no meaning if the government only ratcheted the threat level up and never down. Bush later told me this was one "of the interesting dilemmas I face."

"We need to be alert—what does it mean? You start warning the country—and what does it mean?

"Look, if we had a specific threat on a specific building, you'd never know about it until after the threat passed—because we had put our covert operations around the people, and we had chased down this, and covered this, and sealed that."

However, he added, with "a general threat, where we've got a noise level coming up, we sent a warning out. And it was interesting because the idea was to have somewhat of a chilling effect on the enemy: 'We know.' So, in other words, deterrence.

"But we ran the risk of Chicken Little, crying wolf too much. On the other hand, people needed to know."

He concluded that the American people "believe me" when "I say there is a threat."

"The role of the president is to educate the people about the realities of our day," Bush told me. "I've got to constantly remind people."

Amid this backdrop, CNN marked the first-month anniversary of the bombing campaign with a particularly downbeat report by Bob Franken.

"One month into this new war in Afghanistan, it's almost exclusively a war fought from above Afghanistan. This is how the Pentagon likes to tell the bombing story—through the lens of the airplane nose cameras. But the nose cameras do not show the other part of the bombing story—the misses, the unintended civilian casualties that

U.S. officials say are few and regrettable. The Taliban have tried to exploit the casualties by conducting media tours. Still, the barrage against Taliban troop positions grows more intense daily, two weeks after these memorable words."

Franken then replayed the now familiar clip of Lieutenant General Newbold saying, "The combat power of the Taliban has been eviscerated."

The reporter added, "Pentagon officials wish the word 'eviscerated' had never escaped that general's lips. Rather than being gutted, Taliban forces are still holding their ground. Al Qaeda and its leader, Osama bin Laden, are still presumed to be hiding in the country's vast web of caves. So-called 'bunker buster' bombs have failed to make much of a dent. Air power has limitations."

After the report was concluded, Aaron Brown, host of CNN's prime time show *NewsNight*, asked retired Army colonel David Hackworth for his take on the war's progress. But Hackworth launched into a tirade against the report by Franken, whom he mistakenly called Franklin.

"Well, I think before the American people—in spite of guys like Mr. Franklin, when you read that report and listen to it, it really is discouraging—when the American people slice into their turkey on turkey day, we will see the Taliban no longer in business," Hackworth predicted.

"And that will not be the end of round one. Then it will be, for the next six months or even year, mopping up the Taliban. This is a thirty-round fight. We haven't even got in the middle of round one. It's not World War II. It's not Korea. It's not Vietnam, Desert Storm, or a General Clark Serbian war—a little bit of each.

"But it's an absolutely different kind of war," he concluded. "And that's what the American people must understand. Not that garbage we heard from Franklin."

The next morning, *New York Times* reporter Michael R. Gordon baldly stated on the front page that the administration "underestimated the Taliban's resilience." He wrote that the American military "lacked the intelligence information to carry out the flurry of Special Operations raids it had projected." He complained that the Pentagon "seems content" to let the Northern Alliance "do the dirty work on the ground during the winter.

"For now, the front lines remain largely where they were a month ago," the reporter wrote. "The mountains are already snow-capped and winter is setting in; any military results will have to be achieved soon."

It is impossible to overstate the *New York Times*'s influence on the broadcast media. TV correspondents religiously turned to the paper each morning for guidance in shaping the day's coverage. Producers actually called a senior White House official each evening to ask which members of the administration would be making news in the next morning's edition of the *Times*. The official, while refusing to disclose the nature of the news itself, would nonetheless advise the producers which Bush lieutenants should be booked for the morning shows. The producers then blindly booked these guests, confident that their "news judgment" would be validated when the *Times* hit the streets a few hours later.

So it was no surprise that the broadcast media took their cue from the *Times*'s grim assessments of America's progress on the war front. At the Pentagon press briefing on November 8, CNN correspondent Jamie McIntyre asked General Tommy Franks, who was running the war in Afghanistan, about the mounting press complaints.

"I'm not offering a judgment on this criticism, but we have so little opportunity to address this to you. You're clearly the one who can address this," McIntyre began. "Two areas of criticism: the war plan, and you personally.

"Let me start with the war plan. You hear people inside and outside the Pentagon criticizing the plan as having been too timid in the beginning, fought with half measures, that the sortie rate—roughly 100 sorties a day, give or take—was not as robust as it could have been. Can you answer that criticism? And then I'll follow up with my other one."

Franks, who was making his first Pentagon briefing since the war began, showed no sign of irritation at the question.

"Do I believe that this campaign plan was too timid? Absolutely not," he said. "The campaign plan which we have initiated—I won't say executed, but what we have initiated—is precisely the plan that we intended to begin to initiate, and, as I said, I'm well satisfied with it."

"If I could just follow up," McIntyre said. "The other criticism you hear is that this war, if it's to maintain the support of the American people, needs to have a general commanding it who's accessible to the American people, who helps make the case, along with the secretary of defense and the Joint Chiefs chairman. The comparison is constantly made to Norman Schwarzkopf in the Gulf War. And with all due respect, sir, what you hear is: Tommy Franks is no Norman Schwarzkopf. Your response?"

"Well, I suppose I'd begin sort of at the end: By acknowledging that Tommy Franks is no Norman Schwarzkopf," the general said, drawing laughter in the briefing room.

"Nor vice versa!" interjected Rumsfeld, who was standing at the general's side.

"Nor vice versa," concurred Franks. "The secretary and our president have asked me to do a job. I believe that the American people have every right to expect me to do that job. I believe that it's important for us to think our way through and execute the strategy and the operations which are important to our country.

"And what I have found up to this point is not a shyness for media," he added with a chuckle. "It very simply is an insufficient amount of time to be able to do, sir, what you have suggested."

In other words, Franks had been too busy executing the war in the theater to spend a lot of time jawboning with a lot of know-it-all reporters back in Washington. As for the progress on the battlefield, he was unapologetic that U.S.-backed forces still controlled just 15 percent of Afghanistan.

"We're a bit over a month into this effort," Franks reminded the reporters. "I have described this as an effort that will, in fact, take as long as it takes.

"I've described it as an effort that will be unconventional, rather than linear. This will not, day by day, be all about the establishment or the movement of troops along a line of contact."

Franks made it clear that while the media might be impatient, the military was not. He extolled "the depth of commitment, the depth of resolve, the depth of confidence that our president and the secretary of defense have shown in our command." He also praised the servicemen who were actually prosecuting the war.

"These wonderful young people who, as we speak, are engaged, many of them in harm's way—should give us cause for a great deal of pride," Franks said.

Rumsfeld's growing exasperation at such press criticism was evident during an interview later that day with Jim Lehrer of PBS.

"What do you think of the conventional wisdom?" Lehrer asked. "Support for our military action is beginning to wane."

"I think the impatience you're characterizing is more with the press than it is with the American people," Rumsfeld countered. "I think the American people understand the truth that the president has said, that this is not going to be fast. It's going to take some time. It is a totally different kind of a conflict. There's no road map for it. There's no silver bullet."

Pressed about the criticism, Rumsfeld bristled.

"I mean, it's been a month," he said. "Think of that. I mean, that's amazing. To have moved that many people, to fashion that many countries' involvement, to have—what—some 2,000 sorties have been flown over that country, 300 hours of radio programming, leaflets, and over a million meals of food have been put down by the United States military.

"It is a lot that has been done. And a lot of Taliban people have been killed and a lot of al Qaeda people have been killed. And a lot of tanks have been taken out. If there were navies we could sink, we would sink them. If there were armies we could take on head on, we would. If there were air forces we could shoot down, we would. They aren't there."

Rumsfeld reminded his interviewer that it had been less than sixty days since the terrorist attacks on the United States.

"No one in the world thought we'd be running a war like this," he said. "Imagine, you're sitting in the Pentagon and a plane—one of our planes—is used as a missile to fly into our building and into the World Trade Center. It was beyond one's imagination."

On November 8, Gallup began conducting a poll to measure the public's approval of the major players in the war on terrorism, including the press. The results confirmed what Rumsfeld and the rest of the Bush administration had been saying for weeks—that there was a dramatic disconnect between what the media were saying and what the public was feeling. In fact, the public approved of the performance of all players in the war against terrorism except the press. A whopping 54 percent of Americans disapproved of how the news media were "handling the war on terrorism since September 11," compared with just 43 percent approval, the poll found.

By contrast, there was 80 percent approval for Rumsfeld, 75 percent for Cheney, and 87 percent for Colin Powell. Attorney General John Ashcroft, Congress, and the U.S. Postal Service—which had been hit hard by the anthrax attacks—each garnered 77 percent approval. Topping the list was President Bush himself, whose handling of the war against terrorism—in spite of all the negative coverage—met the approval of a staggering 89 percent of America.

In short, by a more than 2-to-1 margin, the public favored the president's performance over that of the press. As if to add insult to the media's injury, Gallup also found that registered voters would now vote for Bush over Gore by an almost 2-to-1 margin, 61 to 35 percent. So much for the "deeply divided electorate" the press had predicted for Bush's first term.

Another polling organization, the Pew Research Center, found a dramatic drop in the public's opinion of press coverage of the war. Fully 56 percent of Americans who were surveyed in the immediate aftermath of the terrorist attacks—September 13 through 17—viewed the coverage as "excellent." But within a month that number had been cut nearly in half. The public's disgust with the media's blatant negativism kept the figure hovering around 30 percent into November.

Undaunted, the press continued to ridicule the Pentagon's strategy. Reporters insisted aerial bombing and a few hundred Special Operations troops were failing to prop up the Northern Alliance, which was doing most of the "dirty work."

"Just one month into the U.S. war in Afghanistan, military experts increasingly are coming to the same conclusion: Air strikes and commandos won't be enough to rout the Taliban," wrote *USA Today* reporters on November 8. "American ground forces will be needed to finish the job."

"Those calling for a massive deployment of Army soldiers and Marines differ over how many are required," the reporters wrote in their front-page story. "But a common scenario calls for up to 100,000 troops."

"Try 250,000," said *Newsweek*'s Evan Thomas on *Inside Washington*, a syndicated TV talk show. "I think there's a very credible argument that the only way you're ever going to get there is by ground troops. And maybe we should face up to that, and just accept that painful reality."

Fellow panelist Nina Totenberg of National Public Radio agreed.

"Overwhelming force is the only thing that works," she declared. "We'd better damn well win. And if it means ground troops, it means a lot of ground troops—not a few."

Totenberg's comments were echoed by *Baltimore Sun* columnist Jack Germond.

"It's inevitable we're going to have a large ground presence there— it has to happen," he said. "We're not going to be able to fight another one of these antiseptic wars."

"I'm not sure it is inevitable," countered syndicated columnist Charles Krauthammer, the panel's only conservative. "There's a battle going on right now, as we speak, in Mazar-i-Sharif, which is a northern town.

"And if the rebels succeed, it would mean that we may not have to have a large presence on the ground. We have proxies."

President Bush shrugged off the rising chorus of media naysayers and took comfort in the support of the public. As the *New York Times* observed, "Despite threats about anthrax unfolding virtually every day and little discernible progress in the air campaign against the Taliban, Americans are still offering President Bush their over-whelming approval."

On November 8, as the negative coverage reached a crescendo, Bush traveled to Atlanta to give his biggest speech since the joint address to Congress seven weeks earlier. Without mentioning journalists, he expressly rebuked their message of gloom and doom.

"I'm so proud of our military," the president said. "We are destroying training camps, disrupting communications, and dismantling air defenses. We are now bombing Taliban front lines. We are deliberately and systematically hunting down these murderers, and we will bring them to justice."

Determined to set the record straight on alleged atrocities, he added, "We do not target innocent civilians. We care for the innocent people of Afghanistan, so we continue to provide humanitarian aid, even while their government tries to steal the food we send."

As for the notion that Afghan civilians favored the Taliban over America, Bush countered, "When the terrorists and their supporters are gone, the people of Afghanistan will say with the rest of the world: Good riddance."

The president reminded the nation, as well as the press, of the patience he had counseled a mere month earlier.

"We are at the beginning of our efforts in Afghanistan," he said. "And Afghanistan is only the beginning of our efforts in the world."

Bush closed with an acknowledgment that the future was uncertain, but hopeful.

"We cannot know every turn this battle will take. Yet we know our cause is just and our ultimate victory is assured. We will, no doubt, face new challenges. But we have our marching orders.

"My fellow Americans: Let's roll."

Chapter Eleven

Osama Unplugged

OSAMA BIN LADEN WAS SO TALL that he had to hunch slightly as he came through the doorway. Smiling demurely, he surveyed the spartan room. Not a stick of furniture in sight. But floral cushions had been placed on the blue carpet and against the bottom of the white painted walls. A sheet had been tacked over a glass vestibule for privacy. A large map hung on one wall, several posters on another. The chamber was illuminated by a modern electrical fixture that descended from the ceiling and diverged into two glowing globes. That was an encouraging sign. A month of bombing by the infidels had failed to interrupt the flow of electricity, at least to this modest Kandahar safe house.

Clutching his trusty Kalashnikov, bin Laden began working the room. He greeted an adolescent boy, kissed a young man with a mustache, and headed for a paraplegic sitting on a cushion beneath the room's only window. Bin Laden had known Khaled al-Harbi since the 1980s, when they helped drive the Soviets out of Afghanistan. Harbi had gone on to fight alongside Muslims in Bosnia and then Chechnya, where an injury left him paralyzed from the waist down. With a sheet covering his crippled legs, Harbi was now kissing bin Laden's second-in-command, Egyptian surgeon Ayman Al-Zawahiri, who accidentally dislodged the top roll of the paraplegic's turban. Feeling the fabric tumble down his back, Harbi groped his head to assess the damage. By this time, however, bin Laden was crouching in front of him and puckering up. So Harbi placed both hands on bin Laden's turban and the men kissed.

Bin Laden sat cross-legged against a wall, propping his rifle on a cushion between himself and Harbi. The sight of his old acquaintance's disheveled turban prompted bin Laden to check his own. Grasping it with both hands, he tipped it low over his eyes and then settled it back on his pate before stroking the silky white tail that flowed over his camouflage fatigues. Encouraged by this preening, Harbi resumed his own damage assessment, but succeeded only in dislodging another loop of his turban, which now drooped ridiculously below his eyes. With only one loop left, Harbi gave up and removed the whole mess, leaving his hairy head topped only by a skullcap. He plopped the turban into his lap while half a dozen men in the room, some of whom were toting rifles, exchanged greetings and settled themselves on the floor. Then Harbi carefully wound the turban back around his head as he addressed the guest of honor. They were aware that their meeting was being recorded on videotape, which was time-stamped November 9.

"You have given us weapons, you have given us hope, and we thank Allah for you," Harbi began. "We don't want to take much of your time."

Harbi explained that he and his entourage had come here from Saudi Arabia by way of Kabul. Their driver had taken them through the countryside on "a night with a full moon." Along the way, they had encountered Muslims who were inspired by the attacks of September 11.

"People now are supporting us more. Even those ones who did not support us in the past, support us more now," he said. "Everybody praises what you did, the great action you did, which was first and foremost by the grace of Allah. This is the guidance of Allah and the blessed fruit of jihad."

"Thanks to Allah," bin Laden said. Then he asked how religious leaders at the sacred mosques of Mecca and Medina had reacted to the news. It had been a decade since bin Laden set foot in his Saudi homeland.

"Honestly, they are very positive," Harbi said. "Sheikh Al-Bahrani gave a good sermon in his class after the sunset prayers. It was videotaped and I was supposed to carry it with me. But unfortunately, I had to leave immediately."

"The day of the events?" bin Laden said.

"At the exact time of the attack on America, precisely at the time," Harbi assured him. "He told the youth, 'You are asking for martyrdom and wonder where you should go?' Allah was inciting them to go."

But Bahrani's sermon and other expressions of support for bin Laden were evidently not appreciated by Saudi government authorities.

"After he issued the first fatwa, he was detained for interrogation, as you know," Harbi said. "He told them, 'Don't waste my time. I have another fatwa. If you want me, I can sign both at the same time.'"

"Thanks be to Allah," bin Laden said.

"His position is really very encouraging," Harbi said hopefully. "When I paid him the first visit about a year and half ago, he asked me, 'How is Sheikh bin Laden?' He sends you his special regards."

The crippled flatterer then described a second Saudi sheikh who lost his job after praising the September 11 attacks.

"He gave a beautiful fatwa," Harbi said. "Miraculously, I heard it on the Koran radio station. It was strange because he sacrificed his position, which is equivalent to a director. It was transcribed word by word. The brothers listened to it in detail. I briefly heard it before the noon prayers. He said this was jihad and those people were not innocent people."

When bin Laden asked about the reaction of a third Saudi sheikh, Harbi replied, "Honestly, I did not meet with him. My movements were truly limited."

"Allah bless you," bin Laden said.

Harbi went back to describing his trip to this meeting, which he said was facilitated by bin Laden sympathizers, including one from the Saudi religious police.

"They smuggled us and then I thought that we would be in different caves inside the mountains. So I was surprised at the guest house," he said, gesturing to his surroundings. "We also learned that this location is safe, by Allah's blessings. The place is clean and we are very comfortable."

They were also well fed. At one point, the men took a break for a communal meal. Bin Laden leaned forward to scoop food from a bowl into his mouth using his fingers. Others eagerly helped themselves.

Bin Laden recited sayings associated with the prophet Muhammad, including, "I was ordered to fight the people until they say there is no god but Allah, and his prophet Muhammad."

He explained that "those young men" who attacked America on September 11 were following Muhammad's true teachings, not the flawed interpretation of Islam practiced by mainstream Muslims. He said the hijackers' "deeds" were like great "speeches." They were "speeches that overshadowed all other speeches made everywhere else in the world. The speeches are understood by both Arabs and non-Arabs—even by Chinese."

Bin Laden reveled in the outpouring of worldwide support for his cause since the attacks.

"In Holland, at one of the centers, the number of people who accepted Islam during the days that followed the operations were more than the people who accepted Islam in the last eleven years," he said. "I heard someone on Islamic radio who owns a school in America say, 'We don't have time to keep up with the demands of those who are asking about Islamic books to learn about Islam.' This event made people think, which benefited Islam greatly."

"Hundreds of people used to doubt you and few only would follow you until this huge event happened," Harbi said. "Now hundreds of people are coming out to join you."

Smiling serenely, bin Laden proceeded to explain how he used his engineering expertise to inflict maximum damage on the World Trade Center.

"We calculated in advance the number of casualties from the enemy, who would be killed based on the position of the tower. We calculated that the floors that would be hit would be three or four floors. I was the most optimistic of them all," he said. "Because of my experience in this field, I was thinking that the fire from the gas in the plane would melt the iron structure of the building and collapse the area where the plane hit and all the floors above it only. This is all we had hoped for."

He gestured with his right hand as if it were an airplane crashing into the World Trade Center, which was represented by his upraised left hand, the fingers toppling on impact.

"Allah be praised," Harbi said.

Bin Laden made clear that while he had masterminded the attack, he allowed underlings to select the exact date.

"We had notification since the previous Thursday that the event would take place that day. We had finished our work that day and had the radio on. It was 5:30 P.M. our time," he recalled. "Immediately, we heard the news that a plane had hit the World Trade Center. We turned the radio station to the news from Washington. The news continued and no mention of the attack until the end. At the end of the newscast, they reported that a plane had just hit the World Trade Center."

Bin Laden covered his mouth with his hand in an attempt to contain his laughter.

"Allah be praised," Harbi said.

"After a little while, they announced that another plane had hit the World Trade Center," bin Laden added. "The brothers who heard the news were overjoyed by it."

Like everyone else on Earth, Harbi remembered what he was doing when he first learned of the attacks.

"I was sitting," he said. "All of a sudden the news came and everyone was overjoyed. And everyone—until the next day, in the morning—was talking about what was happening. And we stayed until four o'clock, listening to the news—every time a little bit different. Everyone was very joyous and saying, 'Allah is great,' 'Allah is great,' 'We are thankful to Allah,' 'Praise Allah.' And I was happy for the happiness of my brothers. That day the congratulations were coming on the phone nonstop. The mother was receiving phone calls continuously."

Harbi then quoted a verse from the Koran: "Fight them, Allah will torture them, with your hands, he will torture them. He will deceive them and he will give you victory. Allah will forgive the believers, he is knowledgeable about everything."

This led Harbi into a rapturous soliloquy about the September 11 attacks, which he described as nothing short of sublime.

"No doubt it is a clear victory Allah has bestowed on us," he said. "And he will give us blessing and more victory during this holy month of Ramadan. And this is what everyone is hoping for.

"Thank Allah America came out of its caves. We hit her with the first hit. And the next one will hit her with the hands of the believers, the good believers, the strong believers."

Harbi seemed to realize he was getting carried away, but he couldn't help himself.

"I'm sorry to speak in your presence, but it is just thoughts, just thoughts," he said.

"I live in happiness, happiness," he gushed, "I have not experienced, or felt, in a long time."

He went on to scoff at the coalition that America had assembled, a mishmash of Western and Arab infidels whose campaign against bin Laden would surely backfire in the end.

"The day will come when the symbols of Islam will rise up," Harbi vowed. "It will be the greatest jihad in the history of Islam and the resistance of the wicked people."

Gazing at bin Laden with unembarrassed hero worship, he added, "We congratulate you for the great work. Thank Allah."

Bin Laden then quoted an aide who seemed to presage the attacks a year in advance.

" 'I saw in a dream, we were playing a soccer game against the Americans. When our team showed up in the field, they were all pilots!' " the aide had told him. " 'So I wondered if that was a soccer game or a pilot game. Our players were pilots.' "

Bin Laden explained to Harbi, "He didn't know anything about the operation until he heard it on the radio. He said the game went on and we defeated them. That was a good omen for us."

"May Allah be blessed," Harbi said.

Al Qaeda spokesman Sulayman Abu Gaith recalled that he was in a room with his boss on September 11, but then walked into another room to watch television.

"The TV broadcast the big event," the Kuwaiti said. "The scene was showing an Egyptian family sitting in their living room. They exploded with joy. Do you know when there is a soccer game and your team wins? It was the same expression of joy. There was a subtitle that read, 'In revenge for the children of al-Aqsa, Osama bin Ladin executes an operation against America.'"

Gaith said he went back to bin Laden, "who was sitting in a room with fifty to sixty people. I tried to tell him about what I saw, but he made a gesture with his hands, meaning, 'I know, I know.'"

"He did not know about the operation," bin Laden explained to Harbi. "Not everybody knew."

Bin Laden said Muhammad Atta of al Qaeda's Egyptian branch was in charge of the hijackers. This prompted Harbi to praise Atta's performance.

"A plane crashing into a tall building was out of anyone's imagination," Harbi said. "This was a great job. He was one of the pious men in the organization. He became a martyr. Allah bless his soul."

Harbi said the attacks were presaged by a variety of devout Muslims. One man had a vision of dragging an airplane into the desert. Another had a vision of true believers departing for jihad and ending up in Washington and New York, where a plane hit a building. A third swore by Allah that his wife had seen the crash a week before it happened.

"That was unbelievable," Harbi concluded. "My god."

Bin Laden bragged that even the nineteen hijackers were kept in the dark about details of their mission until the last possible moment.

"All they knew was that they have a martyrdom operation and we asked each of them to go to America. But they didn't know anything about the operation, not even one letter. But they were trained and we did not reveal the operation to them until they are there and just before they boarded the planes."

In keeping with al Qaeda's practice of segregating cells of terrorists for security reasons, the hijackers were given very little information about one another.

"Those who were trained to fly didn't know the others," bin Laden said with a giggle. "One group of people did not know the other group."

One of the men in the room then asked bin Laden to tell Harbi about a premonition experienced by an al Qaeda member at a training camp in Kandahar.

"He came close and told me that he saw, in a dream, a tall building in America," bin Laden recalled. "At that point, I was worried that maybe the secret would be revealed if everyone starts seeing it in their dream. So I closed the subject. I told him if he sees another dream, not to tell anybody, because people will be upset with him."

Bin Laden chuckled at the memory. But what he really relished was the moment when all these dreams came true. His followers were beside themselves with jubilation when the news finally broke.

"They were overjoyed when the first plane hit the building, so I said to them, Be patient," he recalled. "The difference between the first and the second plane hitting the towers was twenty minutes. And the difference between the first plane and the plane that hit the Pentagon was one hour."

Harbi interjected that the Americans "were terrified, thinking there was a coup."

Zawahiri, who had been quiet all evening, spoke up to say that this was the first time Americans had felt danger coming at them. He leaned forward to scoop up a final mouthful of food and fell silent again.

Bin Laden, who had celebrated the *Cole* bombing by reciting a poem on Al-Jazeera television, decided the September 11 attacks deserved a similar tribute. Surrounded by his flatterers in this Kandahar safe house, he spoke of a heroic struggle against a bloody tyrant who gets his comeuppance in the end. Bin Laden wagged his finger at his followers as his voice rose for the poem's climax.

> *. . . And over weeping sounds now*
> *We hear the beats of drums and rhythm.*
> *They are storming his forts*
> *And shouting: We will not stop our raids*
> *Until you free our land. . . .*

Chapter Twelve

"Wrong, Wrong, Wrong"

"I WAS WRONG, WRONG, WRONG," said Evan Thomas. "Like a lot of pundits, I was just plain wrong."

The assistant managing editor of *Newsweek* made this remarkable mea culpa exactly one week after insisting on TV that victory in Afghanistan would require no less than a quarter million U.S. ground troops. Thomas had blithely discounted reports of Allied forces over-running the strategic city of Mazar-i-Sharif on November 9.

But he could not ignore dramatic gains over the next few days that put U.S.-backed forces in control of fully half the nation—including the capital, Kabul—by November 13. All this was accomplished with just 250 U.S. ground troops, or a thousand times fewer than the 250,000 Thomas had insisted would be necessary.

At least Thomas was big enough to admit his mistake. The same could not be said for fellow pundit Jack Germond, who had agreed with Thomas insisting, "We're going to have a large ground presence there—it has to happen."

A week later, Germond shrugged: "I don't remember what I said last week and I don't think anybody else does."

"I'll be happy to remind you, Jack," offered panelist Charles Krauthammer.

"The official 'expert' opinion—not the opinion of this panel—was wrong," huffed Germond, who had made no such distinction a week earlier. "I mean, we thought it was going to be a lot tougher to deal with the Taliban than it proved to be."

Nina Totenberg was equally reluctant to retract her week-old call for "a lot of ground troops—not a few."

"Nina, you're ready to eat crow?" asked *Inside Washington* moderator Gordon Peterson.

"Why should I eat crow? I kept saying that this is enough force. I agreed with Charles," she replied with a straight face. "You forget that we agreed on this subject."

But there had been no such agreement. In fact, Totenberg and the rest of the panel had expressly disagreed with Krauthammer when he cautioned, "We may not have to have a large presence on the ground. We have proxies."

Remembering the columnist's prescience, Peterson now offered a victory lap.

"Charles, do you wish to crow?" the moderator said.

"Oh, modesty prevents me, Gordon," Krauthammer said. "But I will point out that I was right."

With the exception of Evan Thomas, most in the press were unwilling to acknowledge they had been "wrong, wrong, wrong" about the war in Afghanistan. Instead, journalists acted as though U.S. commanders were the ones who had miscalculated.

"Stunned by their own sudden success in Afghanistan, Pentagon officials are scrambling to shift military strategy," began a breathless story on the front page of *USA Today* on November 14. "Just last week, Defense Secretary Donald Rumsfeld was deflecting criticism that U.S. forces were being drawn into a Vietnam-style quagmire. But in four days, the war in Afghanistan has taken a remarkable turn in favor of the United States and its Northern Alliance partners."

Incredibly, the story made it sound as though Rumsfeld was somehow to blame for the very criticism he had been "deflecting"—which came from the *press itself*. *USA Today* conveniently neglected to remind readers of its own dire warning just days earlier that "air strikes and commandos won't be enough to rout the Taliban."

The *New York Times* was equally unrepentant about its wrongheadedness.

"The rout of the Taliban from Afghanistan cities continued apace yesterday," began the paper's lead story on November 15. "As much as 80 percent of the country now appeared to be out of the control of the Taliban." Reporter Serge Schemann went on to gush about "the extraordinary pace of developments in the last 48 hours."

Even Johnny Apple, the *Times*'s chief Washington correspondent, managed to forget about his "Another Vietnam?" question from the October 31 front page.

"What a difference a week makes," he blithely began his "Letter from Washington" on November 16.

"Last week, Washington belonged to the naysayers and what-iffers. Spokesmen at the White House were badgered with questions about the campaign against terrorism. The strategy in Afghanistan would never work, people said. It relied too heavily on bombing, they said. Eventually, the armchair Clausewitzes maintained, you would have to use ground troops."

Naysayers? What-iffers? *Armchair Clausewitzes?* Apple was tut-tutting the misguided media as though he were not one of its prime practitioners. Having spent the last month likening the war to a Vietnam "quagmire," Apple now adopted the tone of a sage who had known better all along.

"Not one of the pessimistic prophets would have even entertained the suggestion that forces friendly to the United States would control every major Afghan city by Thanksgiving," he sniffed.

Evidently, Apple had missed David Hackworth's angry TV appearance on October 7. "When the American people slice into their turkey on turkey day, we will see the Taliban no longer in business," the retired army colonel had predicted on CNN's *NewsNight*.

Undaunted, Apple plowed on: "Clearly, as in the war in the Persian Gulf, air power has proved more potent than its critics expected." He did not mention that he had also been one of the chief critics of the Gulf War strategy, comparing it in 1991 to—what else?—Vietnam.

Even now, as Apple acknowledged that Allied forces were routing the Taliban, he could not let go of his gloomy obsession with Vietnam.

"So is this a false dawn, the end of a phase and not the war?" he asked rhetorically. "There was a good deal of talk tonight about a protracted and difficult campaign against Taliban guerrillas by Western commandos. Washington being Washington, that made a lot of people think once more about Vietnam, which haunts the city even when it is giddy."

Apple's story was headlined, "A Shifting Mood, a Haunting Memory." But the rest of the nation did not appear haunted by Vietnam. To the contrary, Americans were thrilled that the Taliban was being unceremoniously deposed from power. They rejoiced when American missionaries were freed from their Taliban captors on November 13. Far from being unhappy with the performance of the U.S. military, Americans reserved their displeasure for the performance of the press.

Nowhere was this abysmal performance more evident than at the televised Pentagon press briefings, where reporters asked questions so fatuous that many viewers shook their heads in disgust. On November 13, a reporter demanded to know why allied forces sweeping across northern Afghanistan were shooting armed Taliban soldiers.

"Mr. Secretary, could you explain the justification for attacking military troops in retreat?" the journalist said.

"They have been obviously offered an opportunity to surrender," Rumsfeld explained. "And they are not surrendering, they're not throwing down their weapons—they're moving their vehicles. And it is a perfectly legitimate and attractive target."

Another journalist asked about "reports from the ground that the Northern Alliance have made atrocities in Mazar-i-Sharif."

"Who's making these reports?" Rumsfeld asked.

"From the ground."

"Who?"

"Witnesses from the ground."

"Who?"

"The reporters," a journalist said. "And UN officials."

"UN officials?" Rumsfeld said. "I don't think there are any UN officials in there."

"Right," the reporter said. "The UN is just representing these as reports 'out of the region.' That's where we're getting them from."

"Well, the reports that we've heard out of the regions have been absolutely lying through their teeth, week after week after week, throughout the entire thing," Rumsfeld spat. "I don't know that it's really useful to repeat unsubstantiated and sensational charges that I can't validate, that you can't validate, and that have not been checked."

The reporter's suggestion that U.S.-backed forces were the bad guys in this conflict struck a raw nerve with Rumsfeld. He said it was part of "a thread I find from time to time" that runs through the media's conventional wisdom.

"The implication is that America is what's wrong with the world, and in fact it's not," Rumsfeld said. "The Taliban have been vicious repressors in that country. They have done enormous humanitarian harm and damage to men, women, and children in that country."

He paused as if mulling whether to continue the lecture.

"That piece of real estate has changed hands dozens and dozens of times throughout history, and the carnage has just been unbelievable. Century after century, people have—in some cases—eliminated entire cities. The last time these places changed hands, the Taliban came in and killed hundreds and hundreds and hundreds of people."

He added, "I'll guess that when this is over, that this probably will prove to have been the change of hands with the least loss of life of any time in modern memory in that country. But there will be loss of life."

Another reporter suggested the rout of al Qaeda would trigger a strike against the United States.

"Some people suggest they may launch some sort of last-gasp terrorist attack," the journalist cautioned.

"They already did," Rumsfeld replied. "They've threatened to do more. They *will* do more—whether we do what we're doing or whether we don't do what we're doing.

"And the idea that you could appease them by stopping doing what we're doing—or some implication that by doing what we're doing, we're inciting them to attack us—is just utter nonsense.

"It's just—it's kind of like feeding an alligator, hoping it eats you last. I mean, it—this is what we need to do. You cannot defend against terrorists. You must take the battles to them. It's self-defense."

Some reporters tried to assuage their guilt over having belittled the war strategy by offering Rumsfeld opportunities to gloat. But the defense secretary avoided this trap, knowing it would appear unseemly to claim vindication at a time when American troops were still in harm's way.

"Mr. Secretary, as you know, about this time last week you were getting skeptical questions and skeptical critiques about the conduct of the war," one journalist offered.

Rumsfeld called this "the understatement of the afternoon," and left it at that. But the next day, when he visited Ground Zero with New York Mayor Rudy Giuliani, a reporter inquired whether "you feel like telling us 'I told you so'?"

"No, I don't," Rumsfeld said. "We still have a ways to go, and I can understand—when things are happening that aren't visible and aren't something that we can remark on—I can understand the impatience."

He added, "It is, needless to say, gratifying to see the Taliban fleeing and the people of Afghanistan getting their country back."

At the Pentagon the next day, Tommy Franks also refused to rise to the bait when a reporter asked, "General, do you feel exonerated after the criticism in the past, last time you were here, that your campaign is too timid?"

"No, sir," Franks replied. "I don't feel exonerated, because I never felt vilified. I am simply a soldier doing his job, and I'll continue to do that."

Later, when Rumsfeld visited Franks's stateside headquarters in Tampa, Florida, a reporter asked how much of the military's success "frankly is a surprise?"

"What was taking place in the earlier phases was exactly as planned," Rumsfeld said. "The conditions were being set for what needed to be done. The air defenses were being taken out. And we were putting people on the ground, so that they could begin assisting with respect to resupply and targeting and the like.

"It looked like nothing was happening. Indeed, it looked like we were in a—all together now—quagmire," he said mischievously. The press chuckled uneasily.

"Sir, I was going to say 'stalemate,'" Franks deadpanned.

"A stalemate, yes," Rumsfeld said, drawing more uncomfortable laughter. "But in fact we were not. It was proceeding along, and pressure was being built, and the capabilities to do what has since occurred were being established."

Bush later told me that he was unfazed by all the carping about "getting into the quagmire. That didn't bother me in the least. It really didn't."

When I asked if it prompted him to wonder whether he had chosen the right strategy, he said, "No, I never wondered that at all." He explained that the initial phase of the counterattack—which entailed tasks like flying "a B-1 out of Diego Garcia and a B-2 out of Missouri, and maybe a refueler"—was much simpler than the next phase, which involved putting "boots on the ground."

"It was the hardest logistical challenge," he said. "You know, we took no time wiping out the first phase, wipe out whatever assets they had. That didn't take long. And that was pretty easy. The degree of difficulty mounted significantly as we then tried to get our troops into the country."

On November 17, *Saturday Night Live* opened its show with a devastating spoof of the Pentagon press corps. An actress portrayed an insipid reporter grilling Rumsfeld, who was played by a squinting, bespectacled actor.

"With our military campaign stalled and the opposition forces seemingly bogged down in a quagmire, isn't there a danger the U.S.

will look like a weakling and thus lose the support of the Afghan people?" the reporter asked.

"Isn't that the same question you asked last week?" Rumsfeld
demanded.

"Oh, I'm sorry," the reporter said. "Okay, with our military moving so rapidly and opposition forces easily overrunning Taliban areas,
isn't there a danger the U.S. will look like a bully and thus lose the
support of the Afghan people?"

The studio audience and viewers around the nation howled with
knowing laughter. They had come to admire Rumsfeld's deft and fearless handling of the press. Once derided as a Bush "retread," the wily
defense secretary was now so popular with Americans that Bush joked
about his new status as a "TV matinee idol." CNN's Larry King called
him a "sex symbol." Vice President Cheney said his televised briefings
were stealing audiences from afternoon soap operas. Now the sixty-
nine-year-old defense secretary was receiving the ultimate tribute of
American pop culture—a *Saturday Night Live* spoof that portrayed
him not as the object of ridicule, but as the put-upon protagonist. The
reporters, the very baby boomers who had mocked Rumsfeld before
September 11, were now the ones being skewered as clueless.

"We're getting reports of U.S. Special Op forces being dropped into
Taliban areas with camouflage and night-vision goggles," one fictional reporter said to the fictional Rumsfeld. "This means the Taliban soldiers won't be able to see our troops, but we'll be able to see
them. Is that fair?"

Another reporter said, "We're being told that Northern Alliance
forces are firing back at Taliban troops who have fired on them, even
though the Taliban troops missed. Does the U.S. condone that?"

"Now what kind of question is that?" the Rumsfeld character
demanded.

"Thought-provoking?" the reporter offered.

"No."

"Incisive?"

"No," Rumsfeld said. "Remember what I said about your question the other day?"

"That it was idiotic?"

"And?"

"And that I am an embarrassment both to myself and to my newspaper?"

"That's right."

The following week, at the conclusion of the real Pentagon press briefing, a reporter said, "What did you think of your portrayal on *Saturday Night Live*?"

"When I want to discuss *Saturday Night Live*, I'll bring it up," Rumsfeld cracked as he walked away from the podium.

Saturday Night Live's parody had not been far from the truth. America's disgust with the press was so pervasive it sometimes bordered on outright hostility. This was evidenced on November 18, when ABC's Peter Jennings visited a Dallas Cowboys tailgate party as part of his national tour to gauge the post-September 11 "mood."

"The president's approval rating is high in his home state," the anchorman observed to one football fan.

"George Bush, so far, has done an unbelievable job," the man replied.

"Many of us in the media don't get the same high marks," Jennings said before turning to a second man. "Can you tell me how the mood is in Dallas these days?"

"Nobody likes you," the man replied matter-of-factly.

Jennings explained to his TV audience, "This man told us our reporting in these days is unpatriotic and cannot help the nation get back to business."

Oblivious to such feedback, the press continued its grim negativism. The *Washington Post* ran a front-page story claiming the Pentagon called off a number of military strikes against al Qaeda leaders because the explosions might have killed nearby civilians. The story also anonymously quoted a four-star general who said Rumsfeld was micromanaging the war, which the source derided as "military amateur hour."

CNN Pentagon Correspondent Jamie McIntyre decided to give a wider audience to the anonymous allegations by bringing them up at the next day's televised press briefing.

"Secretary Rumsfeld, despite the success that you've enjoyed in this military campaign, I'm sure you won't be surprised to know that there are still critics," McIntyre said.

"Can you believe this?" Rumsfeld said with mock indignation.

"If we are to believe the *Washington Post*, some of these critics are right here in this building. Could I just get your reaction to the *Post* story of yesterday, which said that red tape was in some cases preventing effective targeting? And apparently, one anonymous four-star general accused you of micromanaging the war."

"You mentioned that one of the people was unidentified. There was *no one* identified in the story," Rumsfeld chuckled. "Not just the one you happen to be quoting."

He called the story "a world-class thumb-sucker, with all respect to the *Post*, mind you."

Having long been criticized for bombing too many civilians, Rumsfeld now found himself defending Tommy Franks's efforts to minimize such casualties.

"He has to balance the question of doing the maximum amount to kill people on the ground—who might be part of the al Qaeda and Taliban leadership—against trying to avoid so much collateral damage," Rumsfeld said.

"And my attitude is: Tommy Franks is doing a darn good job," he concluded. "And I think most of the people in this building believe that. And the fact that there are one or two anonymous people who seem to at some point have observed something that they might have done differently ought not to surprise you at all—an expert like you, Jamie."

Impervious to these ironic rebukes, the press kept at it. A favorite topic was the president's executive order giving the United States the option to try foreign terrorists in military tribunals. Although such tribunals had not been used since World War II, Bush wanted the option in case Allied forces captured bin Laden or other top al Qaeda leaders. The American Civil Liberties Union went ballistic, insisting Bush was trying "to circumvent the requirements of the Bill of Rights." The press agreed, arguing that bin Laden should be brought to the United States, given a lawyer, and put on trial in a civilian court.

"Why the military rather than civilian?" a reporter demanded of Rumsfeld at the Pentagon. "Is this the idea of summary court-martials and executions?"

"Charlie, what is this 'summary court-martials and executions'!" Rumsfeld exclaimed. "I'm shocked that those words even came out of your mouth."

A military tribunal, he explained, was "a mechanism that has been used throughout the history of this country. And we will approach it in a manner distinctly different from that which you've suggested."

New York Times columnist William Safire went apoplectic in a column headlined "Kangaroo Courts." He railed that these "Star Chamber tribunals" would deny "traditional American human rights" to foreign terrorists. This "try-'em-and-fry-'em" approach was Bush's way of assuming "dictatorial power," Safire groused.

Over at the White House, similarly skeptical journalists attacked the proposal from a variety of angles.

"Why wasn't Congress informed?" demanded a reporter in the press briefing room.

"Well, the president—in his authority as commander in chief—has wide powers to act as he thinks is appropriate for the nation at a time where national security is of paramount interest," Ari Fleischer explained. "It is not always the role of the administration to consult with all parties."

Another reporter asked, "What criteria will the president use in his identification and selection of individuals for trial by military commission?"

"He will make that determination on the basis of what he believes is in the national security interest," Fleischer said.

"That's very broad."

"It is very broad," the spokesman agreed.

"Just whatever he thinks the national security requires?"

"Under the law and under the Supreme Court precedence, the president has that authority," Fleischer said.

"How can he take that authority?"

"He has reserved it to himself, as opposed to delegating it to the secretary of defense," Fleischer explained.

Rumsfeld said "shrill" journalists were engaging in "ready, fire, aim" analysis of the tribunals.

Vice President Cheney, when questioned about the tribunals, emphasized historical precedents.

"This is the way we dealt with the people who assassinated Abraham Lincoln and tried to assassinate part of the cabinet back in 1865—they were tried by military tribunals," he said.

"In 1942, we had German saboteurs land on the coast up in Long Island and down in Florida," Cheney said. "President Roosevelt signed an order, established a tribunal, had these individuals tried. They were given a fair trial, prosecuted under this military tribunal, and executed in relatively rapid order. And that procedure was upheld by the Supreme Court when it was challenged later on. So there's ample precedent for it.

"The basic proposition here is that somebody who comes into the United States of America illegally, who conducts a terrorist operation killing thousands of innocent Americans—men, women, and children—is not a lawful combatant. They don't deserve to be treated as a prisoner of war. They don't deserve the same guarantees and safeguards that would be used for an American citizen going through the normal judicial process. They will have a fair trial, but it'll be under the procedures of a military tribunal."

In the Oval Office, ABC's Terry Moran reminded Bush that some civil libertarians, law professors, and members of Congress considered military tribunals "an abandonment of traditional American principles."

"We're fighting a war, Terry, against the most evil kinds of people," Bush replied. "And I need to have that extraordinary option at my fingertips. I ought to be able to have that option available should we ever bring one of these al Qaeda members in alive."

He added, "This government will do everything we can to defend the American people within the confines of our Constitution. And that's exactly how we're proceeding. And so, to the critics I say: I made the absolute right decision."

Another reporter pressed Bush: "Are you concerned with the amount of dissent over your decision to establish military tribunals?"

"Not the least bit concerned," the president replied. "It makes sense for the protection of potential jurors. It makes sense for homeland security."

The proposal, which would allow for the execution of convicted terrorists, prompted European opponents of the death penalty to balk at extraditing suspects to the United States.

"A lot of people in Europe, and also in Norway, sir, are very worried about the military tribunals that you're proposing," a Norwegian reporter admonished Bush. "Many people are saying that when you want to save democracy, then this might be—part of the way—undermining democracy itself."

"Well, I appreciate that question and I want the people of the world to understand that our great nation will never forgo the values that have made us unique; that we believe in democracy and rule of law and the Constitution," Bush said. "But we're under attack. Every morning I wake up and read the threat assessments. The evil ones still intend to harm America."

He explained that the tribunals were designed to protect Americans, not undermine democracy.

"If we capture an al Qaeda representative, if we capture a murderer, and in order to convict that murderer it would require us giving means of how we knew he was guilty that would jeopardize the security of the United States, he'll be tried in a military tribunal," Bush said. "And I, in order to get a conviction of a murderer, will not jeopardize the people of the United States. I will not show our secrets. I will not tip our hand. I will not let the world at large—particularly our enemy—understand how we put a case together if it's going to jeopardize and compromise national security secrets of the United States of America.

"My job is to protect the United States people from further attack," he concluded. "And that's exactly what I'm going to do and, at the same time, bring al Qaeda to justice."

The public sided with Bush, according to a poll conducted on November 27 for ABC News and the *Washington Post*: 6 in 10 Americans wanted suspected terrorists tried in military tribunals. Only 39 percent preferred civilian courts.

Although the *Post* published the poll results on its front page, the rest of the press continued to emphasize criticism of the tribunals.

"You people just don't get it," a C-SPAN caller scolded *New York Times* publisher Arthur Sulzberger Jr., a guest on *Washington Journal* the day after the poll was published.

Moderator Brian Lamb explained to Sulzberger, "I think he's suggesting that the newspapers and the media care more about this tribunal issue than the public at large."

Sulzberger had not seen the *Post* poll.

"I don't read any other newspaper on a regular basis," he sniffed. But he added: "There's a reason that we have trial by jury in this country and not summary execution."

An even larger majority of Americans—73 percent—supported a decision by Attorney General John Ashcroft to allow the FBI to eavesdrop on jailhouse conversations between suspected terrorists and their lawyers. The new rule applied to only about a dozen prisoners and had built-in safeguards to make sure their rights were not violated.

The poll also showed that 79 percent of Americans supported Ashcroft's plans to have federal prosecutors interview some five thousand Middle Eastern men visiting the United States on temporary visas. And nearly 9 in 10 poll respondents said Ashcroft was justified in detaining six hundred foreign nationals for breaking immigration laws.

Yet the media seemed firmly opposed to all these measures. Reporters had long distrusted Ashcroft more than any other member of Bush's cabinet. For years, they had caricatured him as a teetotaling pro-lifer, a devout Christian who even frowned on public dancing. Now that he was taking steps to protect Americans from terrorist attacks, the press went on the offensive.

"An expanding coalition of lawmakers and civil liberties groups is complaining that Attorney General John D. Ashcroft's campaign against terrorism had gone too far," reported the *Washington Post* in a front-page story.

Coverage grew even more ominous when Ashcroft began promoting a preexisting program that gave special immigration status to foreigners who provided useful information about terrorists. Although the Responsible Cooperators Program had long enjoyed broad bipartisan support on Capitol Hill, the press suddenly decided it smacked of Stalinism.

"Does it not make the administration uncomfortable to be promulgating a program that bears at least passing similarity to what totalitarian societies like East Germany and the Soviet Union used to do, which is to say to people: Turn informant, and you'll get rewarded?" a reporter asked Fleischer at the White House briefing room. "Isn't the essential bargain the same?"

"Absolutely not," Fleischer replied. "The essential bargain is only the same if you believe in moral equivalence between totalitarian governments and the government of the United States. And I don't."

"So you're suggesting that it is somehow morally superior if we do it here?" the reporter pressed.

"I think that people here understand that when they help catch people who are committing crimes, they help to protect freedom," Fleischer said.

The attack on the Responsible Cooperators Program continued the next day, when a reporter invoked the gods of political correctness.

"One of the main Arab-American organizations in the country says that the word 'cooperator' has a very negative connotation in the Arabic language, that it suggests something more akin to collaborator, someone who sells out, in fact, and that this is likely to inhibit cooperation among Arab-Americans in the program," the reporter said. "Is there any thought being given to reconsider the name of this program?"

"This program was named by the Department of Justice," Fleischer punted. "So if you have any questions about the nomenclature, I'd refer you to Justice."

"Well, but this has happened twice before—the use of the word 'crusade,' which created some ripples in the Arabic world, and also 'Infinite Justice,'" the reporter persisted. "There have been two gaffes of this kind. This appears to be the third one. Is there any concern about this?"

Fleischer demurred: "Well, again, I would refer you to Justice, to see if it fits that category."

Over at the Justice Department, Ashcroft was growing increasingly irritated with criticism not only from the press but also from Democrats such as Senator Patrick Leahy of Vermont, who summoned the attorney general before the Senate Judiciary Committee for questioning.

"We need honest, reasoned debate, and not fear mongering," Ashcroft testified. "To those who scare peace-loving people with phantoms of lost liberty, my message is this: Your tactics only aid terrorists, for they erode our national unity and diminish our resolve. They give ammunition to America's enemies, and pause to America's friends. They encourage people of goodwill to remain silent in the face of evil."

Ashcroft said those who believed there would not be another terrorist attack against the United States "were living in a dreamworld." Holding up an al Qaeda training manual, he added, "Terrorists are taught how to use America's freedoms as a weapon against us."

This was too much for liberals in the press, who immediately accused Ashcroft of McCarthyism.

"Here is a guy who says people who disagree with the policies of this administration are aiding and abetting terrorism—that's the kind of thing McCarthy used to say," Jack Germond fumed on *Inside Washington.*

"He is a right-wing extremist himself," Germond added. "He was a religious, fundamentalist extremist as a senator and a governor. He is not the man with clean hands in this thing. He was a terrible choice."

Al Hunt, executive editor of the *Wall Street Journal*, agreed.

"What John Ashcroft and George Bush propose is to trample all over fundamental principles," he said on CNN's *Capital Gang.* He said for Ashcroft to imply that his critics "are somehow un-American, are giving aid and comfort to the enemy, is a smear worthy of Joe McCarthy."

Liberal columnist Anthony Lewis of the *New York Times* actually likened Ashcroft to bin Laden. Troubled by the attorney general's moral clarity, Lewis concluded: "Certainty is the enemy of decency and humanity in people who are sure they are right, like Osama bin Laden and John Ashcroft."

While these debates were raging in Washington, the war was still raging in Afghanistan. U.S. commandos were trying to help the Northern Alliance take Kunduz, the last Taliban stronghold in the north. U.S. marines began moving into southern Afghanistan on November 25 to help Pashtun tribes prepare for the siege of Kandahar, the last stronghold in the south. Meanwhile, the accuracy of U.S. bombing raids had improved dramatically.

"When we bomb, we bomb precisely—if we have accuracy as to the targets," Bush told me later. "And the war changed when we were able to get our troops on the ground, get eyes on targets, get the capacity to have the human beings dial in the necessary coordinates, to then effect the war. That included both CIA and Special Forces troops."

Some of these troops actually rode horseback over rugged terrain to more precisely direct the air strikes from U.S. bombers. It was an unlikely amalgam of warfare techniques from the nineteenth and twenty-first centuries.

"We fought the first cavalry charge of the twenty-first century—Special Forces and CIA agents on wooden saddles with some of the most sophisticated technology developed by mankind," Bush marveled.

The CIA agents performed other tasks as well, including the interrogation of captured members of al Qaeda. During one such interrogation, CIA agent Johnny "Mike" Spann encountered a prisoner who turned out to be from the United States. John Walker Lindh, twenty, had left his suburban Marin County, California, home a year earlier to join al Qaeda's fight against America. Captured by Allied forces, Lindh found himself in a prison teeming with hundreds of other al Qaeda members and Taliban soldiers five miles outside Mazar-i-Sharif.

"Where are you from?" Spann asked Lindh in the prison courtyard on November 25. "You believe in what you're doing here that much, you're willing to be killed here? How were you recruited to come here? Who brought you here? Hey!"

Spann, thirty-two, snapped his fingers in front of Lindh's face, but the "American Taliban" said nothing.

"What's your name? Hey. Who brought you here? Wake up! Who brought you here to Afghanistan? How did you get here?"

"What, are you puzzled?" Spann said after several moments of silence. "You gotta talk to me. All I want to do is talk to you and find out what your story is. I know you speak English."

A CIA agent named Dave walked over to play the role of "bad cop" to Spann's "good cop." The exchange, which was captured on videotape by an Afghan cameraman, took place within earshot of Lindh.

"He needs to decide if he wants to live or die—and die here," Dave said. "We're just going to leave him, and he's going to f—ing sit in prison the rest of his f—ing short life. It's his decision, man. We can only help the guys who want to talk to us. We can only get the Red Cross to help so many guys. If they don't talk to us, we can't—"

"Do you know the people here you're working with are terrorists, and killed other Muslims?" Spann said to Lindh. "There were several hundred Muslims killed in the bombing in New York City. Is that what the Koran teaches? I don't think so. Are you going to talk to us?"

"That's all right, man," Dave told Spann. "He got his chance."

But it was Spann, not Lindh, who would perish in the prison that afternoon. Shortly after this fruitless interrogation, prisoners overpowered their guards and staged a bloody uprising. Spann was killed almost immediately in the fierce fighting that ensued. He was the first American combat fatality in Afghanistan.

Lindh fled to the prison basement, where he hid until the raging battle ended seven days later. Finally forced from his hiding place when Allied forces flooded the basement with water, Lindh was placed in a bed and given medical attention by several doctors. While this was going on, he granted an interview to CNN. Filthy and weak, the holy warrior who had refused to answer questions from CIA agent Mike Spann now had no compunction about answering questions from CNN correspondent Robert Pelton.

"Is this what you thought it would be?" Pelton asked. "Was this the right cause or the right place?"

"It is exactly what I thought it would be," Lindh replied.

"Have you thought of fighting jihad in places like Chechnya?"

"Any Muslim that's concerned for the affairs of Muslims," Lindh said, "has considered this."

"But you chose Afghanistan, and one thing that I always wondered was: You have Muslims fighting Muslims here," Pelton observed.

"That's a question that's actually addressed in the Koran itself," Walker said. "There are certain situations in which Muslims, by necessity, are fought—for example, if a group of Muslims were renegades against the Islamic state."

"I'm an author of a book called *The World's Most Dangerous Places*," Pelton said. "And I traveled with you jihad groups through various places, and—"

"Yourself a Muslim?" Walker inquired.

"No, unfortunately, I'm not," Pelton allowed. "But I respect the cause and I respect the call."

So much for journalistic detachment. Pelton's astonishing profession of "respect" for jihad set the tone for the media's coddling coverage of the American Taliban. The sympathy was subtle at first, with reporters taking pains to refer to the twenty-year-old as a "young man," as if this somehow mitigated his decision to wage armed conflict against the United States.

"Do you know what you're going to do with him?" a reporter asked Rumsfeld at the Pentagon briefing room.

"He is being provided medical attention," Rumsfeld said. "He's being visited with by the people in close proximity to him, and we'll get to that in good time."

"Has the Pentagon yet heard from the attorney that his family hired?" another reporter said. "And you said that you would, quote, 'deal with him in good time.' But if he's an American citizen, in fact he would, one supposes, have some rights to due process. So what instructions are you giving the military about what 'in good time' really means?"

"Well, I have no knowledge of a lawyer. We found a person who says he's an American, with an AK-47, in a prison with a bunch of al Qaeda and Taliban fighters," Rumsfeld said. "And you can be certain he will have all the rights he is due."

The White House press corps was even more sympathetic to Walker.

"The young Taliban," a reporter began. "How much credibility do you assign to this young guy, who did not seem to be in the senior al Qaeda leadership?"

The reporter went on to argue that it was "difficult to believe that some guy in the middle levels or at lower levels of the Taliban" could know very much, since, after all, even the hijackers had been kept in the dark about their mission until the last possible moment.

But Walker admitted to U.S. investigators that he had met with senior al Qaeda officials, including Osama bin Laden himself. He acknowledged his membership in al Qaeda and told investigators he had been trained in bin Laden's camps to use poisons and explosives. He also learned how to carry out operations at American airports without attracting attention. None of this, however, stopped the press from coddling the American Taliban.

"Ari, John Walker has now been in custody—U.S. custody—for more than a week, and interrogated pretty regularly," said ABC's Terry Moran. "As an American citizen, he has a constitutional right, in that he's facing very serious criminal charges, to talk to a lawyer. He hasn't. Why not?"

"The facts are still being gathered to ascertain what, if any, charges will be brought," Fleischer said.

"Is this an indication of the kind of due process that people caught up in these terrorist investigations are going to face? Because as an American citizen facing—as the attorney general and others have said—very serious criminal charges, he has a constitutional right to see a lawyer, and he hasn't."

"I don't think this is the typical case," Fleischer said. "This is a case where an American citizen is found in a country abroad which was doing battle with the United States. It's not as if there's a lawyer on the street corner who was available at that moment. So, of course, constitutional rights will be obeyed."

"But is he being denied legal help?" asked Helen Thomas of Hearst Newspapers. "Lawyers aren't that few around. You could get one to him."

Moran added, "Should the authorities refrain from interrogating him and placing him in jeopardy of incriminating himself?"

Fleischer did his best to deflect such queries, but they intensified the next day.

"Is Walker considered a prisoner of war?" a reporter asked. "Is he considered a prisoner of war?"

"He is considered, under the Geneva Convention regarding the treatment of prisoners of war, a battlefield detainee," Fleischer said.

"And how is that different?"

"That affords him the protections of the Geneva Convention," the spokesman explained.

"Are we so primitive that we would ship this man in a box, deny him legal rights, deny him the right to see a lawyer, deny him the right to see his parents?" Thomas demanded. "I mean, is that America?"

"Helen, under the Geneva Convention regarding treatment of prisoners of war, the military and intelligence agencies may question prisoners for information," Fleischer said. If the information has "military value" in the "conduct of war," the questioning can be done "without the presence of a lawyer," he added.

"You ship him in a box?" Thomas asked.

"The Geneva Convention is being followed in this case."

"So it trumps his constitutional right?"

"No," Fleischer said. "This is done consistent with the Constitution."

"He can't see his parents?" Thomas said. "He's not allowed to see his parents?"

"He has been given medical care—which he was not receiving under the Taliban," Fleischer said. "And he has received the protection of the United States Armed Forces in a very dangerous battlefield condition."

"And he's being interrogated without a lawyer. Is that fair?"

"He is being given all his rights, which are far more than the rights the Taliban or the al Qaeda extended to anybody living there," Fleischer said.

"Well, we're not comparing ourselves, are we?"

"He is being treated as someone who fought against the United States in an armed conflict," the spokesman said. "And he is being treated well."

The media's sympathy for Walker was even more obvious the next day.

"This is an individual American who is in an extraordinary situation, really," one reporter told Fleischer. "Is he still being deprived of a lawyer?"

"Do you know if he's been Mirandaized?" said another.

"At what point can he have a lawyer?"

"Do you have any knowledge as to whether or not he's able to receive mail?"

"I just wanted to ask you if the president might consider a Christmas-season visit to Walker by his parents?"

Not bloody likely. The president later told me he considered Lindh "a pathetic figure. I was angry at anybody who took up arms against America. But I want to know whether or not he killed the CIA guy, that's what I want to know. I want to know whether he murdered one of our fine citizens."

He added, "Had he done so, we would have thrown the ultimate book at him. But our people, our prosecutors don't feel that's the case."

So Lindh, who was eventually brought back to the United States to stand trial, was instead allowed to plead guilty to being an armed member of al Qaeda, an outlawed terrorist organization. As Lindh accepted his prison sentence of twenty years, his father let reporters know they had been wrong all along. He said his son never claimed to have been mistreated in the slightest by the American soldiers he once fought against.

"A pathetic figure," Bush repeated. "And now he gets to spend twenty years, no parole. And the decision he made puts him away for a long time."

In late autumn, long before this sentence was handed down, Allied forces were completing their rout of the Taliban in Afghanistan. Kunduz, the last major enemy stronghold in the north, fell on November 26. Kandahar, the last stronghold in the south, fell on December 7, although Mullah Muhammad Omar, the head of the Taliban, seemed to slip away in the confusion, and the hunt for Osama bin Laden continued in the cave-riddled mountains near Tora Bora.

But virtually all of Afghanistan had been liberated a mere two months after the American counterattack began. From one end of the bombed-out nation to the other, Afghan men happily shaved their beards and women shed their burkas. Music and television, which had been outlawed, once again blared in streets and homes. Girls were allowed to go to school.

The Taliban's reign of terror, which had begun five years earlier with a multimillion-dollar cash infusion from bin Laden, was suddenly over. This had been accomplished using a force of American ground troops that now numbered just 2,500, a sustained air assault, and a ragtag mix of Northern Alliance soldiers and southern Pashtun tribes. There had been only a handful of U.S. deaths, including three soldiers who were accidentally killed December 5 by an errant American bomb.

In two months, the United States achieved what the Soviet Union had failed to do in a decade—take control of Afghanistan. But unlike the Soviets, America staked no claim to the land it had liberated. On December 5, four Afghan factions met in Bonn and signed a pact creating an interim government. Hamed Karzai, a moderate,

Westernized Afghan who had long opposed the Taliban, was named interim leader. After two decades of bloody warfare that claimed the lives of countless millions, peace finally seemed possible again in Afghanistan.

President Bush marked the sixtieth anniversary of the attack on Pearl Harbor by visiting the USS *Enterprise*, which was docked in Norfolk after a tour of duty in the Afghan conflict. Although he was far from declaring an end to the War Against Terrorism, he derided the scattered Taliban and al Qaeda fighters.

"Not long ago, that regime controlled most of Afghanistan. Today, they control not much more than a few caves," Bush said, drawing raucous laughter and applause from sailors crowded on deck. "Not long ago, al Qaeda's leader dismissed America as a paper tiger. That was before the tiger roared. Throughout history, other armies have sought to conquer Afghanistan, and they failed. Our military was sent to liberate Afghanistan, and you are succeeding.

"We're a long way from finished in Afghanistan. Much difficult and dangerous work is yet to come. Many terrorists are still hiding in heavily fortified bunkers in very rugged territory. They are said to be prepared for a long stay underground. But they are in for a sudden change of plans. Because one by one, we're going to find them. And piece by piece, we'll tear their terrorist network apart."

At 8:46 A.M. on December 11, precisely three months after bin Laden's monstrous act of terror against the United States, Bush stood in the East Room of the White House and implored the nation to remember.

"A great writer has said that the struggle of humanity against tyranny is the struggle of memory against forgetting," he began. "When we fight terror, we fight tyranny; and so we remember.

"We remember the perfect blueness of the sky that Tuesday morning. We remember the children traveling without their mothers when their planes were hijacked.

"We remember the cruelty of the murderers and the pain and anguish of the murdered. Every one of the innocents who died on September the 11th was the most important person on earth to somebody. Every death extinguished a world.

"We remember the courage of the rescue workers and the outpouring of friendship and sympathy from nations around the world. We remember how we felt that day. Our sadness, the surge of love for our country, our anger, and our determination to right this huge wrong.

"Today, the wrong is being righted and justice is being done. We still have far to go. And many dangers lie ahead. Yet there can be no doubt how this conflict will end.

"Our enemies have made the mistake that America's enemies always make. They saw liberty and thought they saw weakness. And now, they see defeat.

"In time, this war will end. But our remembrance never will. All around this beautiful city are statues of our heroes, memorials, museums, and archives that preserve our national experience, our achievements and our failures, our defeats and our victories.

"This republic is young, but its memory is long. Now we have inscribed a new memory alongside those others. It's a memory of tragedy and shock, of loss and mourning. But not only of loss and mourning. It's also a memory of bravery and self-sacrifice, and the love that lays down its life for a friend—even a friend whose name it never knew.

"We are privileged to have with us the families of many of the heroes on September the 11th, including the family of Jeremy Glick of Flight 93. His courage and self-sacrifice may have saved the White House. It is right and fitting that it is here we pay our respects.

"In time, perhaps, we will mark the memory of September the 11th in stone and metal—something we can show children as yet unborn to help them understand what happened on this minute and on this day.

"But for those of us who lived through these events, the only marker we'll ever need is the tick of a clock at the 46th minute of the 8th hour of the 11th day. We will remember where we were and how we felt. We will remember the dead and what we owe them. We will remember what we lost and what we found.

"And in our time, we will honor the memory of the 11th day by doing our duty as citizens of this great country—freedom's home and freedom's defender."

Chapter Thirteen

"George Bush's Recession"

"I DON'T THINK ANYBODY will ever forget the last date we were here," James Carville chuckled in the Mount Vernon Room of the St. Regis Hotel on December 10.

There was an awkward pause.

"When was that?" eighty-six-year-old Budge Sperling finally asked. "I forget."

"Nine. Eleven. Oh-one...?" Carville reminded him.

"I got a cell phone call...?" Bob Shrum added helpfully.

"Ohhh," Sperling said as the memory flooded back.

"It was *something* that we were here," Carville marveled. "We walked in here in one world and walked out in another—*in one hour.*"

Corporal Cueball's prophecy at the conclusion of that hour—*"this changes everything"*—had proven true, at least for a while.

"We held our fire for some time," Stanley Greenberg explained as reporters gorged themselves on yet another free breakfast. "For decency. And unity. And our own sense of, you know, commitment to this effort."

And fear, to be honest about it—although Greenberg didn't mention this particular motivation. Yet it had been Carville himself who explained at the last Sperling Breakfast that Washington "is a city that operates on fear. And the Democrats don't fear Bush." Back then, the Ragin' Cajun observed that Bush had yet to win the support of anyone beyond his own Republican base. "And until he can do that, the Democrats are not gonna be scared," Carville had gloated. Well, Bush was now enjoying the support of virtually every Republican in America and massive numbers of Democrats to boot. In fact, the support was so overwhelming that Democracy Corps—the supposedly fearless cabal of partisan Democratic firepower, forged in the anger of impeachment and Florida—had decided to hold its fire. Only instead of attributing this cease-fire to "fear," it was now giving itself points for "decency."

Democracy Corps's sense of decency lasted exactly sixty-three days. Then, on November 13, it released a controversial manifesto entitled "Politics After the Attack." The document counseled Democrats to praise Bush for his handling of the war against terrorism, but to savage him on the faltering economy.

"With America's nerves very raw, many have suggested that Democrats step back," said the manifesto, issued the day Kabul fell. "But we disagree on the politics of the moment."

The document—written by Carville, Shrum, and Greenberg—urged Democrats not to despair over "the shift of the president's fortunes." The authors assured the party faithful that voters still had misgivings about Bush but were temporarily suppressing them "because they want and need for him to succeed."

"While George W. Bush is popular, voter doubts are close to the surface," they wrote. "We should not give voice to these doubts in this period, but we should be prepared to highlight issues that allow those doubts to emerge later."

On Capitol Hill, Democrats viewed "Politics After the Attack" as a hot potato. For two weeks, they resisted its call to arms. With U.S. forces still battling the Taliban and al Qaeda, Democrats feared it would be political suicide to attack the commander in chief, even on domestic issues.

They were emboldened on November 26, however, when the National Bureau of Economic Research (NBER) announced that America was officially in a recession. Although this group of economists usually waited for two consecutive quarters of decline in the Gross Domestic Product (GDP) before declaring a recession, this time they waited for just one. They also retroactively pegged the recession's starting point to March.

For the next seventy-two hours, Democrats deliberated over whether to attack Bush on the economy. Unnerved by the president's stubbornly stratospheric approval ratings, they finally decided he could no longer be given a free pass. The first shot would be fired by Representative Nita Lowey of New York, chair of the Democratic Congressional Campaign Committee (DCCC), the group dedicated to retaking control of the House. On November 29, Lowey met with journalists from *USA Today* and other Gannett papers to officially break the cease-fire in partisan politics, which had lasted all of seventy-nine days.

"The time is right to make an issue of the just-confirmed recession," Lowey declared. "The bottom line is: This is George Bush's recession."

Lowey unveiled the Democrats' first political ad campaign since September 11, a series of TV spots suggesting it was "unpatriotic" for the president to be cutting taxes at a time when workers were being laid off.

That same day, House Minority Leader Richard Gephardt accused Bush of "mismanaging" the economy. Within twenty-four hours, Senate Majority Leader Tom Daschle added his voice to the rising Democratic chorus.

"We're virtually in a recession. We are facing deficits of a magnitude we haven't seen in many, many years," Daschle said. "And that's a direct result of the Bush policies enacted last spring."

Daschle was referring to the president's $1.35 trillion tax cut, the centerpiece of his economic policy. But Bush did not sign the tax cut until June 7, or three months after the recession began. And it was a ten-year, phased-in plan, with most of the cuts not taking effect until the latter part of the decade. Besides, even if Bush had somehow been able instantaneously to enact the entire $1.35 trillion cut upon inauguration, the notion that he could single-handedly reverse ten years of uninterrupted economic expansion in less than ten weeks of governance was not taken seriously by economists. It takes months and even years for any president's policies to manifest themselves fully on the U.S. economy. Even Democrats acknowledged the slowdown had begun in March 2000, a full ten months before Clinton left office. Although the economy continued to falter for the first eight months of the Bush term, it did not nosedive until September 11.

"Before the attacks, it is possible that the decline in the economy would have been too mild to qualify as a recession," the NBER economists wrote in their declaration of recession. "The attacks clearly deepened the contraction and may have been an important factor in turning the episode into a recession."

With the war and recession so inextricably intertwined, Democrats were taking an enormous risk by attacking Bush on the economy. Hundreds of thousands of airline employees and other workers felt they had been thrown out of work by Osama bin Laden, not George W. Bush. To many of them, blaming the president for the recession was tantamount to blaming him for the terrorist attacks.

Still, Democrats were tantalized by the memory of Bush's father, whose record-breaking popularity after the Gulf War evaporated amid Democratic claims that he let the economy drift into recession while trying to craft a new world order. Inspired by Carville's campaign mantra—"It's the economy, stupid"—Clinton had gone on to vanquish the seemingly unbeatable Bush. He and Gore did it by insisting, right up until election day in November 1992, that America was in the throes of "the worst economy since the Great Depression."

In reality, the economy had begun expanding in March 1991— nearly two full years before Clinton took office. But whenever this was pointed out during the 1992 campaign, Clinton and the press (89 percent of whom voted for him) retorted, "Tell that to the poor guy who's out of work and is struggling to feed his family." The NBER didn't exactly help matters. It waited until the month after the election to officially announce the recovery, retroactively pegging its starting point to March 1991. These economists, who normally declared an expansion after two consecutive quarters of GDP growth, had waited until deep into the seventh consecutive quarter to acknowledge the turnaround. By then, of course, it was too late for the elder Bush. In the ten weeks between Clinton's election and inauguration, the press lauded the economic expansion as if it were a wholly new creation. Some news accounts even attributed the turnaround to the psychological impact of Clinton's victory.

In February 2000, when the expansion broke the old record of 106 consecutive months, set in 1969, Clinton and Gore bragged about presiding over the longest boom in U.S. history. But to make this claim meant taking credit for the recovery that had begun roughly midway through the elder Bush's term. The only newspaper that bothered to point this out was the *Washington Times*.

The younger Bush, who worked on his father's 1992 campaign, never forgot this injustice, which he believed cost "41" the White House.

"The economy was recovering as he lost the election, but people didn't know it," George W. Bush wrote in his memoirs. "Bill Clinton managed to convince people, I think unfairly, but nonetheless convincingly, that he had a plan to improve the economy but my father did not."

The Democrats now sought to argue that the ten-year "Clinton-Gore" expansion was bookended by Bush recessions. As far as the Democrats were concerned, the only element needed to complete the son's reenactment of the father's failure was a flip-flop on taxes.

"There's an old taboo in American politics that goes back to Ronald Reagan now, which is: You can never say postpone a tax cut; you can never say cancel a tax cut," Shrum said.

"Ask George Bush," said Carville, referring to "41."

"It's just unthinkable, can't be done—that's what Bush thinks from his father's experience," Shrum continued. "But the truth is that post-September 11th—even though that may not be the reason why the tax cut's bad—post-September 11th, people are very ready to say we ought to cancel it, we ought to postpone it."

The strategists hoped that such a flip-flop, combined with the recession, would kill Bush's popularity regardless of how well he prosecuted the war.

"We have real-life, historical experience—the Persian Gulf War," Greenberg said. "The numbers drive up, and then they go back toward the original position, the default position. I'm confident that these numbers have driven up to their highest point."

"Can you attack this president directly on the economy now?" asked Sperling.

"Sure," Carville said. Why not? Of course you can."

"You can attack his tax cut," he added. "Let me try: This tax cut, that this president supported, was a bad idea. And we oughta delay it or get rid of it. It's a bad idea, it's bad policy, it's bad economics. Now there it is. I just did it. Guess what?

"Whoops, there's Ashcroft!" Carville joked. "Cuff me, cuff me! Hit me, hit me! Am I giving Omar—or whatever it is—am I giving him solace by saying that this tax cut's a bad idea? Cuff me, baby!"

The Ragin' Cajun laughed diabolically as the reporters cut glances at one another and chuckled. Liberal columnist Mark Shields demanded to know why no Democrats had called for "holding the tax cut in abeyance." Nor had Democrats denounced the tax rebate checks mailed out over the summer.

"It took a David Broder column—I mean, David Broder's not queen of the bomb-throwers," Shields said. "Could I ask you why the Democrats have been so timid? I mean, they haven't made that a central issue. What is it? Are they cowed by the numbers?"

"They're trying to get their footing here, okay?" Carville said. "We've been a little slow here, but I think we're starting to find our footing."

The Ragin' Cajun became even more defensive when a journalist invoked the name of his former boss—Bill Clinton.

"There's a lot of talk in Congress about having hearings to find out why 9/11 happened and who was responsible," the reporter said.

"Do you guys fear that there's a hidden vulnerability of the Clinton administration?"

"Why would there be a vulnerability of the Clinton administration?" Carville said. "I don't understand. What was the difference between the Clinton administration and the Bush administration up to 9/11?

"I don't know of any difference," he added. "Let's see: The counterterrorism director? No, it's the same one Clinton had. Wait, the CIA director—that must be it. No, come to think of it, that's the same one. Gee, uh—"

"The military," Greenberg interjected. "Different military?"

"Yeah, different military?" Carville said.

"The Republicans aren't gonna listen to me, but they ought to let this go," Shrum added. "The country has no interest in going back, in my view, and bashing Clinton. But ever since 1992 it's been their favorite sport. And it's their reaction to everything."

Greenberg agreed.

"People moaned in the focus groups on trying to explore responsibility—and that goes beyond the Clinton question," he said. "That includes the CIA; that includes intelligence failures. People were proud of the fact that we had united as a country. They thought that made us strong, rather than weak. They thought that the investigative side of this served no purpose, that going back in history served no purpose. It would weaken the country."

"What are you gonna say about this president and the way he's handling the war?" Sperling said.

"That he's doing a good job," Carville replied. "We've got a team on the field; I wanna win the game. We'll deal with the coach's contract in 2004."

Although Carville vowed not to criticize the president's prosecution of the war publicly, he couldn't resist noting that historically, such criticism has paid handsome political dividends.

"Look, Franklin Roosevelt lost a ton of seats in 1942," he said. "Fifty! And guess what? The Republicans attacked him! You know that? And after Pearl Harbor! And you know what was happening in the war? We were in bad shape. That was the zenith of Axis expansion. And guess what? They attacked him. We have the First Amendment."

But not even the First Amendment could embolden Democrats to speak out against Bush's handling of the war against terrorism. Shrum felt it was hard enough just getting them to challenge the president on domestic issues.

"The Democrats just have to be bold enough to say what they're doing, what their reason is, and to stand their ground," he said. "And you win the debate. You don't win the debate if the debate's not held."

Carville agreed, saying Democrats could learn a lot from the fierce unity of Republicans.

"We just don't look tough enough," he moaned. "America will never trust a party to defend it that won't defend itself. And I think there's a real good case to be made for the fact that we have to hit back and hit hard—and we don't do that. They do that a lot better than us."

Francine Kiefer of the *Christian Science Monitor* now posed a question.

"You all point out that terrorism is still a top concern, but it's receding and the economy is taking over as the top concern," she said. "Why is terrorism receding? Why is that fading?"

"One, I suspect that in people's individual lives, there's less personal fear," Greenberg ventured. "And two, I think there's a sense that the administration and the country is handling this well."

In fact, the strategists hoped Bush's strong performance on the war would be his undoing on the domestic front.

"There's a kind of interesting one-way ratchet here," Shrum explained. "To the extent that the administration does well in this war, and to the extent that it does well on security, the concern over terrorism recedes and the attention goes back to other issues. And the alternative to that, by the way, is not thinkable."

"Yeah, I think it's good politics to win this war—and fast," Carville translated. "It's good for Democrats. I'm all for it. I'm cheerin', man—let's have the parade."

"And you're for it on patriotic grounds too, James," Shrum reminded his colleague.

"Right, right," Carville added perfunctorily.

"If there's a definitive moment—bin Laden's captured or there's some definitive moment of victory—I think the shift back to domestic terrain will probably be a little bit more dramatic," Greenberg said. "If the conflict there goes on, then it's a different situation."

While an ongoing conflict would shoot down Greenberg's hopes for a swift return to domestic priorities, he tried to look on the bright side: it might also herald a return to the era of big government.

"If it goes on like we really are in a new Cold War, we have to wage a whole different kind of conflict," he said. "But the Cold War produced highway programs, education programs, to-the-moon programs, produced a whole range of things that were related to that war. I don't know what this produces. What I do know is that people think it's a new, serious moment, requiring lots of serious expenditures—you know, military, domestic security, other domestic needs."

When a reporter asked about the politics of the John Walker Lindh case, Carville played up the man's youthfulness. Still, not even the

Ragin' Cajun could fathom how the Taliban held any allure for the youth of America.

"All right, they get drugs—it's kind of around the school or something. Or sex—you can kind of understand how a seventeen-year-old, eighteen-year-old gets involved in that kind of thing, or whatever. How in the hell do you get involved with the damn Taliban?" he said, drawing laughter from the reporters. "I mean, it's not like they're recruitin' you out there, or somethin'. Heh-heh-heh. I mean, it's an extraordinary journey. I mean, I never—I mean, most parents don't worry about their kids goin' off with the Taliban, you know what I mean?"

"Uncle Omar needs you!" cried Shrum amid much merriment.

Sperling tried to wrestle the discussion back to more serious matters.

"I can remember during the campaign and over at the convention," he said. "We talked about Mr. Bush at that time, what kind of a candidate and guy he was. And as you saw him—and maybe a lot of other people too—as a rather second-rate candidate with a rather second-rate mind. Certainly not a great leader or anything. Hasn't he surprised you a little bit?"

"Sure," said Shrum. "Oliver Wendell Holmes, when he met Franklin Roosevelt, described him as a first-rate temperament and second-rate mind. I don't know whether that was a fair description or not. Roosevelt was certainly an extraordinary leader.

"This crisis came to the president. And the president has, on the whole, over an extended period of time, reacted very well in terms of terrorism and security and handled the thing very well," he added. "I don't think any of us are going to dispute that."

"But did that surprise you?" Sperling pressed. "Isn't this a little bit of a different guy, though, than you thought was going to be in there?"

"I don't know that if you had presented this scenario to me, I would have said that he would not have handled this well," Shrum said. "In fact, I think, basically, he and Al Gore would have done exactly the same things about the September 11th attacks."

"Hasn't he become a rather formidable political force now?" Sperling asked.

"Sure," Shrum acknowledged.

"He's not a political force on domestic issues," Carville interjected.

"Prior to September 11th, there was not a single Democratic gathering where you didn't hear that George Bush thinks fettuccine Alfredo is a place in Italy," Shields added to journalistic laughter. "I mean, they all said this disparaging and minimizing stuff. And now the stature gap is permanently closed."

"I agree with that," Shrum said. "Look, in our last poll, 48 percent of the people believed he was not up to the job of being president—that's gone. People think he *is* up to the job of being president. That doesn't mean that they want to vote for him or vote for his domestic priorities."

"I don't know how to make it any clearer," Carville said. "He's doing a good job on the war. The Democrats ought to support him on the war. That doesn't mean that this translates into support for his domestic policies."

"But has he surprised you?" Sperling persisted. "That's what I asked."

"Has he surprised us? Yes," Carville said. "He's doing better on the war than I would have suspected under the circumstances. I don't think it's like a total surprise—I never thought he would be a bad American or anything. And he's doing probably worse on economic and domestic issues than I would have thought."

"Now that the stature gap is closed, hasn't that hurt Gore?" a reporter asked.

"No," said Greenberg. "Given his experience as vice president and experience with the military, I think he could be helped by it."

Another reporter made the mistake of referring to Gore as "the person who lost the electoral vote to Bush."

"No," Carville insisted. "He didn't lose it."

"Excuse me?" the reporter said.

"Clearly, he didn't lose it," Carville said. "He lost a count that was stacked against him."

But even the journalists weren't eager to rehash yet again the Florida recount wars. Mark Shields took the conversation to the broader swath of American history.

"From 1940 to 1990, basically the job description of the president began with commander in chief," he said. "From FDR to Ike and all the way through, you had to have that credential. It ended with the end of the Cold War. I mean, Bill Clinton could win in 1992 with a rather spotty military record."

"And so could George Bush," said Shrum, equating Clinton's draft dodging and Vietnam protests to Bush's service in the Texas Air National Guard.

"And so could George W. Bush in the year 2000," Shields agreed. "But I mean, isn't it a distinct possibility that in 2004, George W. Bush now meets the commander in chief test? He's been there and been commander in chief—in a plausible sense. Is it a distinct possibility that in 2004, Democrats better have somebody who meets that?"

"Democrats won a lot of elections between 1940 and 1990," Carville said. "But I think you're right. I agree that the threshold for both parties, on the issue of commander in chief, is raised beyond what it was in 2000."

Of course, September 11 had raised something much more profound in America, although Carville wasn't sure it could last.

"Historians are going to have an interesting time with this period in American history, because we all wanted to believe that people would line up to volunteer for the armed forces, or there were going to be fewer divorces, or more people were going to church, or there was just something rolling across the country," he said. "And yet the more evidence that rolls in, the more people's lives, in some ways—"

But he trailed off without finishing the sentence. Not even the Ragin' Cajun could bring himself to rain on America's parade of patriotism and purpose—at least not in front of the press.

"I think a lot of things have changed since September 11th," Corporal Cueball concluded. "I don't think *everything* has changed."

Chapter Fourteen

Bob Beckwith, Celebrity

BOB BECKWITH, NOW SEVENTY, was every bit as trim as he had
been when he first joined the New York City Fire Department at age
thirty-two. So he had no trouble whatsoever fitting into his "dress
blues" uniform, which is what he was wearing when he walked into
the West Wing on February 25. The White House had called the old-
timer weeks earlier and invited him to an Oval Office ceremony. The
bullhorn from Ground Zero was going to be turned over to a father-
son exhibit at the elder Bush's presidential library in Texas.

"I says sure, I'll come," Beckwith recalled. "That's very nice,
thank you. Can I bring my—well, I have nine grandchildren, and I
knew I was pushin' it then—but I asked them, could I bring one of
my sons? They said yes. I said could I bring my daughter? They said
yes. I said could I bring my daughter's husband? He's a fireman in the
Garden City Fire Department. And two of my grandchildren? They
said okay.

"And so we went down and I stayed at my sister-in-law's in Maryland and then the next morning we went to the White House. We
went through security—the bomb-sniffin' dog, the whole bit. I parked

right on the grounds. I was in uniform and I went into the West Wing with my family.

"This one's gonna rip you," Beckwith told me. "I walk in—I'm nobody, right?—I walk in and these eight guys are comin' down and walkin' out a door maybe fifteen feet away from me. And I'm lookin' at this one guy. And he turns and he looks at me and he comes over and he says, Nice job, Bob. And he shakes my hand.

"You know who it was? *Donald Rumsfeld!* A busy man like that comes over to shake my hand. Isn't that awesome?"

Indeed, Rumsfeld had been a busy man. Although it had been eleven weeks since the liberation of Afghanistan, the defense secretary had increased the number of U.S. troops on the ground in an effort to maintain order while the fledgling Afghan government took shape. There were still pockets of Taliban and al Qaeda resistance that periodically engaged the Americans in dangerous firefights. The United States had apprehended 158 of these fighters and brought them to a detention camp in Guantanamo Bay, Cuba. Mistakenly believing the press would applaud the capture of terrorists from an organization that had perpetrated the most heinous attack against America since Pearl Harbor, the Pentagon released photographs of the prisoners kneeling on the ground with hoods over their heads—the hoods being a temporary security precaution in transporting men who were trained killers. The European press, however, went ballistic, seizing on the photos as evidence of U.S. "torture." Not to be outdone, the American press assailed Rumsfeld with yet another barrage of inane questions at a Pentagon press briefing on January 22, just days after two marines were killed in a helicopter crash in Afghanistan.

"You say these prisoners are being treated humanely," scoffed NBC's Jim Miklaszewski. "That's certainly not the perception in some quarters. Is there a concern that the U.S. will somehow lose the high moral authority in this war on terrorism by the treatment of the detainees?"

The high moral authority! As if the killers who had snuffed out the lives of some three thousand innocent men, women, and children on that perfect day in September were remotely capable of seizing the high moral authority from the United States of America. How profane! Such effrontery! And yet Rumsfeld kept his cool.

"Well, I guess I think the truth ultimately wins out, and the truth of the matter is, they're being treated humanely," he replied. "You know, it's perfectly possible for anyone to stand up and say, 'Henny Penny, the sky's falling, isn't this terrible what's happening?' and say that; and have someone else say, 'Gee, I view with alarm the possibility that the sky's falling!' And then it gets repeated. And then some breathless commentator repeats it again. And then it goes on for three days. Now, does that make it so? No. At some point does the air come out of that balloon? You bet."

In the upside-down world inhabited by the Pentagon press corps, Rumsfeld felt compelled to explain why the U.S. forces were the good guys and al Qaeda forces were the bad guys. He also found it necessary to remind the reporters that the prisoners, when you got right down to it, never had it so good.

"The more than 150 detainees have warm showers; toiletries; water; clean clothes; blankets; regular, culturally appropriate meals; prayer mats and the right to practice their religion; modern medical attention far beyond anything they could have expected or received in Afghanistan; exercise; quarters that I believe are something like eight-by-eight and seven-and-a-half feet high; writing materials; and visits by the International Committee of the Red Cross.

"These men are extremely dangerous, particularly when being moved, such as loading or unloading an aircraft, buses, ferries, movements between facilities, movements to and from showers and the like. During such periods, the troops, properly, take extra precautions. Lest we forget, in Mazar-i-Sharif, the al Qaeda prisoners broke loose in a bloody uprising. They killed one American and they killed a number of Afghan troops, and some prisoners were carrying grenades under their clothing."

In case the memory of CIA agent Johnny "Mike" Spann's death was not enough to shame the media, Rumsfeld added, "At least one detainee now in Cuba has been threatening to kill Americans. Another has bitten a guard. This is not wonderful duty. It's difficult duty. To stop future terrorist attacks, we have detained these people, and we have and will be questioning them to gather additional intelligence information."

Incredibly, the reporters began grousing that there was no air-conditioning for the prisoners.

"As you know, in a few months it's going to be very, very hot down there," said AP reporter Thelma LeBrecht. "And there is going to be more complaints about them being held in open conditions like that."

Rumsfeld was stupefied.

"I don't know how many times I've been to Guantanamo Bay, but it's a lot, and it frequently was in the summer when I was a Navy pilot, and that was back in the days before air-conditioning," he said. "And it's just amazing, but people do fine. I mean, there are a lot of people in Cuba with no air-conditioning. I know that will come as a surprise. But I was in Washington before there was air-conditioning and *the windows used to open!* It's amazing!"

Another reporter whined: "I grew up in South Florida, and my mom never turned on the air-conditioning, and I'm here to tell you it was torture."

"Would you please refrain from using that word?" Rumsfeld pleaded. "Look at you! You've survived admirably."

"Yeah, I moved up north," the woman muttered.

Reuters, the London-based news agency that banned the word "terrorist," ran a story that was openly skeptical of Rumsfeld's insistence that the prisoners were being treated humanely in Cuba. "He did not mention the disease-carrying mosquitoes on the Caribbean island," the story sniffed.

"I'm used to people, the elite in Europe, hollering about my administration," Bush told me later. "People don't understand we're at war and these are killers."

He added, "I knew that if anybody ever took the time to find out the facts, they'd find we don't torture people. And as far as whether or not they've got air-conditioning, I like that argument. I represent the American people, that's who I represent. I'm leading a nation which is willing to make sacrifices necessary to win a war for freedom and for civilization itself.

"You know, I learned some lessons, one great lesson from Ronald Reagan: When you speak, you speak to the people. You don't worry about a cadre of elites. So that's my constituency—particularly the American people. People are making great sacrifices in this war. So I know what their attitude is. You know, sitting around saying, 'Are we going to get them air-conditioned cells for people who just tried to destroy America and/or kill three thousand Americans?' isn't going to fly."

One American who did not have air-conditioning was Beckwith, which was perhaps why he was hitting it off so well with Rumsfeld. As the two men chatted in the West Wing, Beckwith's family noticed Colin Powell climbing into his limousine and departing the White House.

The secretary of state had been every bit as busy as Rumsfeld in recent weeks, although the two were not always on the same page. In fact, Powell disagreed with Bush's January 18 decision, which was supported by Rumsfeld, to classify the prisoners in Cuba as "battlefield detainees." Powell, along with human rights groups and left-leaning European politicians, wanted them classified as prisoners of war, which would give them greater rights under the Geneva Convention. He was worried that America's enemies would retaliate by capturing GIs and denying them full rights under the Geneva Convention.

"The secretary of state has requested that you reconsider that decision," White House Counsel Alberto Gonzales wrote in an internal memo to Bush on January 25.

A copy of the memo was obtained that same day by Pentagon reporter Rowan Scarborough, who reprinted it the next morning on the front page of the *Washington Times*.

"The memo provides a rare glimpse of a major dispute inside the Bush White House on what has become one of the most contentious issues in the war in Afghanistan," Scarborough wrote. "Mr. Powell wants the president to reverse his position. But Mr. Gonzales and most, if not all, members of the president's national security team are urging him not to retreat, according to the memo."

The *Times* also reprinted a memo from National Security Advisor Condoleezza Rice to Powell, Rumsfeld, Cheney, and other top administration officials, asking for their opinions and alerting them that the dispute would be discussed with Bush at a meeting of the National Security Council.

The story sent shock waves through the rest of the media world, which for months had been trying to portray Powell as the administration's odd man out. The premise had been explored in numerous speculative thumb suckers, none of which were supported by any hard evidence. Suddenly that evidence materialized in, of all places, the *Washington Times*. The memos were a veritable smoking gun. The *New York Times* seized on Scarborough's story as evidence of a rift that had existed all along. But the truth of the matter was that on most major issues involving the war against terrorism, Powell and Rumsfeld and Bush pretty much agreed with one another.

Chief among these was a shared aversion to the Vietnam model of warfare. Bush and his lieutenants were loath to send soldiers into battle hamstrung by onerous political considerations. Sure, there were political considerations to the war against terrorism. But the president felt he and Powell could manage them through aggressive diplomacy. That would allow Rumsfeld maximum flexibility to execute the military mission—namely, blasting the Taliban to kingdom come.

The night before Scarborough's story broke, Bush watched the film *Black Hawk Down*, which graphically recreates the killing of eighteen American soldiers by Somalis linked to Osama bin Laden. The scenes of jubilant Somalis dragging a dead GI through the streets of Mogadishu repulsed Bush. But a scene that recreates the planning meeting for that fateful 1993 mission repulsed him even more.

"I had requested light armor and AC-130 Spectre gunships," Major General William Garrison tells the soldiers just before sending them into battle. "But Washington, in all its wisdom, decided against this. Too high-profile. So Black Hawks and minibirds will provide the air cover."

"No Spectre gunships," muttered one of the soldiers after the meeting. "Down on the street, it's unforgiving."

Bush shook his head in disgust when recounting this scene to Ari Fleischer as they choppered from Camp David to the White House later that weekend. That a commander requesting armor from Washington could be turned down for political reasons disgusted Bush's sense of priorities; if Bush sent men into harm's way, he wanted them to have the military hardware they needed. Clinton, like Bush, had been warned that too much firepower might roil the "Arab street" in the larger Muslim world. But Bush, unlike Clinton, had discounted such warnings and given his defense secretary carte blanche to prosecute the war.

When Rumsfeld finished talking with Beckwith in the West Wing, he turned the fireman over to Karl Rove. It had been Rove who told Beckwith to jump up and down on the crushed pumper at Ground Zero and ordered him to climb down as soon as the president climbed up. Now Beckwith and Rove reminisced about that fateful day when Bush exclaimed, "I can hear *you!*"

At the conclusion of that electrifying speech, Bush and Beckwith had a brief conversation as the crowd chanted "USA! USA!"

"You been pretty busy the last coupla days," the old-timer remarked to the president.

"Yeah," Bush replied. "You know it."

"Well, don't get yourself sick over this," said Beckwith, who later reproached himself for presuming to advise the most powerful person on the planet.

"Who am I to tell the president what to do?" he muttered. "I didn't even like it when those ironworkers were calling him by his first name. I thought it was very disrespectful, myself. I'm seventy years old, and when I was brought up, you respected people."

After Bush departed the scene, Beckwith remained perched on the pumper for a few moments. Spotting New York Governor George Pataki right in front of him, the old-timer tapped him on the shoulder in order to say hello. But instead of shaking Beckwith's hand, the governor turned around, grabbed him around the legs in a bear hug, and picked him up off the pumper.

"You're gonna hurt yourself," Beckwith cautioned.

"Not me," said Pataki as he placed the fireman gently on West Street.

Pataki, like everyone one else on the scene, had been energized by the president's call to arms.

"I tell ya, there wasn't a guy out there that wasn't floatin' two feet off the ground," Beckwith recalled. "He really gave us the shot in the arm that we needed. Nobody said anything, but everybody went right back to work."

Actually, Beckwith's return to the bucket brigades did not last long.

"I'm goin' back to work and I get a tap on the shoulder," he said. "I turn around and it's a Secret Service guy. He says, The president's been lookin' for you. I look at him and I says, The president's been lookin' for me? What's the president been lookin' for me for? What'd I do? He says, He wanted you to have this flag."

The agent handed Beckwith the small American flag that Bush had waved at the conclusion of his remarks. Beckwith didn't know it at the time, but a photo of the president brandishing the flag in one hand and embracing the old fireman with the other would make the cover of *Time* magazine. Beckwith never noticed the news cameras amid the throng of chanting hardhats. Oh, there were a couple of print reporters who came over to him afterward and asked him to spell his name. But Beckwith was confident they would never go to the trouble of actually publishing it. He assumed the scene with Bush had been largely a private moment for the rescue workers. Any press coverage would surely focus on the president's inspirational remarks, not some old-timer who happened to be standing around.

"He gave it to me and I says, Gee, that's nice. And I roll it up and stick it in my back pocket. But then I think to myself, Why am I goin' back to work? Somebody's gonna cop this thing outta my pocket while I'm workin' or I'm gonna break it. So I says, Ahh, it's gettin' late and I'm a little tired. And I'm fightin' with myself—should I go back to work? And I says, Nah, I'm not goin' back. It's like 5:30 at night and I'm kinda beat anyway, so I figure maybe I should start moseyin' home. I got the flag and I start to walk back to the firehouse, which is about ten, eleven blocks. And all these things were goin' through my head. I walk all the way back to where my car is. And I throw my gloves against the hydrant that I see down there, 'cause they were, you know, touchin' parts, and I don't want to bring that inside.

"And I go back and I pay my condolences to the night crew there, and I thanked them for lettin' me park there. I went outside and I'm lookin' at the candles—it was the day people came out with candles—and they had the pictures of their four firemen that were killed.

"And I'm drivin' home, and I'm sayin' to myself, Who the hell's gonna believe that I was with the president today? I'm gonna get home and tell my kids that I was with the president. But my kids ain't gonna believe me.

"Anyway, I get home and I pull up into my driveway and the neighbors are comin' outta their houses, carryin' candles. The women and the guys are comin' out and they says, Oh, we saw you. And I says, What are you talkin' about? They says, We saw you on the television. I says, Get outta here.

"And then a guy across the street, a cop, comes over, shakes my hand and says, Aww, thanks a lot, Beck, for goin' down—they call me Beck—thanks a lot, Beck, for goin' down.

"They're sayin' thank you to me. And I said, How did yas know? They said, Ya kiddin? You were on television. And I said, There was no TV cameras there.

"And then I came in. And since my wife didn't know if I was comin' home that night, she didn't make supper. So we went out to a diner.

"And they had it on TV in the diner. And people were lookin', 'cause I was still in my scroungy clothes. And people came over to me and were talkin'. They said, Wow, thanks for goin' down. You're an old-timer and you went down. And they were very nice. And a guy comes over to me and says, Aren't you the guy on TV? And I says, yeah. And they ripped up my check."

Bob Beckwith began to realize that his life had been bifurcated. There was the old phase—those sixty-nine years of growing up in New York City, joining the Navy, toiling for UPS and the fire department, hustling side jobs as a window washer and a house painter, getting married, raising kids, becoming a grandfather, and retiring in relative anonymity. And then there was this new phase of his life, which entailed being something of a—well, celebrity.

From the minute Beckwith's weather-beaten face appeared on TV, the phone never stopped ringing in his modest little saltbox-colonial out on Long Island, the one with the wrought-iron bench chained and padlocked to a tree in the front yard. When he and his wife Barbara were away, the messages piled up on the telephone answering machine, the old-fashioned kind that still used a tape recorder. One was from the wife of a Florida retiree named Buddy who had worked with some of the Cantor Fitzgerald employees killed in the World Trade Center.

"We've gone through a helluva week," the woman said on the tape, which Barbara couldn't bring herself to erase. "So many people that

Buddy knew. Worried about my own sons—and they're fine. And when we see Bob on TV, I can't tell you what it does for us. Thank you."

Beckwith, who spent the next several days working at Ground Zero, found himself recognized by more and more strangers on the streets of New York. Some even knew his name.

"They said, Aren't you Bob Beckwith, the guy with the president? Thank you for what you did. I says, What are you thankin' me for? There's eight thousand guys down here."

Eventually, the firemen at Ground Zero agreed with Beckwith's family that he was too old to be digging through the smoldering heap, which they simply called The Pile. They told him to instead attend the funerals and memorials of the firemen, 343 of whom had been killed in the attacks. Beckwith acquiesced and began showing up at two or three services a day. After a while, they all seemed to run together in a nightmarish blur of sorrow and depression. When he confided to a fellow old-timer that he was growing weary of this endless parade of death, the man reproached him and pointed out that these firemen had given up their very lives. How could anyone complain about something as trivial as fatigue? So Beckwith apologized and kept going to the funerals. He fantasized that one day he would wake up and discover that it had all been a bad dream. But of course that never happened.

Meanwhile, he was finding his new status as a celebrity unsettling.

"What happened was, after September 11, after the meeting with the president, people called me up—*Good Morning America*, Diane Sawyer, Rosie O'Donnell. I turned 'em all down. I didn't want to get involved in any of that kinda stuff. I'm a retired old man. People don't know me.

"So a friend of mine in Manhattan calls me up and says how come you're turnin' 'em all down? I says, I don't need it. She says look, I'm gonna have a friend of mine from Harvard University call you and talk to you about it. So this guy calls me up and says, I understand you're turnin' down everything and you're a little depressed right now. But if you don't go on these shows, someone's gonna go in your place."

Beckwith decided to give it a try. He granted a live TV interview to John Seigenthaler on MSNBC.

"I was a nervous wreck," he recalled. "I'm not a public speaker. But every time you do it, it gets a little easier."

He was more relaxed for an interview with David Asman on the Fox News Channel. He was starting to get the hang of the routine.

Before long, Beckwith was granting interviews to news organizations all over the world. He and his wife were flown several times to Europe, where they got the star treatment, complete with limousines and first-class accommodations. Several German news networks offered him $6,000 for appearances, but he told them to send the money directly to the New York Firefighters Burn Center Foundation. Beckwith began giving speeches and fundraisers on behalf of the charity. Elected officials in Ireland gave him the VIP treatment. He was given the key to a city in Mississippi. He was asked for autographs when he appeared at New York schools to talk to students. He was mortified to begin receiving things called "courage awards."

"I tell ya, I got newspapers from Israel, I got newspapers from Japan, comin' over my house to take pictures," he said. "I just don't want it goin' to my head."

During one interview, he mistakenly explained that the man who had asked him to help the president up on the fire truck was a Secret

Service agent. He later received a tongue-in-cheek letter from Karl Rove, thanking him for the compliment. Rove invited Beckwith and his wife Barbara to the White House. Then he received a phone call from a West Wing aide inviting him to attend the bullhorn ceremony at the Oval Office on February 25.

And now here he was talking with Rove in the West Wing. His wife, Barbara, was chatting with White House Counselor Karen Hughes. Their daughter, Christine, was exchanging greetings with Attorney General John Ashcroft. Christine's husband, Peter, was talking with General Richard Myers, chairman of the Joint Chiefs of Staff. Beckwith's son, Bobby, was over in the corner, chatting with EPA Administrator Christie Todd Whitman. Over there was National Security Advisor Condoleezza Rice. And there was White House Press Secretary Ari Fleischer.

Beckwith couldn't believe the scene all around him. Here he was with his family in the White House, hobnobbing with the most important people in government. Not bad for a guy whose dad warned him against ending up on the Bowery.

By and by, he was ushered into the Oval Office.

"Bob, you made me famous that day," President Bush joked as the old-timer walked in.

They shook hands in the center of the room, directly beneath the presidential seal, which was set in low relief into the ceiling. Then Bush gave the Beckwith family a guided tour of the most famous office in America. Above a gray marble fireplace hung a portrait of Washington in his Continental Army uniform. Off to one side was a portrait of Lincoln, the great emancipator. Bush took particular pride in an oil painting of a horseman charging up a rough trail. The painting, by Western illustrator W. H. D. Koerner, is *A Charge to Keep*, a phrase Bush liked so much that he used it as the title of his memoirs. The president then pointed out the oval rug beneath their feet, a custom-woven masterpiece that spread like cream in every direction, nearly to the edges of the hardwood floor. He explained that every president designed his own rug and that he, along with Laura, had come up with this particular design, an uplifting pattern of sunbeams emanating from the presidential coat of arms in the center.

The same coat of arms had been carved, at FDR's request, into the kneehole of an imposing oak desk that Bush now used as the nerve center for his ongoing war. The desk was hewn from the timbers of the HMS *Resolute*, a ship recovered by American whalers in the Arctic in 1855. It was a piece of furniture so richly carved, so luxuriously detailed, that it practically begged you to run your fingers over it. The eagle on its coat of arms clutched thirteen arrows in one set of talons and an olive branch in the other. From the raptor's beak fluttered a banner proclaiming "E Pluribus Unum"—from many, one. Bush explained that this was the desk in the famous photograph of President Kennedy working while his toddler son, John-John, scampered through the kneehole. It was also the desk used by Ronald Reagan.

"I don't know why my dad didn't choose it," Bush remarked. "It's a beautiful desk."

The president then posed for group and individual pictures with the seven members of the Beckwith family. They chatted for a while as the room began to fill up with various people, including Governor Pataki, who had hoisted Beckwith off the fire truck, and his wife, Libby. When Ari Fleischer showed up, the president decided this would be a good time to show his visitors the White House press corps.

"Let the press pool in," Bush commanded.

A slightly curved door that blended seamlessly into the wall suddenly opened. In walked a dozen journalists, schlepping cameras, boom microphones, lights, cables, stepladders, tape recorders, notebooks, and anything else they seemed capable of carrying. When they were done rustling and rooting and banging around, the president stood by his desk and began to speak.

"Listen, I want to—I want to welcome Bob Beckwith to the Oval Office, and his wife, Barbara, and his two grandchildren and son and daughter who are here, and son-in-law.

"As you may remember, I met Bob on the heap of a burnt-out fire engine in New York. And he didn't know and I didn't know that we were going to meet on that day, and I had—I was traveling there with George Pataki and Rudy Giuliani and it was my chance, after the National Prayer Service, to go to New York City and tell the good people of that town, that city, how the nation stood with them. I had a chance to go and see the firefighters and the police officers who had been giving every ounce of their energy to rescue their fellow citizens.

"And I was given a bullhorn. And it turned out to be one of those moments where I had a chance to speak to the world on behalf of the citizens of New York. And Bob was standing there by my side. I told Bob when he came in, You made me famous that day. But I want to thank you, Bob, for coming back."

Bush then talked about the fate of the famous bullhorn.

"There's a father-and-son exhibit that's going to go on at the Bush Library, Bush 41 Library, at Texas A&M, and this will be one of the key parts of the exhibit. It's an historic, really an historic memento. Something we didn't choose, but it's one of those days that I'll never forget, and I want to thank you."

"I'll never forget," Beckwith said.

"It was an amazing experience," Bush said. "You know, I didn't realize at the time that you and I walked up on the heap of a burnt-out fire engine. I didn't realize that. And what's interesting, as a result of that, some people in Louisiana saw us standing on the fire engine and went and raised money for a new fire engine for New York. So that event had a lot of interesting ramifications."

Pataki presented the bullhorn to the president, who then fielded a series of unremarkable questions from the press, which was eventually herded back outside. When the curved door was finally shut, Bush spent some time talking with Beckwith's grandchildren and even wrote a note to Joe Clancy, the boy who had been clipped by a car on September 11. Today just happened to be Joe's fifteenth birthday.

"Happy Birthday," Bush wrote on a piece of White House stationery. "A day you'll never forget."

"Are you gonna write us absentee notes?" Joe asked after Bush handed him the birthday greeting.

"Huh?" Bush said.

"Oh, we took off school to be here today," said Joe's eleven-year-old sister, Megan. The girl had initially been nervous around the president, but now was completely at ease.

"And I guess that requires a note from me," said Bush, who opened a drawer in the Resolute desk and took out some more paper.

Using his black Sharpie marker, Bush wrote notes to the children's teachers, explaining that they had spent the day with the president and asking for them to be excused. Libby Pataki suggested the kids turn in photocopies of the notes and keep the originals for their scrapbooks. Joe would explain his absence the next day to a history teacher, who sighed, "Well, now I've heard everything," before being shown the note.

"Why don't we go see the Rose Garden outside?" Bush said after writing the notes and chatting with Beckwith some more.

They stepped outside and the First Arborist pointed out the trees that had been planted by various presidents. Then he pointed to the residence and explained where he and Laura lived.

"That's where my wife's sitting room is," he said, pointing to a window. "And there's Laura's office. And over there is the kitchen. Well, we don't really use it much."

"Where are your dogs?" Megan asked.

"They're taking their morning nap," Bush replied.

The president pointed out the prototypes of hybrid electric cars on the driveway of the South Lawn, where they were parked for an event promoting alternative energy sources. He told Megan he would like to see such cars sold by the time she was old enough to drive.

At length, an aide came over and said the president had another meeting. So the Beckwiths bade goodbye to Bush and departed the Oval Office. Bob went to a bank of microphones in the driveway of the North Lawn, known as the stakeout, to answer a few questions from reporters. He was getting used to being a media personality. While he was talking, the rest of the family gathered in an office of the West Wing and watched themselves in the background of Bush's chat with the press, which was now being shown on TV. Afterward, the Beckwiths drove away.

"He spent about forty-five minutes with my family," Beckwith marveled. "I mean, we're at war and he found time. What a gentleman."

"Isn't that unbelievable?" he added. "And the rest is history."

Chapter Fifteen

"Bush Knew"

THREE DAYS AFTER BOB BECKWITH'S visit to the White House, Senate Majority Leader Tom Daschle became the first major Democrat to openly criticize the president's prosecution of the war against terrorism. Ignoring the advice of Carville, Shrum, and Greenberg—who were still urging Democrats to limit their criticism of Bush to domestic policy—Daschle told reporters the president's war lacked direction, was too open-ended, and would be a failure unless the top Taliban and al Qaeda leaders were captured. It was a direct challenge to the administration's insistence that the war's scope was so broad that its success or failure could not be measured by the fate of any individual terrorist. "We've got to find Mohammed Omar, we've got to find Osama bin Laden, and we've got to find other key leaders of the al Qaeda network, or we will have failed," the South Dakotan declared. "We're not safe until we have broken the back of al Qaeda. And we haven't done that yet."

Daschle was skillfully exploiting the public's unease about the fate of bin Laden. The terrorist appeared gaunt and perhaps injured in a videotape that was aired on Al-Jazeera in late December. But he was alive, wasn't he? The tape showed him gloating some more about the September 11 attacks and taking responsibility for the 1998 bombings of U.S. embassies in Africa. Defiant even in defeat, he vowed: "If I live or die, the war will continue."

Ironically, Bush couldn't agree more. Although he wanted bin Laden killed or captured, the president was not about to let the terrorist's fugitive status preclude the administration from prosecuting the war in other parts of the world. The Pentagon had already sent advisors to the Philippines and other nations to train local armies on how to fight domestic and international terrorism.

Besides, in an odd way, the lack of information about bin Laden's status had an up side for Bush. It allowed him to continue prosecuting the war without being accused of overkill. Bin Laden's elusiveness merely added to his mystique as the shadowy "Evildoer," a mythical figure of such unspeakable malevolence that he might even strike again. As long as this monster remained at large—amid sketchy reports of sightings and ominous hints of more videotapes—the public was not about to withdraw its support for the war. Greenberg himself had said it best: The capture of bin Laden would be seen as a "definitive moment of victory," which would be followed by a dramatic shift in the public's focus away from the war and onto domestic policies, precisely the terrain on which Bush was most vulnerable.

But Daschle had grown impatient waiting for such a moment to arrive. Democrats had been attacking the president on domestic issues for three months—ever since Nita Lowey broke the cease-fire in partisan politics by announcing "George Bush's recession"—and had gained precious little traction. The press and public remained stubbornly focused on the open-ended war. Democrats were concerned that White House adviser Karl Rove was herding congressional

Republicans onto a "war platform" for the mid-term elections. With Democrats clinging to a one-vote edge in the Senate, Daschle was not about to wait around until some strategist told him it was finally safe to criticize the president on the only subject that seemed to matter—the war. So he pronounced it a failure. The blowback from Republicans was swift and severe.

"How dare Senator Daschle criticize President Bush while we are fighting our war on terrorism, especially when we have troops in the field," said Senate Minority Leader Trent Lott, Mississippi Republican. "He should not be trying to divide our country while we are united."

House Majority Whip Tom DeLay was even more blunt. The Texas Republican issued a statement containing exactly one word: "Disgusting."

Daschle's criticism turned out to be badly timed. Two days later, American soldiers launched their biggest ground assault of the war—Operation Anaconda—against hundreds of Taliban and al Qaeda troops who had massed in eastern Afghanistan for a last, desperate counterattack against allied forces. Almost immediately, tragedy befell the Americans.

"It was very tough terrain," Bush told me. "We lose a soldier—a SEAL comes out of the back of a chopper that's trying to take off. Our rule as Americans: We value every life. We send the men back in to get, to pick up the body, and lose seven more."

He added of the Taliban, "But they've lost hundreds." The pride in the president's voice was unmistakable.

Suddenly, Daschle's criticism seemed terribly unpatriotic. Under mounting pressure to retract his words, he hastily crafted a resolution declaring that the Senate "stands united with the president in the ongoing effort to destroy al Qaeda." His flip-flop made the front page of the *Washington Times* on March 6, the day Carville, Shrum, and Greenberg addressed yet another Sperling Breakfast. It prompted Shrum to complain that Republicans were intentionally stifling dissent.

"The reason why, whenever a Democrat starts to do it, they go into a full court attack mode, is because they want to deter Democrats from doing this," he said. "Their whole strategy is to have a kind of quiescent Democratic Party."

He added, "They lose on domestic issues if we're out there arguing in a serious, substantive, big-idea way. They know that. And so what they want to do is conflate the support for the war into support for the president and Republicans generally. And our challenge is to separate those two—to be able to support the war, support the president on the war, but also stand up for the things we believe in."

Carville fretted that the president's stubbornly persistent popularity was paralyzing the Democratic Party.

"Do you think people in the party have been intimidated by President Bush?" a reporter asked.

"Yes," Carville muttered. "Yes. Of course I do. You'd have to be an *idiot* to think otherwise."

The Ragin' Cajun's frustration was understandable. After all, according to the polls, Bush had passed James Carville's test of successful politicians—namely, winning the support of at least some people from the opposition party. The Gipper had rounded up "Reagan Democrats" in places like Macomb County, Michigan. Clinton had wooed "soccer moms" from traditionally Republican suburbs. And now Bush was garnering the support of a new species of swing voter—post-terror patriots. People like Gwendolyn Tosé-Rigell, the black school principal in Sarasota who initially considered the president a "phony." People like Bob Beckwith, the old fireman at Ground Zero, who had supported Democrats all his life but now planned to vote for Bush in 2004. No question about it. The president was winning over large numbers of Democrats who had voted for Al Gore. Before the war against terrorism, it was the "one thing Bush has never been able to do," Carville had bragged to the reporters at that fateful Sperling Breakfast on September 11. Now these same reporters were throwing it back in his face.

"Why have they been so reticent?" one of them asked about Democrats.

"They've always been that way; there's nothing new. We got run over in Florida," Carville groused. "I have no idea. It's, it's, it's—it's part of the genetic composition of being a Democrat!"

When I asked Bush about Carville's definition of a successful politician and my own theory about "post-terror patriots," he sought to frame the issue in a context larger than politics.

"What the American people want at this point in history is somebody who knows where to lead, somebody who's got a vision. And I've got a vision of peace based upon a plan to fight those who want to take our freedoms away from us. I think it's a leadership issue. I think that's what the people want. In times of war, they want somebody to lead. And in order to lead, I think you have to speak real plainly and clearly."

He added, "'Axis of evil' is pretty clear. 'Saving the world from weapons of mass destruction' is clear. 'History has called us into action' is a clear statement."

Ironically, the very quality that had once made Bush such a ripe target for ridicule—his Texan plain spokenness that some regarded as simplistic—was now resonating with a public starved for moral clarity.

"Some find it not diplomatic to speak 'good and evil,'" the president told me. "I don't know how you say this the right way: I feel like I represent how the American people feel. It doesn't matter whether you're Republican or Democrat. I'm not talking about how they do their politics; I'm talking about how they feel instinctively.

"And the American people know that these are evil people. And I think they appreciate a president saying that. And they also know that if we're tough and strong, that we can achieve some incredible good. There's a great optimism about the American people that's true and real. And they want somebody to call upon the better instincts and somebody to lead that optimism."

Democrats like Carville couldn't help noticing that the war against terrorism had enabled Bush to shake his reputation as a foreign policy lightweight. The man who was once mercilessly mocked for not being able to recite the names of foreign leaders was now considered a respected and formidable player on the world stage.

"Argentina now has its fifth president in two weeks," Jay Leno cracked on the *Tonight Show*. "Hey, I have a little advice for the people over there in Argentina: Give your guy a chance. Sometimes when we elect a new president, he doesn't turn out to be as dumb as he originally appeared to be."

With even late-night comics now praising instead of mocking George W. Bush's intellectual firepower, things were looking desperate indeed for the Democrats. Perhaps that's why they waited just over a month after Daschle's ill-fated comments to resume their attack. In early April, Congresswoman Cynthia McKinney, a hard-left Democrat from Georgia, called for an investigation into whether Bush had advance notice of the September 11 attacks and simply let them happen.

"We know there were numerous warnings of the events to come on September 11th," she told a Berkeley, California, radio station. "What did this administration know and when did it know it, about the events of September 11th? Who else knew, and why did they not warn the innocent people of New York who were needlessly murdered?"

She added ominously, "What do they have to hide?"

Incredibly, McKinney insinuated that the attacks were allowed to proceed so that Bush's big-business cronies could engage in war profiteering.

"Persons close to this administration are poised to make huge profits off America's new war," she asserted.

When the *Washington Post* called her office for an interview, McKinney refused. But she issued the following statement: "I am not aware of any evidence showing that President Bush or members of his administration have personally profited from the attacks of 9/11. A complete investigation might reveal that to be the case."

Fellow Democrats treated McKinney as if she had leprosy. Surely no other Democrat was kooky enough to endorse such a ludicrous conspiracy theory.

But on May 15, the press seized on the revelation that Bush had been told in his morning CIA briefing on August 6 that al Qaeda might be planning to hijack U.S. jetliners. There was no inkling of when these hijackings might occur. Moreover, there was no clue that the terrorists would turn the planes into missiles against American landmarks—an almost unimaginable evil, outside the realm of thriller fiction, in the pre-September 11 world. Taken in the context of the deluge of vague threats the administration received from all over the globe on a daily basis, the generalized indications that al Qaeda might be planning to hijack U.S. jetliners were roughly akin to generalized indications that the sun might rise in the morning. Still, the press went into a feeding frenzy. CNN's Judy Woodruff took an enormous leap by baldly asserting, "President Bush knew that al Qaeda was planning to hijack a U.S. airliner and he knew it before September the 11th." The Associated Press put out a breathless dispatch headlined, "Bush Was Warned of Hijacking Plot."

On May 16, ABC's Charlie Gibson began *Good Morning America* by suggesting Bush had been downright negligent.

"It may put the president under a lot of heat today as the public learns that he knew, through his daily CIA intelligence briefings, that bin Laden had potential terror attack plans underway," Gibson said. "It also calls into question what happened when Andy Card, Andrew Card, the White House chief of staff, that morning went and whispered in the president's ear, as the president was talking to a group of school students in Florida. Was the President really surprised?"

A second plane hit the second tower. America is under attack. The press was now insinuating that Bush had been *expecting* Card's stunning words all along. Paula Zahn opened CNN's *American Morning* by crowing, "The White House admits the terrorist attack on 9/11 was not a complete surprise." Over at CBS, Bryant Gumbel wanted to know, "How embarrassing to the president? How injurious to the administration?" Katie Couric, like virtually every other news anchor, opened ABC's *Today* show by invoking the specter of Watergate.

"What did he know and when did he know it?" she railed. "The Bush administration admits the president was warned in an intelligence briefing last summer of the possibility that Osama bin Laden's terrorist network might hijack American planes, raising more questions about whether the attacks on America could have been prevented."

The press was throwing around ominous phrases like "could have been prevented" and loaded words like "admits" because they implied wrongdoing. *What did he know and when did he know it?* The sacred battle cry from the Holy Grail of American journalism— Watergate. Words that seemed so ludicrously conspiratorial when uttered by Cynthia McKinney a mere month earlier were now on the lips of every major news anchor in America.

"What did the president know and when did he know it in the days before 9/11?" NBC's Tom Brokaw demanded at the top of his newscast that evening. "At the White House tonight, it is all hands on deck as the administration tries to cope with a storm of criticism."

Over at CBS, anchorman Dan Rather demanded to know "why the president never shared what he knew with the public."

Reporters began to piece together disparate shreds of intelligence that, when viewed with the benefit of hindsight, suggested Bush had dropped the ball. They discovered that an FBI agent in Phoenix had written a memo in July warning that al Qaeda members might be training in U.S. flight schools.

The agent, Kenneth Williams, later testified that he never envisioned the kinds of attacks that were carried out on September 11. He insisted that none of the information in his memo could have possibly allowed investigators to prevent the attacks. But no matter. The media hounds were in full battle cry. They linked this FBI memo, along with the president's CIA briefing, to the report on al Qaeda that the administration had prepared for Bush to read when he returned from his education trip to Florida. Although journalists had known about the existence of this detailed briefing paper for months, they suddenly began reporting it as if it were the very Pentagon Papers.

Peter Jennings hyperventilated on ABC, "All over the country today people are wondering whether the White House knew more about the possibility the country would be attacked by Osama bin Laden's terrorists."

On May 16, 2002, New York Senator Hillary Rodham Clinton marched to the floor of the United States Senate and brandished a newspaper with an enormous front-page headline that screamed: "BUSH KNEW." A scant eight months after the most heinous terrorist attacks in history killed three thousand innocent men, women, and children, an influential member of the Democratic Party was lending credence to an excitable media's conspiracy theory that the president of the United States had advance knowledge of this unspeakable evil and did nothing to stop it. Clinton realized she was taking a major political risk. Carville, Shrum, and Greenberg—the men who had saved her husband's bacon more times than she cared to remember—were still advising Democrats to praise Bush on the war while criticizing him on the economy. But that was getting harder to do. The Gross Domestic Product had declined in exactly one quarter—*the one in which the terrorists struck*—and then grown in the two subsequent quarters, which was the textbook definition of recovery.

Hillary Clinton assumed that with the media attacking Bush on his handling of September 11 and its aftermath, it was finally safe for Democrats to do the same. The major media players couldn't all be wrong, could they?

Actually, they could. The next day, on *Inside Washington*, Evan Thomas of *Newsweek* admitted the "what did he know and when did he know it?" story was "phony" and "bogus."

"The media beast was so happy to have a scandal here, that we jumped up and down and waved our arms and got all excited about it," he said.

"Well, that's because the media beast thinks—the media beast is starting to worry it's giving a pass for too long," said Nina Totenberg of NPR. "It really is a secretive administration."

Amazingly, these influential journalists were admitting on TV that the press had invented a monstrous story insinuating the commander in chief could have stopped the terrorist attacks. Why? Because reporters were tired of giving Bush a "pass" on the war and were shamelessly "happy to have a scandal."

Totenberg went a step further by acknowledging the press was leading Democrats around by their noses on this story.

"Nobody in the political establishment said, 'What did they know and when did they know it?' That was us in the media," she confessed.

"It was us," Thomas agreed.

"It really was us," Totenberg concluded.

But these mea culpas came a day too late for Clinton, who had already leveled her enormous accusation against the president on the floor of the United States Senate. Such was the media's power of suggestion over the Democratic Party. It had prompted a high-profile senator to embrace a newspaper that had long savaged her (the *New York Post*), ignore the advice of her party's most trusted strategists, and lend credence to an accusation that was unthinkable when those planes first slammed into the World Trade Center, the Pentagon, and a field in Pennsylvania—"BUSH KNEW."

"The president knew what?" she demanded. "My constituents would like to know the answers to that and many other questions. Not to blame the president or any other American. But just to know. To learn from our experience."

Bush aides were livid. They couldn't believe that in a mere eight months, things had come full circle. Back on September 11, members of Congress stood on the steps of the Capitol and sang "God Bless

America" in a bipartisan display of national unity. And now a leading Democrat was on the Senate floor, insinuating the president had advance knowledge of the most heinous assault on America in generations. Although White House Press Secretary Ari Fleischer normally eschewed political paybacks from the podium of the James S. Brady briefing room, he made an exception in Hillary's case.

He compared her unfavorably with New York Mayor Michael Bloomberg, who had telephoned the White House to be disabused of the offending headline's veracity.

"I have to say, with disappointment, that Mrs. Clinton, having seen that same headline, did not call the White House, did not ask if it was accurate or not," Fleischer told reporters. "Instead, she immediately went to the floor of the Senate, and I'm sorry to say that she followed that headline and divided."

Fleischer made it clear that Hillary had gone too far.

"I think that anytime anybody suggests or implies to the American people that this president had specific information that could have prevented the attacks on our country on September 11th, that crosses the lines," he said. "I don't think that's a fair thing to say. And I think the American people will be very wary of any politician who seeks to turn the sorrow of victims into their own political gain."

Bush agreed.

"It bothered me," he told me. "What bothered me was the fact that somebody would be so irresponsible and kind of stirring up a bunch of wonderful Americans that somehow I wouldn't have done what was necessary. Yes, it bothered me.

"I also understand how the news cycles work. Bits of news kind of churn through our system quite quickly," he added. "It wasn't the truth. The truth is what really matters, and I think the American people understand that."

No wonder the president had mixed feelings about the press. Oh, he was disciplined enough to engage reporters in ironic, good-natured banter whenever possible. But he made no attempt to hide his suspicion that the media were fundamentally biased against conservatives. In fact, when former CBS journalist Bernard Goldberg published a tell-all book exposing the liberal leanings of network news, Bush made a point of carrying it around in full view of the White House press corps. Aware that he would be photographed from his right side as he walked across the South Lawn one day, Bush carefully clutched Goldberg's book in his right hand so that its prominent title, *Bias*, would be captured by the cameras. He later acknowledged, "Sometimes, when a president holds a book, it promotes sales." Indeed, *Bias* became a runaway bestseller.

The president was even more explicit about his disdain for the press ten days after the "BUSH KNEW" incident. During a joint press conference with French President Jacques Chirac in Paris, NBC's David Gregory asked Bush, "I wonder why it is you think there are such strong sentiments in Europe against you and against this administration? Why, particularly, there's a view that you and your administration are trying to impose America's will on the rest of the world, particularly when it comes to the Middle East and where the war on terrorism goes next?"

Turning to Chirac, Gregory added in French, "And, Mr. President, would you maybe comment on that?"

"Very good," Bush said sardonically. "The guy memorizes four words, and he plays like he's intercontinental."

"I can go on," Gregory offered.

"I'm impressed—*que bueno*," said Bush, using the Spanish phrase for "how wonderful." He deadpanned, "Now I'm literate in two languages."

Roars of laughter filled the ornate Palais de l'Elysée.

"So you go to a protest, and I drive through the streets of Berlin, seeing hundreds of people lining the road, waving," the president continued derisively. "I don't view hostility here. I view the fact we've got a lot of friends here. And I'm grateful for the friendship. And the fact that protesters show up, that's good. I mean, I'm in a democracy. I'm traveling to a country that respects other people's points of view. But I feel very comfortable coming to Europe; I feel very comfortable coming to France. I've got a lot of friends here."

"Sir, if I could just follow—" Gregory began.

"Thank you," Bush shot back dismissively, cutting off the question.

Chirac then continued this extraordinary, public dressing-down of a high-profile network correspondent.

"These demonstrations are really marginal demonstrations," the French leader scolded. "You shouldn't give too much credit to these demonstrations. They do not reflect a so-called natural aversion of such-and-such a people in Europe to the president of the United States or to the U.S. people as a whole."

Chirac said the bond between America and Europe is "an increasingly important relationship, and it would be the sign of shortsightedness to refuse to acknowledge that."

After Chirac completed his rebuke of the reporter, he concluded the press conference.

As Bush stepped away from the podium, he called to Gregory, "As soon as you get in front of a camera, you start showing off."

During that same European trip, Bush and Vladimir Putin signed the Treaty of Moscow, an agreement to slash the nuclear arsenals of the United States and Russia by two-thirds over the next decade. Although Democrats and the press had long warned that Bush would spark a new arms race if he insisted on unilaterally withdrawing from the 1972 Anti-Ballistic Missile Treaty in order to build a missile defense shield, precisely the opposite occurred. Bush pulled out of the treaty and then took unilateralism a step further by pledging to reduce America's nuclear stockpile—no strings attached.

"It's hard to have an arms race when you have one of the main competitors saying, 'We're going to reduce our arsenal by a significant number,'" the president told me. "I mean, an arms race requires two people. And had he chosen to go through an arms race, he would have been the winner. On the other hand, we had enough nuclear warheads on missiles to protect ourselves."

The gamble paid off. Putin voluntarily offered to match Bush's move by slashing Russia's nuclear arsenal. He also agreed, after much cajoling from his American counterpart, to mute his criticism of Bush's withdrawal from ABM. Bush later shrugged off my suggestion that these historic developments had been accelerated by the war against terrorism.

"I said in the campaign: Elect me, the ABM Treaty is over. The ABM Treaty was over the minute I swore in as president," he insisted. "My first meeting with Vladimir Putin, I told him, I said, 'Vladimir, we're out of the ABM Treaty—that's no longer an issue. But you have to know, you need to be comfortable with that because you're not our enemy. And so let's get rid of this thing that says we're enemies.' And that's when we started the discussion about where to go from there."

Bush acknowledged that it took a few of those discussions to bring Putin on board. He also agreed that Democrats and the press had a much milder reaction to his abrogation of the ABM Treaty than had been widely expected. He mischievously attributed this collective yawn to the liberals trusting Putin, a former Communist, more than they trusted the American president.

"I one time facetiously told Putin," he revealed to me, " 'there's a handful of United States senators who trust your judgment on the ABM Treaty more than they trust mine.'

"That's kind of a unique aspect of democracy. And so those who are likely to object to removal of the ABM Treaty took their cue not from me, but from Putin."

Bush said once the Russian president was on board, liberal Democrats could no longer squawk about the death of ABM.

"If he'd been raising heck about it, then it might have had a different resonance," Bush marveled, "amongst a handful—not many—in our own country, and Europe."

Prior to September 11, Democrats had ridiculed Bush for naively gushing about gazing into the "soul" of Putin, a former KGB agent. But it turned out that Bush had been quietly enlisting Putin in his effort to mitigate Democratic opposition to the abrogation of the ABM Treaty.

The irony was nothing short of exquisite.

Chapter Sixteen

"How Great Presidents Are Made"

A PAIR OF CHINOOK TRANSPORT helicopters appeared over the tree line and swooped down on a vast plain of mowed grass, disgorging a platoon of heavily armed soldiers dressed in tan desert fatigues. The infantrymen fanned out and hurled their bodies to the ground, taking aim with high-tech rifles as the choppers lifted off and disappeared over the horizon. Moments later, a pair of Black Hawks materialized over the other end of the field, carrying howitzers on long steel cables. They deposited these big guns on the grass as teams of artillery soldiers hustled over to swing the massive barrels in the direction of the trees. Each howitzer was fired three times, emitting clouds of white smoke that hung languidly in the humid summer air. Then the artillery soldiers, dressed in green camouflage fatigues, turned and began sprinting across the field. The infantrymen jumped to their feet and began running as well. They converged and formed a neat semicircle, two soldiers deep, around a man they believed had earned the title of commander in chief.

President Bush clearly enjoyed this military exercise, which replicated the movement of troops in Operation Anaconda. Many of these soldiers had helped destroy the Taliban in Afghanistan before redeploying here to Fort Drum, the sprawling military base in upstate New York. All those months of difficult and dangerous duty now seemed worthwhile to these members of the storied 10th Mountain Division as they got to shake hands and exchange a few words with the president himself. When the last man had been greeted, Bush stepped back to address the entire group on this, the 312th day of the war against terrorism.

"I'm proud of you guys," he said.

"Hoo-ah," the soldiers said in their all-purpose expression of approval.

"The enemy made a bad mistake."

"Hoo-ah!"

"They didn't understand you all. They didn't understand us."

"Hoo-ah!"

"We're staying after them," Bush concluded, "until we get all of them."

"HOO-AH!"

The president headed for another field, this one jammed with thousands of black-beret-wearing soldiers and their family members. He shucked his suit jacket and rolled his sleeves halfway up his forearms before stepping behind the presidential podium, known as the "blue goose." It was July 19 and he was less than twenty-four hours away from completing his first eighteen months as president.

"Can't imagine what the enemy was thinking," Bush mused. "They must have thought we were so weak, so feeble a nation that we might, after September 11th, file a lawsuit or two."

It was a point he had been making for months, sometimes by saying the enemy must have formed its impression of America by watching the *Jerry Springer Show*, which celebrated the depraved and dysfunctional.

"They didn't understand what I know—the character and the strength and the courage of the men and women of the United States military," he said, drawing wild applause.

"This war came upon us suddenly," the president said. "Within days, you stepped forward to guard against further attacks on the homeland. Within weeks, soldiers from Fort Drum were guarding bases in Uzbekistan and moving in to defeat a brutal regime in Afghanistan.

"You fought beside our allies in cold and rugged terrain, against trained and resourceful killers. You met the enemy half a world away in its own element. Yet the terrorists discovered no bunker could protect them—"

A roar of applause filled the air.

"—darkness couldn't conceal them—"

Another roar.

"—and there was no cave deep enough to save them."

The soldiers cheered wildly, even when the president warned them that they might be deployed to new hot spots.

"In some parts of the world, there will be no substitute for direct action by the United States. That is when we will send you, our military, to win the battles that only you can win," Bush said. "We're prepared for any enemy—any enemy of freedom."

"Let's get Saddam!" a soldier hollered.

Bush smiled wryly at this reference to Iraqi dictator Saddam Hussein as the soldiers cheered again. He counseled patience to these gung-ho fighting men.

"This new war is going to take some time. We're in this for the long haul," he said. "We fight against a shadowy network that hides in many nations and has revealed its intention to gain and use weapons of mass destruction."

This was a reference not only to Iraq but also to Iran and North Korea, which the president had long ago collectively branded an "axis of evil"—much to the consternation of the press.

"We're threatened by regimes that have sought these ultimate weapons, and hide their weapons programs from the eyes of the world—the same regimes that have shown their true nature by torturing and butchering their own people.

"These tyrants and terrorists have one thing in common. Whatever their plans and schemes, they will not be restrained by a hint of humanity or conscience.

"The enemies of America no longer need great armies to attack our people. They require only great hatred, made more dangerous by advanced technologies.

"Against such enemies, we cannot sit quietly and hope for the best. To ignore this mounting danger, is to invite it. America must act against these terrible threats before they're fully formed. We will use diplomacy when possible, and force when necessary. We will prepare deliberately and act decisively.

"Our commitment should be clear to all, to friend and enemy alike: America will not leave the safety of our people, and the future of peace, in the hands of a few evil and destructive men."

This was Bush's way of explaining what amounted to a sea change in U.S. foreign policy—proactively attacking enemies before they could attack America. The president viewed this as crucial not just in a strategic sense, but also for humanitarian purposes.

"In this war we fight against the advance of terror, and its agents, we also fight for the advance of freedom and human dignity. We do more than oppose an ideology of violence and hatred. We offer a vision of democracy, a development that can overcome resentment and despair in every part of the earth.

"Seldom have the ideals of freedom been under greater threat. Seldom have the ideals of freedom had greater appeal.

"This nation, this generation, you all have been entrusted with the ideals and with their defense. This is a charge we bear. This is a charge we shall keep.

"As we prepare our military for action, we will protect our military from international courts and committees with agendas of their own. You might have heard about a treaty that would place American troops under the jurisdiction of something called the International Criminal Court.

"The United States cooperates with many other nations to keep the peace, but we will not submit American troops to prosecutors and judges whose jurisdiction we do not accept.

"Our nation expects and enforces the highest standards of honor and conduct in our military. That's how you were trained. That's what we expect. Every person who serves under the American flag will answer to his or her own superiors, and to military law, not to the rulings of an unaccountable International Criminal Court," he declared.

The crowd convulsed with wild cheering and applause. Crawling into caves after terrorists was difficult enough without having to worry about being subjected to some sort of anti-American starchamber. The Bush administration had threatened to withdraw peacekeeping troops from Bosnia and other hotspots unless the United Nations permanently exempted American soldiers and diplomats from the tribunal, which began operations July 1 in The Hague. Although the White House later softened its demands and contented itself with a patchwork of temporary exemptions, the effect was the same. The court couldn't touch Americans.

"Your duties will take you many places, and some places you and your fellow soldiers may be the only representatives of justice and order," Bush said.

"As members of our military you will stand between American citizens and grave danger. You will stand between civilization and chaos. And you will stand for liberty and tolerance and truth, the ideals of America and the hope of the entire world.

"Soldiers of the 10th Mountain Division, and men and women of the armed forces, I'm honored to serve with you. This is a decisive moment in the history of freedom.

"As your commander in chief, I leave you this message: Be proud, be strong, and be ready. May God bless you all, and God bless America."

The president's last words could barely be heard above the din of the crowd. Soldiers who had faced death in Afghanistan lunged forward and shouted their praise of the president. Bush descended from the stage and worked the perimeter of the crowd, shaking hands until he finally extracted himself and headed for the motorcade.

Back on Air Force One, he settled behind his desk in his cabin near the front of the plane and munched red grapes from a plate on the window ledge. He motioned for me to sit down across from him for the last in a series of extensive interviews about September 11 and its aftermath. During our talks on Air Force One and in the Oval Office, Bush reflected on the momentous events that had shaped history and bifurcated his presidency.

He covered a lot of ground in these sessions. He began by taking me back to September 10, to the dinner with his brother Jeb and their political supporters at the Colony Beach & Tennis Resort on Longboat Key, Florida. He recounted the laughter and conversations they shared on that last night of innocence. He spoke wistfully about the predawn jog with "Stretch" on September 11, the way he felt "purged" by the glorious Florida humidity. He recalled the drive to Emma E. Booker Elementary School in the Sarasota ghetto. The rapid-fire reading drill in the second-grade classroom. The way he could *sense* Andy Card approach before actually seeing him.

"I feel his presence out here," the president recalled, gesturing with his right arm. "And I kind of look over. And he whispers in my ear."

America is under attack.

Three years earlier, Bush had begun his memoirs by writing, "Most lives have defining moments. Moments that forever change you. Moments that set you on a different course. Moments of recognition so vivid and so clear that everything later seems different."

Certainly this had been one of those moments for George W. Bush.

"I'm talking too much," the president remarked after a while.

And yet he seemed determined to recount each event in as much detail as possible. He vividly described images that stuck in his mind during those first frantic hours. Like the way well-wishers, unaware of the tragedy, blithely lined the roadway to smile and wave at their president as he was hustled to the Sarasota airport. Or the sight of F-16s appearing off the wings of Air Force One during that frenetic hopscotch of the nation. Or his wife's inability to see without her contact lenses during the late-night dash to the White House bunker.

Bush reconstructed crucial turning points and moments of high drama in the days after September 11. That first, tearful cabinet meeting. The emotional prayer service at the National Cathedral. The surreal visit to Ground Zero. The electrifying encounter with Bob Beckwith and the hardhats. The wrenching session with the lost souls at the convention center. The way Arlene Dillon pressed her son's police badge into his hand. The fact that he still never travels without it.

The president also spent some time looking back on his administration's response to the terrorist attacks.

"Everybody had a task to do," he said. "And they did it brilliantly. I think, in retrospect, when you look back, history will say, Wow, these people did their job.

"Secretary Powell's job was to assemble a coalition, and he did. And bringing, by the way, Pakistan into the coalition, which was a significant move. A lot of people—I think if you would have said before September 11th: Gosh, would the United States and Pakistan be able to work together? No way.

"Secretary Rumsfeld's job, of course, was to prepare—pick a commander and prepare to move," he recalled. "Rumsfeld had no problem saying, Tommy, you're it. He trusted him and developed a plan quickly."

Bush also seemed to take some measure of satisfaction in proving his naysayers wrong.

"You've got to remember, Bill, that a lot of people were saying, You can't fight a conventional war in Afghanistan. Nobody else had been able to do it," he said. "It looked easy, in retrospect. But we understood the degree of difficulty."

He added, "We had a military strategy that was really well thought out. And it was the ability to win a guerrilla war using conventional forces—something nobody else had been able to do."

Having just witnessed a partial reenactment of Operation Anaconda, the commander in chief reflected on the historical significance of that battle, which claimed eight American lives in a single tragic incident. But hundreds of Taliban and al Qaeda fighters were also killed because they made the mistake of massing for a conventional battle instead of splitting up and waging guerrilla warfare.

"Operation Anaconda was like a counterattack on their part. They foolishly grouped up. They bunched. They were going to make this 'We'll show them.' And we *hammered* them," Bush recalled. "People will need to look back at that battle. It was a significant American victory—and a coalition victory—in a very tough terrain."

It also significantly changed al Qaeda's battle strategy from that day forward, which, in turn, changed America's strategy.

"They're wiser now. There's not as many of them and they realize if they clump up we're going to get them," the president explained. "The nature of the hunt has kind of shifted, but it still goes on."

He added, "I don't know if the press fully understands when I say we're hunting people down one by one. That *is* the strategy. That's *what's happening*. And, therefore, I'm not so sure a lot of people who follow this—including some of the American people—understand the nature of the war."

Bush explained that while the routing of the Taliban resulted in "thousands of people captured and thousands of others dead," even greater numbers were still on the loose. He said between 50,000 and 100,000 people had been trained in the terrorist camps set up by Osama bin Laden's al Qaeda network over the years. But it was almost impossible to determine how many of those trainees turned out to be "hardcore al Qaeda" and how many ended up drifting away from the cause.

"It's kind of interesting," he told me. "If thousands have been captured and thousands have been killed, you're wondering how many are left. And, of course, that depends upon how many of their soldiers are the kind of people that these young packs that will maybe train, but turn out to be, you know—need to go back to their mothers.

"So the fundamental question is—and the story that's hard to tell is—how many of the al Qaeda seniors are loose? And where are they and how come we haven't heard from them if we don't have them? And that's a hard story to report, I readily concede."

But, he added, "The role of the president is to educate the people about the realities of our day. I've got a lot of work to do. I've got to constantly remind people."

He was especially keen about reminding people that victory in Afghanistan is not the same as victory in the larger war against terrorism.

"This is the first battle of a lot of other battles. It's a good one to get behind us," he told me. "The first battle is to get rid of the Taliban and we did it. We destroyed a lot of al Qaeda."

But he cautioned, "The liberation of Afghanistan is not complete yet, because we've still got a government to worry about; we had a vice president recently assassinated; we've got many clamoring for international peacekeepers all over the country of Afghanistan. As you know, my position is we don't need any more targets of opportunity for people that are still very dangerous that we need to go get first. As well as we need to help Afghanistan train her own army. And we've got quite a ways to go to get to that part of the liberation."

Bush said he understood that deployed soldiers and their families can sometimes feel that the war is taking "forever." "But we've only been fighting a war, the first war of the twenty-first century, a war of chaos versus civilization—and I believe those words; I'm not exaggerating—we've been at it for ten months. There's no telling where the next battlefields will be. As a matter of fact, we are engaged in other battlefields."

He rattled off a list of nations where U.S. forces are training local armies to root out terrorists—places like Yemen and the Philippines.

"Today we've got troops training in Georgia. And there are some pretty bad characters in Georgia. It may seem insignificant to most Americans, but it's pretty darn significant, I can assure you, to those troops—American troops in Georgia."

The president added that while Americans are cognizant of the continued threat of terrorism, it was normal for them to eventually return to their pre-September 11 lives.

"They're all not going to go into the fetal position," he told me. "We're a courageous people."

When I asked if he feared another attack, Bush said, "Do I fear it? Yes. I worry about it; I'm concerned about it. Yes."

But he was less concerned that such an attack would be personally orchestrated by Osama bin Laden.

"Do you hate him?" I asked the president about bin Laden. "Do you think of him as a formidable adversary? What are your thoughts?"

"That's an interesting question," Bush said. "Well, first of all, let me answer your question this way: I don't hear much from him. And neither does the world. I remember right after the attacks there was all this speculation about how people would rally around this man. And now he's nothing, as far as I'm concerned."

Bush talked of bin Laden's "sense that it's okay to kill in the name of false religion and kill in the name of truly tyrannical thought. And that's how I view him. I view him as one of a group of misled, misguided killers."

He added, "I don't believe we can rehabilitate them. I don't believe we can negotiate with them. I know that we're going to run them down. They are misguided people who have hijacked a great religion."

The president was indeed covering a lot of ground in these interviews. But throughout the process, I kept thinking back to that chilly December morning when he was showing Tommy Franks around Prairie Chapel Ranch as a pair of turkey buzzards circled overhead. Like many journalists, I was still vexed by the question of how much the events of September 11 had changed George W. Bush.

Chris Matthews, the hyperkinetic host of CNBC's *Hardball*, tackled the subject while interviewing presidential historian Michael Beschloss.

"Many have made the comparison—me included—that he's gone from being a kind of a Prince Hal to Warrior King Henry," Matthews said. "He's grown up—maybe not overnight—but he's certainly a grownup now. Tell me about, historically, do you think he has?"

"No, I think these qualities were always there," Beschloss countered. "It's just the era now that really brings out the things that are really wonderful about him. . . .

"You know, Franklin Roosevelt was wonderful in the '30s and the '40s—economic depression, World War II. He would have been a disastrous president of the 1920s, when the people didn't want a president to do very much.

"In George Bush's case, this is a guy who's decisive, knows how to call on talent, feels comfortable not being the person who knows the most in the room about a particular subject. And also, when he talks, you don't hear pollsters in the background; you don't hear consultants.

"This is a guy who means what he says. That helps to get the American people to follow him. Also, it helps him to warn our enemies that worse things could be ahead."

Matthews, a Democrat who previously worked for President Carter and House Speaker Tip O'Neill, hinted that Bush's anti-intellectual image was an asset for the war against terrorism.

"This war we're fighting now, both at home and abroad against the terrorists—al Qaeda and all the rest of them—isn't some intellectual's war," he said. "It's not some pencil-neck's war thought up by think-tank people. This is a blue-collar, regular guy's, regular woman's war, where the average American wants to fight this war. And they know why."

Beschloss, who worked on Democratic Senator Ted Kennedy's presidential campaign in 1980, suggested the terrorist strikes reflected poorly on Clinton. Previously, Beschloss had expressed admiration for Clinton and even dined with him in the White House.

"We've had all sorts of warnings about terrorism for years," the historian said. "When you're looking at the presidency of Bill Clinton—I don't want to single him out—but this changes the way we look at a past presidency. Because, for instance, in 1929, after the crash in the stock market, Calvin Coolidge looked different. One of the big questions you'll ask about Bill Clinton is going to be: What did he do to avert this?"

"Let's talk about *this* president," Matthews said. "How long is his line of credit right now? How long can he go in pursuing the evil ones around the world? Can he go to three or four other countries like Yemen, Somalia, Sudan? Does he risk his line of credit with the American people if he extends this war too broadly?"

"I don't think he does, as long as he makes the case and tells us in advance exactly what's going to happen," Beschloss said. "The impressive thing about Bush is that in September, he didn't shade what he was saying. He said, Look, this war could take a long time. You may get impatient. There could be months where we don't see a visible victory. There could be casualties.

"He told us at the beginning that this might not be very much fun. That's one reason why, I think, the people have said, We appreciate that. We'll stick with you."

"Why do people like George W. Bush?" Matthews said. "And they do."

"I think in the pit of their stomachs they think he's real and they feel that he's ethical," Beschloss said. "And they also feel that when he's making decisions about something like this war, he's not going to make it based on the polls."

"Some of our presidents love domestic policy," Matthews observed. "Other presidents can't wait to bite into the rich melon of foreign policy, as it's been called. George Bush seemed to lack a mission. And I have very mixed feelings about the guy. I like him in a lot of ways. But I felt he lacked a mission. He was down at the Texas ranch in August. This hell came upon us, and he leaped to it.

"Do you think this is the kind of thing that he needed to be a great leader? Because domestic policy would always just be tax cutting and fighting with the liberals. Whereas here's a chance for him to be a leader of everybody."

"I think it is," Beschloss said. "And the interesting thing is that Bush, I think, did not have this enormous aspiration for a great legacy, as you saw with Bill Clinton and other presidents. A lot of the campaign was: Let's downsize the presidency, downsize government—modesty. This has changed all of that. So he's been presented with both a crisis and a big, national need. That's the way great presidents are made."

Incredibly, this televised conversation about whether Bush would be regarded as a great president took place a mere ten months into his first term in office. It would be years, perhaps decades, before historians could even begin to assess whether Bush had made the cut. And yet, in this age of instant information, the media could not possibly bear to wait that long.

"I don't spend a lot of time worrying about my standing—I truly don't," the president told me. "I appreciate it. It's a lot nicer to go through a crowd and people are saying, We love you, Mr. President, rather than them saying, We hate you. Or ride the streets and they're waving, as opposed to gesturing. Obviously, that makes a person feel better.

"But I'm really not—I don't spend a lot of time analyzing things. I know what I need to say. I try to say it in a way that I'm comfortable with."

Nor was Bush willing to judge Clinton when I asked him whether his predecessor had done enough to combat terrorism.

"The job of historians," he told me, "is to put it all in perspective. And we'll let others make all the judgments [and] piece all the bits of the puzzle together. And in order to do it right, there's going to have to be enough time passed to understand not only the immediate eight years to mine, but years before that, as well.

"So I cast no stones. We were just presented with a different hand, and that is an outright attack on America. These people had been in the country for a period of time. I think all the second-guessing is harmful, so I won't do that."

Clinton, however, had no compunction about second-guessing the elder Bush's track record on terrorism. In fact, he insinuated that the old man was somehow responsible for the Somalia debacle that killed eighteen U.S. soldiers—even though it was Clinton who initiated the mission in August 1993. Nine years later, Clinton tried to shift blame to his predecessor when asked by a reporter about a completely different subject—the fact that corporate scandals now exploding on the younger Bush's watch had begun during the Clinton years.

"These people ran on responsibility, but as soon as you scratch them they go straight to blame," Clinton said. "Now, you know, I didn't blame his father for Somalia when we had that awful day memorialized in *Black Hawk Down*. I didn't do that."

But the younger Bush had never blamed Clinton for the corporate scandals in the first place. In fact, when asked at a news conference whether Clinton was responsible for the lax accounting procedures that helped fuel the false prosperity of the 1990s, Bush gave a one word answer: "No."

As my time with the president wound down, I couldn't resist taking one last shot at the nagging question of whether he, as Matthews put it, had undergone a Shakespearean transformation from Prince Hal to Warrior King Henry.

"I tried to get you to answer this down in Crawford in late December," I ventured. "You must be changed a little bit. I mean, we were *all* changed a little bit."

"Yes, we are changed," the president acknowledged.

"What I have come to realize is . . . the role of a president," he said. "I instinctively knew this; I now know it firsthand. And the role of a president is to seek great objectives for the country, big goals."

Bush said the events of September 11 caused him to focus on two big goals that he believed the nation could achieve.

"One is peace. And I mean not only peace for America, I mean peace around the world. This country, if we lead and we're strong and we're tough, I believe we can achieve a peace. I believe we can achieve the peace in the Middle East. And I believe we can achieve a peace in South Asia. It's going to take a while, going to have to be patient. But we've got a chance. See, I view this as an opportunity that we will seize.

"And at home," he added, "the cultural shift toward personal responsibility is going to enable us to better deal with those who could be left behind."

As evidence, Bush cited the bravery of Todd Beamer and other passengers who forced Flight 93 into a Pennsylvania field instead of letting it slam into the White House. The president was inspired by Beamer's courageous exhortation, "Let's roll."

"Flight 93 is, admittedly, the most significant example of serving something greater than yourself in life. I believe it's had an impact on our culture. And one of my jobs is to seize this opportunity, to encourage its impact on our culture. Because I think the sacrifice on Flight 93 is a great example of what I mean by loving your neighbor like you'd like to be loved yourself."

Animated by the power of his own words, the president leaned forward and invoked the legacy of a predecessor whose greatness was assured long ago—Abraham Lincoln.

"He understood that in order to achieve big goals for the country, the nation had to be united. And so one of my jobs is to keep this nation united, to achieve those two big objectives.

"The presidency is much bigger than budget battles and political squabbles. The presidency and the job of a president is to elevate the sights of the country.

"And you can't do that," concluded George W. Bush, "unless the country is united."

Acknowledgments

First and foremost, I would like to thank my wife, Becky, and our children, Brittany, Brooke, Ben, Billy, and Blair, for their incredible support and understanding as I undertook this project. I also appreciate the flexibility and support of everyone at the *Washington Times*, especially publisher Douglas Joo, editor in chief Wes Pruden, managing editor Fran Coombs, national editor Ken Hanner, fellow White House correspondent Joe Curl, and researcher John Sopko. My friends at Fox News Channel, starting with Roger Ailes, Brit Hume, Kim Hume, and Jacqueline Pham, demonstrated remarkable patience. So did Llewellyn King and Linda Gasparello at *White House Weekly*. A special thanks to publisher Al Regnery for championing this book and editors Harry Crocker and Miriam Moore for guiding it to publication. Finally, this project would not have been possible without the generous cooperation of President Bush and many members of his administration.

Index